Introduction to
ARCHITECTURAL SCIENCE
The Basis of Sustainable Design

Introduction to
ARCHITECTURAL SCIENCE
The Basis of Sustainable Design

Steven V. Szokolay

Second edition

AMSTERDAM • BOSTON • HEIDELBERG • LONDON • NEW YORK • OXFORD
PARIS • SAN DIEGO • SAN FRANCISCO • SINGAPORE • SYDNEY • TOKYO

Architectural Press is an imprint of Elsevier

Architectural Press is an imprint of Elsevier
Linacre House, Jordan Hill, Oxford OX2 8DP, UK
30 Corporate Drive, Suite 400, Burlington, MA 01803, USA

Second edition 2008

British Library Cataloguing in Publication Data
Szokolay, S. V.
   Introduction to architectural science : the basis of sustainable design. – 2nd ed.
   1. Architectural design 2. Buildings – Environmental engineering 3. Sustainable architecture
   I. Title
   721'.046

Library of Congress Catalog Number: 2008924601

ISBN: 978-0-7506-8704-1

For information on all Architectural Press publications
visit our website at: www.architecturalpress.com

Typeset by Charon Tec Ltd., A Macmillan Company. (www.macmillansolutions.com)

Printed and bound by Uniprint

08 09 10 11   11 10 9 8 7 6 5 4 3 2 1

CONTENTS

PREFACE TO THE SECOND EDITION

Much has changed in the 3 years since the first edition of this book.

The physics of heat, light, sound and energy is still the same, so there is little change in the first three parts. Apart from the correction of a few errors, a few new developments are mentioned, some new methods are included and statistics updated.

Part 4 has many new elements that reflect societal changes, especially changes in public attitudes. Three years ago there were many who denied global warming or who regarded renewable energy technologies as 'kids' stuff'. Today only a few of these survive. Global warming is recognized as a fact by politicians as well as the general public. As the general public is better informed, politicians are forced to pay at least lip service to sustainability. Some actions have also been taken, albeit rather timidly.

There is significant progress in renewable energy technologies, both at the scientific and at the practical engineering level. Real life projects are multiplying and increasing in size. Numerous large wind farms and solar power stations are already operating and many are being developed. It is most encouraging that private capital started funding large renewable energy projects. There is also a large increase in small scale, 'distributed' power generation. Architects and the building industry started moving in the direction of sustainable practice as well.

What I said in the original 'Introduction' is just as valid now, as it then was, but the importance of having a critical attitude is even greater now than it was 3 years ago. Unfortunately there are many charlatans around, many use the label of 'sustainable' without the substance, some are ignorant or downright fraudulent. Few dare to say to them that the 'emperor has no clothes'.

I can only hope that this book, besides assisting the designer or the student will also contribute to developing such a critical attitude, thus lead to a progressive improvement.

INTRODUCTION

Four chains of thought lead to the idea of this book and to the definition of its content:

1 It can no longer be disputed that the resources of this earth are finite, that its capacity to absorb our wastes is limited, that if we (as a species) want to survive, we cannot continue our ruthless exploitation of the environment. Where our actions would affect the environment, we must act in a sustainable manner. There are many good books that deal with the need for sustainability (e.g. Vale, 1991; Farmer, 1999; Roaf, 2001; Smith, 2001; Beggs, 2002). This book assumes that the reader is in agreement with these tenets and needs no further persuasion.

2 Architecture is the art and science of building. There exists a large literature on architecture as an art, on the cultural and social significance of architecture – there is no need for discussing these issues here.

3 The term 'bioclimatic architecture' has been coined by Victor Olgyay in the early 1950s and fully explained in his book *Design with climate* (1963). He synthesized elements of human physiology, climatology and building physics, with a strong advocacy of architectural regionalism and of designing in sympathy with the environment. In many ways he can be considered as an important progenitor of what we now call 'sustainable architecture'.

4 Architecture, as a profession is instrumental in huge investments of money and resources. Our professional responsibility is great, not only to our clients and to society, but also for sustainable development. Many excellent books and other publications deal with sustainable development in qualitative terms. However, professional responsibility demands expertise and competence. It is this narrow area where this work intends to supplement the existing literature.

The book is intended to give an introduction to architectural science, to provide an understanding of the physical phenomena we are to deal with and to provide the tools for realizing the many good intentions. Many projects in recent times are claimed to constitute sustainable development, to be sustainable architecture. But are they really green or sustainable? Some new terms started appearing in the literature, such as 'green wash' – meaning that a conventional building is designed and then claimed to be 'green'. Or 'pure rhetoric – no substance', with the same meaning.

My hope is that after absorbing the contents of this modest work, the reader will be able to answer this question. After all, the main aim of any education is to develop a critical faculty.

Building environments affect us through our sensory organs:

1 The eye, i.e. vision, a condition of which is light and lighting; the aim is to ensure visual comfort but also to facilitate visual performance.
2 The ear, i.e. hearing, appropriate conditions for listening to wanted sound must be ensured, but also the elimination (or control) of unwanted sound, noise.
3 Thermal sensors, located over the whole body surface, in the skin; this is not just a sensory channel, as the body itself produces heat and has a number of adjustment mechanisms but it can function only within a fairly narrow range of temperatures and only an even narrower range would be perceived as comfortable. Thermal conditions appropriate for human well-being must be ensured.

What is important for the designer is to be able to control the indoor environmental conditions: heat, light and sound. Rayner Banham (1969) in his *Architecture of the well-tempered environment* postulated that comfortable conditions can be provided by a building (passive control) or by the use of energy (active control), and that if we had an unlimited supply of energy, we could ensure comfort even without a building. In most real cases it is a mixture (or synergy) of the two kinds of control we would be relying on.

In this day and age, when it is realized that our traditional energy sources (coal, oil, gas) are finite and their rapidly increasing use has serious environmental consequences (CO_2 emissions, global warming, as well as local atmospheric pollution), it should be the designer's aim to ensure the required indoor conditions with little or no use of energy, other than from ambient or renewable sources.

Therefore the designer's task is

1 to examine the given conditions (site conditions, climate, daylight and noise climate)
2 to establish the limits of desirable or acceptable conditions (temperatures, lighting and acceptable noise levels)
3 to attempt to control these variables (heat, light and sound) by passive means (by the building itself) as far as practicable
4 to provide for energy-based services (heating, cooling, electric lighting, amplification or masking sound) only for the residual control task.

The building is not just a shelter, or a barrier against unwanted influences (rain, wind, cold), but the building envelope should be considered as a selective filter: to exclude the unwanted influences, but admit the desirable and useful ones, such as daylight, solar radiation in winter or natural ventilation.

The book consists of four parts

1 **Heat: the thermal environment**
2 **Light: the luminous environment**
3 **Sound: the sonic environment**
4 **Resources**

In each part the relevant physical principles are reviewed, followed by a discussion of their relationship to humans (comfort and human requirements). Then the control functions of the building (passive controls) are examined as well as associated installations, energy-using 'active' controls. The emphasis is on how these can be considered in design. The first part (Heat) is the most substantial, as the thermal behaviour of a building has greatest effect on energy use and sustainability and its design is fully the architect's responsibility.

Each part concludes with a series of data sheets relating to that part, together with some 'methods sheets', describing some calculation and design methods

PART 1 HEAT: THE THERMAL ENVIRONMENT

CONTENTS

SYMBOLS AND ABBREVIATIONS

		Units
asg	alternating solar gain factor	–
b	breadth, thickness	m
clo	unit of clothing insulation	
dTe	sol–air excess temperature (difference)	K
er	evaporation rate	kg/h
f	response factor	–
g	vapour quantity	
k	linear heat loss coefficient	W/m K
met	unit of metabolic heat ($58.2 W/m^2$)	
mr	mass flow rate	kg/s
p	pressure	Pa
pt	total atmospheric pressure	Pa
pv	vapour pressure	Pa
pv_s	saturation vapour pressure	Pa
q	building conductance (specfic heat loss rate)	W/K
qa	total admittance	W/K
qc	envelope conductance	W/K
qv	ventilation conductance	W/K
h	surface conductance	$W/m^2 K$
h_c	convective surface conductance	$W/m^2 K$
h_r	radiative surface conductance	$W/m^2 K$
sM	specific mass (per floor area)	kg/m^2
sQ	swing in heat flow rate (from mean)	W
sT	swing in temperature (from mean)	K
t	time	h
v	velocity	m/s
vr	volume flow rate (ventilation rate)	m^3/s, L/s
vR	vapour resistance	$MPa s m^2/g$
y	year	
A	area	m^2
AH	absolute humidity	g/kg
ALT	solar altitude angle	°
AZI	solar azimuth angle	°
C	conductance	$W/m^2 K$
CDD	cooling degree-days	Kd
CoP	coefficient of performance	–
CPZ	control potential zone	
Cd	conduction, conducted heat (from body)	W
Cv	convection, convected heat (from body)	W
D	daily total irradiation	Wh/m^2, MJ/m^2
D_v	daily total vertical irradiation	Wh/m^2, MJ/m^2
DBT	dry-bulb temperature	°C
DEC	solar declination angle	°

		Units
DD	degree-days	Kd
Dh	degree-hours	Kh
DPT	dew-point temperature	°C
DRT	dry resultant temperature	°C
E	radiant heat emission	W
EnvT	environmental temperature	°C
Ev	evaporation heat transfer (from body)	W
ET*	new effective temperature	°C
G	global irradiance	W/m^2
GT	globe temperature	°C
H	enthalpy (heat content)	kJ/kg
HDD	heating degree-days	Kd
H_L	latent heat content	kJ/kg
H_S	sensible heat content	kJ/kg
HSA	horizontal shadow angle	°
Htg	heating requirement	(kWh) Wh
HVAC	Heating, Ventilation and Air Conditioning	–
INC	angle of incidence	°
Kd	kelvin-days	Kd
Kh	kelvin-hours	Kh
L	length (linear thermal bridges)	m
LAT	geographical latitude angle	°
M	metabolic heat production	W
MRT	mean radiant temperature	°C
N	number of air changes per hour	–
ORI	orientation angle	°
Q	heat flux or heat flow rate	W
Qc	conduction heat flow rate	W
Qe	evaporative heat loss rate	W
Qi	internal heat gain rate	W
Qs	solar heat gain rate	W
Qv	ventilation heat flow rate	W
R	resistance	$m^2 K/W$
R_{a-a}	air-to-air resistance	$m^2 K/W$
R_c	cavity resistance	$m^2 K/W$
Rd	radiation, radiated heat (from body)	W
RH	relative humidity	%
R_s	surface resistance	$m^2 K/W$
R_{si}	internal surface resistance	$m^2 K/W$
R_{so}	outside surface resistance	$m^2 K/W$
SD	standard deviation	
SET	standard effective temperature	°
SH	saturation point humidity	g/kg
SI	système International (of units)	
T	temperature	°C
Tb	balance point (base~) temperature	°C
TIL	tilt angle	°
T_i	indoor temperature	°C
Tn	neutrality temperature	°C

(Continued)

SYMBOLS AND ABBREVIATIONS (Continued)

		Units				Units
T_o	outdoor temperature	°C	τ	transmittance		
T_s	surface temperature	°C	ϕ	time lag	h	
T_{s-a}	sol–air temperature	°C	σ	stefan–Boltzmann constant	W/m^2K^4	
U	air-to-air (thermal) transmittance	W/m^2K	Σ	sum of ...		
V	volume	m^3	Δp	pressure difference	Pa	
VSA	vertical shadow angle	°	ΔS	rate of change in stored heat	W	
WBT	wet-bulb temperature	°C	ΔT	temperature difference, interval or	K	
Y	admittance	W/m^2K		increment		
α	absorptance or thermal diffusivity	–				

Subscripts to G and D:

δ	vapour permeability	$\mu g/m\,s\,Pa$	First	b		beam~
ε	emittance	–		d		diffuse~
η	efficiency	–		r		reflected~
θ	solar gain factor	–	Second	h		horizontal
θ_a	alternating solar gain factor	–		v		vertical
κ	conductivity correction factor	–		p		on plane p
λ	conductivity	$W/m\,K$	For G only	n		normal to
μ	decrement factor	–				radiation
π	vapour permeance	$\mu g/m^2\,s\,Pa$				
ρ	density or reflectance	kg/m^3 or –				

LIST OF FIGURES

(Continued)

LIST OF FIGURES (Continued)

(Continued)

LIST OF FIGURES (Continued)

LIST OF TABLES

LIST OF WORKED EXAMPLES

LIST OF EQUATIONS

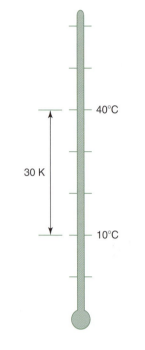

1.1.

Temperature scale and interval.

1.1 PHYSICS OF HEAT

1.1.1 Heat and temperature

Heat is a form of energy, contained in substances as molecular motion or appearing as electromagnetic radiation in space. Energy is the ability or capacity for doing work and it is measured in the same units. The derivation of this unit from the basic MKS (m, kg, s) units in the SI (Système International) is quite simple and logical, as shown in Table 1.1.

Temperature (T) is the symptom of the presence of heat in a substance. The Celsius scale is based on water: its freezing point taken as 0°C and its boiling point (at normal atmospheric pressure) as 100°C. The Kelvin scale starts with the 'absolute zero', the total absence of heat. Thus 0°C = 273.15°K. The temperature interval is the same in both scales. By convention, a point on the scale is denoted °C (degree Celsius) but the notation for a temperature difference or interval is K (Kelvin), which is a certain length of the scale, without specifying where it is on the overall scale (Fig. 1.1). Thus 40 − 10°C = 30 K, and similarly 65 − 35°C is 30 K but 15°C, as a point on the scale, is 288.15°K.

The **specific heat** concept provides the connection between heat and temperature. This is the quantity of heat required to elevate the temperature of unit mass of a substance by one degree, thus it is measured in units of **J/kg K**. Its magnitude is different for different materials and it varies between 100 and 800 J/kg K for metals, 800–1200 J/kg K for masonry materials (brick, concrete) to water, which has the highest value of all common substances: 4176 J/kg K (see data sheet D.1.1).

Table 1.1. Derivation of composite SI units for thermal quantities

Length	m	(metre)
Mass	kg	(kilogram)
Time	s	(second)
Velocity, speed	**m/s**	That is unit length movement in unit time. The everyday unit is km/h, which is 1000 m/3600 s = 0.278 m/s or conversely: 1 m/s = 3.6 km/h
Acceleration	**m/s^2**	That is unit velocity increase in unit time: (m/s)/s
Force	**kg m/s^2**	That which gives unit acceleration to unit mass named newton (**N**)
Work, energy	**kg m^2/s^2**	Unit work is done when unit force is acting over unit length i.e. N × m named joule (**J**)
Power, energy flow rate	**kg m^2/s^3**	Unit energy flow in unit time or unit work done in unit time i.e. J/s named watt (**W**)
Pressure, stress	**kg/m s^2**	Unit force acting on unit area (kg m/ s^2)/m^2 i.e. N/m^2 named pascal (**Pa**)

SI unit symbols, derived from personal names, are always capitalized.

EXAMPLE 1.1

Given 0.5 L (=0.5 kg) of water at 20°C in an electric jug with an 800W immersion heater element (efficiency: 1.0 or 100%). How long will it take to bring it to the boil?

Requirement: 0.5 kg × 4176 J/kg K × (100 − 20) K = 167 040 J

Heat input 800W, i.e. 800 J/s, thus the time required is

167 040 J/800 J/s = 208 s ≈ 3.5 min

Latent heat of a substance is the amount of heat (energy) absorbed by unit mass of the substance at change of state (from solid to liquid or liquid to gaseous) without any change in temperature. This is measured in J/kg, e.g. for water:

latent heat of fusion (ice to water) at 0°C = 335 kJ/kg
latent heat of evaporation at 100°C   = 2261 kJ/kg
                        at about 18°C = 2400 kJ/kg

At a change of state in the reverse direction the same amount of heat is released.

Thermodynamics is the science of the flow of heat and of its relationship to mechanical work.

The *first law* of thermodynamics is the principle of conservation of energy. Energy cannot be created or destroyed (except in sub-atomic processes), but only converted from one form to another. Heat and work are interconvertible. In any system the energy output must equal the energy input, unless there is a +/− storage component.

The *second law* of thermodynamics states that heat (or energy) transfer can take place spontaneously in one direction only: from a hotter to a cooler body or generally from a higher to a lower grade state (same as water flow will take place only downhill). Only with an external energy input can a machine deliver heat in the opposite direction (water will move upwards only if it is pumped). Any machine to perform work must have an energy source and a sink, i.e. energy must flow through the machine: only part of this flow can be turned into work.

Heat flow from a high to a low temperature zone can take place in three forms: conduction, convection and radiation. The magnitude of any such flow can be measured in two ways:

1 as *heat flow rate* (Q), or heat flux, i.e. the total flow in unit time through a defined area of a body or space, or within a defined system, in units of J/s, which is a watt (W) (The most persistent archaic energy flow rate or power unit is the *horsepower*, but in fully metric countries even car engines are now rated in terms of kW.)

2 as *heat flux density* (or density of heat flow rate), i.e. the rate of heat flow through unit area of a body or space, in W/m². The multiple kW (kilowatt = 1000 W) is often used for both quantities. (The term 'density' as used here is analogous with, for example, population density: i.e. people

Black body radiation (handwritten margin note)

per unit area, or with surface density: i.e. kg mass per unit area of a wall or other building element.)

A non-standard, but accepted and very convenient unit of energy is derived from this heat flux unit: the watt-hour (Wh). This is the amount of energy delivered or expended if a flow rate (flux) of 1 W is maintained for an hour. As 1 h = 3600 s and

$$1 W = 1 J/s$$
$$1 Wh = 3600 s \times 1 J/s = 3600 J \quad or \quad 3.6 kJ (kilojoule)[1]$$

The multiple kWh (kilowatt-hour) is often used as a practical unit of energy (e.g. in electricity accounts) 1 kWh = 3 600 000 J or 3600 kJ or 3.6 MJ (megajoule).

1.1.2 Heat flow

As water flows from a higher to a lower position, so heat flows from a higher temperature zone (or body) to a lower temperature one. Such heat flow can take place in three forms:

1 *Conduction* within a body or bodies in contact, by the 'spread' of molecular movement.

2 *Convection* from a solid body to a fluid (liquid or gas) or vice versa (in a broader sense it is also used to mean the transport of heat from one surface to another by a moving fluid, which, strictly speaking, is 'mass transfer'). The magnitude of convection heat flow rate depends on

   a area of contact (A, m^2) between the body and the fluid
   b the difference in temperature (ΔT, in K) between the surface of the body and the fluid
   c a convection coefficient (h_c) measured in W/m^2K, which depends on the viscosity of the fluid and its flow velocity as well as on the physical configuration that will determine whether the flow is laminar or turbulent (see Section 1.1.2.2 below).

3 *Radiation* from a body with a warmer surface to another which is cooler. Thermal radiation is a wavelength band of electromagnetic radiation, normally taken as 700–10 000 nm[2] 10 μm)[3]

'short infrared': 700–2300 nm (2.3 μm) (see note in 1.3.1.2a) and
'long infrared': 2.3–10 μm (some suggest up to 70 μm)

The temperature of the emitting body determines the wavelength. The sun with its 6000°C surface emits short infrared (as well as visible and ultraviolet (UV)), bodies at terrestrial temperatures (<100°C) emit long infrared radiation. (Fig. 1.2 shows these bands in relation to the full electromagnetic spectrum).

In all three forms the magnitude of flux (or of flux density) depends on the temperature difference between the points (or surfaces) considered, whilst the flux (heat flow rate) in conduction also depends on the cross-sectional area of the body available.

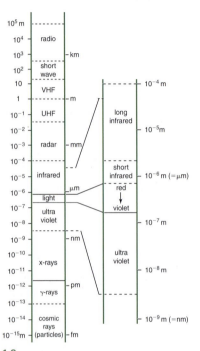

1.2.
The full electromagnetic spectrum and its solar segment.

Wave-band summary	
< 280 nm	UV 'C'
280–315	UV 'B'
315–380	UV 'A'
380–780	light
Overlap with thermal:	
700–2300	short IR
2300–10 000	long IR

---

[1]For all prefixes used with SI units see Table 4.1.
[2]1 nm (nanometre) = 10^{-9} m
[3]1 μm (micrometer) = 10^{-6} m

1.1.2.1 Conduction

Conduction depends also on a property of the material known as *conductivity* (λ), measured as the heat flow density (W/m^2) in a 1 m thick body (i.e. the length of heat flow path is 1 m), with a one degree temperature difference, in units of $W m/m^2 K = \mathbf{W/m\,K}$.

As insulating materials are fibrous or porous, they are very sensitive to moisture content. If the pores are filled with water, the conductivity will increase quite drastically. Take a porous, fibrous cement insulating board:

	Density (kg/m³)	Conductivity (W/m K)
Dry	136	0.051
Wet	272	0.144
Soaked	400	0.203

Materials with a foam (closed pore) structure are not quite as sensitive.

Some conductivity values are given in data sheet D.1.1. Note that these are 'declared values', based on laboratory testing. The operational conditions in transportation and on building sites are such that damage to insulating materials is often inevitable, reducing their insulating properties. Before using such λ values for *U*-value calculations, they should be corrected by one or more conductivity correction factors: κ (kappa), which are additive:

$$\lambda_{design} = \lambda_{declared} \times (1 + \kappa_1 + \kappa_2 \ldots)$$

If from data sheet D.1.1, for expanded polystyrene (EPS) $\lambda_{declared} = 0.035$ and it will be used as external insulation over a brick wall, with cement rendering applied directly to it (with a wire mesh insert), from Table 1.2: $\kappa = 0.25$, then

$$\lambda_{design} = 0.035 \times (1 + 0.25) = 0.0438 \text{ W/m K}$$

Conductivity is a material property, regardless of its shape or size. The corresponding property of a physical body (e.g. a wall) is the *conductance* (*C*) measured between the two surfaces of the wall. For a single layer it is the conductivity, divided by thickness (λ/b). It is a rarely used quantity. *Transmittance*, or *U*-value includes the surface effects and it is the most frequently used measure. This is the heat flow density (W/m^2) with 1 K temperature difference (ΔT) between air inside and air outside (see Fig. 1.3), in units of $\mathbf{W/m^2K}$.

For *U*-values see data sheets D.1.2 and D.1.3.

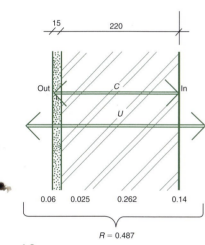

1.3.
Example wall section: *C* and *U* and resistances which are additive.

Table 1.2. Conductivity correction factors

Material	Condition of use	κ
Expanded polystyrene	Between cast concrete layers	0.42
	Between masonry wall layers	0.10
	n ventilated air gap (cavity)	0.30
	With cement render applied	0.25
Mineral wool	Between masonry wall layers	0.10
Polyurethane	In ventilated air gap (cavity)	0.15

(If ΔT is always taken as $T_o - T_i$ then a negative value – thus also a negative Q – will indicate heat loss, whilst a positive value would mean heat gain.)

EXAMPLE 1.2

If the outside temperature is $T_o = 10°C$ and the inside is $T_i = 22°C$, thus $\Delta T = 10 - 22 = -12\,K$ (the negative indicating a heat loss).

Over a 10 m² brick wall ($U = 1.5\,W/m^2K$) the heat flow rate will be

$$\boxed{Q = A \times U \times \Delta T} \tag{1.1}$$

$$Q = 10 \times 1.5 \times (-12) = -180\,W$$

It is often useful to do a 'dimensional check' for such expressions:

$$m^2 \times \frac{W}{m^2K} \times K = W$$

The reciprocal of the *U*-value is the air-to-air *resistance* (R_{a-a}, in m²K/W) which is the sum of component resistances: resistances of the surfaces and of the body of the element (wall, roof, etc.), e.g. for a wall of two layers:

$$R_{a-a} = R_{si} + R_1 + R_2 + R_{so} \tag{1.2}$$

The *R*-value of any homogeneous layer is its thickness (b^4 for breadth) in m, divided by the conductivity of its material:

$$R = \frac{b}{\lambda} \tag{1.3}$$

The reciprocal of this resistance is *conductance*, *C* in W/m²K.

Layers through which heat flows, can be represented as resistances in series, thus the resistances of layers are additive (see Fig. 1.56).

Various elements of an envelope are heat flow paths (with resistances) in parallel, and in this case the (area weighted) conductances (transmittances) are additive (see Fig. 1.55 in Section 1.4.3.1).

For example Fig. 1.3 shows a 220 mm brick wall ($\lambda = 0.84\,W/mK$), with a 15 mm cement render ($\lambda = 0.6\,W/mK$) and surface resistances of $R_{si} = 0.14$ and $R_{so} = 0.06$ m²KW (values taken from data sheets D.1.1 and D.1.4):

$$R_{body} = \frac{0.220}{0.84} + \frac{0.015}{0.6} = 0.287 \quad \text{thus}$$

$$C = \frac{1}{R_{body}} = \frac{1}{0.287} = 3.484\,W/m^2K$$

$$R_{a-a} = 0.14 + \frac{0.220}{0.84} + \frac{0.015}{0.6} + 0.06 = 0.487 \quad \text{thus}$$

$$U = \frac{1}{R_{a-a}} = \frac{1}{0.487} = 2.054\,W/m^2K$$

---

[4]'*b*' is used for thickness (breadth) to distinguish it from '*t*' for time and '*T*' for temperature.

Handwritten margin notes:

Q – heat loss (W)

A – surface area (m²)

U – transmittance (W/m²K)

ΔT – change in Temp. (K)

$W = m^2 \cdot \frac{W}{m^2 K} \cdot K$ ✓

$q_K = -kA \frac{dT}{dx}$ Heat conductivity q_K

$\frac{W}{m^2} = m^2 \frac{W}{m K} \cdot \frac{K}{m}$

$q_K = -kA \frac{dT}{dx}$

The surface resistance depends on the degree of exposure and – to some extent – on surface qualities.

The surface resistance combines the resistances to convection and radiation, thus it is affected by radiation properties of the surface, as discussed below in the radiation section.

1.1.2.2 Convection

Convection heat transfer is a function of the *convection coefficient*, h_c (in W/m²K):

$$\boxed{Q_{cv} = A \times h_c \times \Delta T} \quad m^2 \times W/m^2K \times K = W \tag{1.4}$$

The magnitude of h_c depends on the position of the surface, the direction of the heat flow and the velocity of the fluid, e.g.

- for vertical surfaces (horizontal heat flow) $h_c = 3\,W/m^2K$
- for horizontal surfaces
  - heat flow up (air to ceiling, floor to room air) 4.3 W/m²K
  - heat flow down (air to floor, ceiling to room air) 1.5 W/m²K
  (as hot air rises, the upward heat transfer is stronger).

In the above still air is assumed (i.e. air flow is due to the heat transfer only). If the surface is exposed to wind, or mechanically generated air movement (i.e. if it is forced convection), then the convection coefficient is much higher:

- $h_c = 5.8 + 4.1v$
  where v is air velocity in m/s.

1.1.2.3 Radiation

Radiation heat transfer is proportional to the difference of the 4th power of absolute temperatures of the emitting and receiving surfaces and depends on their surface qualities:

reflectance (ρ) is a decimal fraction indicating how much of the incident radiation is reflected by a surface.

absorptance (α) is expressed as a fraction of that of the 'perfect absorber', the theoretical black body (for which $\alpha = 1$), and its value is high for dark surfaces, low for light or shiny metallic surfaces. For everyday surfaces it varies between $\alpha = 0.9$ for a black asphalt and $\alpha = 0.2$ for a shiny aluminium or white painted surface.

For any opaque surface $\rho + \sigma = $ **1**.

Emittance (ε) is also a decimal fraction, a measure of the ability to emit radiation, relative to the 'black body', the perfect emitter. For an ordinary surface $\alpha = \varepsilon$ for the same wavelength (or temperature) of radiation, but many surfaces have selective properties, e.g. high absorptance for solar (6000°C) radiation but low emittance at ordinary temperatures (<100°C), e.g.:

$$\alpha_{6000} > \varepsilon_{60}$$

The expression for radiant heat transfer between two opposed parallel surfaces is

$$Q = A \times \sigma \times \varepsilon$$
$$\times \left[\left(\frac{T'}{100} \right)^4 - \left(\frac{T''}{100} \right)^4 \right]$$

where $\sigma = 5.67\,W/m^2K^4$ (it is the Stefan–Boltzmann constant) and T is in °K (°C + 273) and ε is the effective emittance

$$\frac{1}{\varepsilon} = \frac{1}{\varepsilon'} + \frac{1}{\varepsilon''} - 1$$

for everyday calculations a radiation (h_r) coefficient can be derived

$$h_r = 5.7 \times \varepsilon$$
$$\times \frac{(T'/100)^4 - (T''/100)^4}{t' - t''}$$

then $Qr = h_r \times A \times (t' - t'')$
Typically $h_r = 5.7 \times \varepsilon$ at 20°C
$\quad h_r = 4.6 \times \varepsilon$ at 0°C
$\quad \varepsilon = 0.9$ for ordinary building
$\qquad$ surfaces
$\quad \varepsilon = 0.2$ for dull aluminium
$\quad \varepsilon = 0.05$ for polished
$\qquad$ aluminium

In the above T is in °K and t is in °C.

Such *selective surfaces* are useful for the absorber panels of solar collectors, but the reverse is desirable where heat dissipation (radiation to the sky) is to be promoted:

$$\alpha_{6000} < \varepsilon_{60}$$

White paints (especially a titanium oxide) have such properties.

A shiny metal surface is non-selective:

$$\alpha_{6000} = \varepsilon_{60}$$

(reflectance, ρ may be the same for a white and a shiny metal surface, but emittance $\varepsilon_{white} > \varepsilon_{shiny}$, so, for example, in a hot climate a white roof is better than a shiny one).

The calculation of radiant heat exchange is complicated, but it is quite simple for the effect which is most important for buildings: solar radiation. If the flux density of incident radiation is known (referred to as global irradiance, G) then the radiant (solar) heat input rate will be

$$\boxed{Qs = A \times G \times \alpha} \qquad m^2 \times W/m^2 \times \text{non-dimensional} = W \qquad (1.5)$$

1.1.3 Humid air: psychrometry

(Not to be confused with 'psychometry', which means psychological measurement; this one has an 'r' in the middle.)

Air is a mixture of oxygen and nitrogen, but the atmosphere around us is humid air, it contains varying amounts of water vapour. At any given temperature the air can only support a limited amount of water vapour, when it is said to be saturated. Figure 1.4 shows the basic structure of the psychrometric chart: dry-bulb (air-) temperature on the horizontal axis and moisture content (or *absolute humidity*, AH) on the vertical axis (in units of g/kg, grams of moisture per kg of dry air).

The top curve is the *saturation line*, indicating the maximum moisture content the air could support at any temperature, which is the *saturation humidity* (SH). Each vertical ordinate can be subdivided (Fig. 1.5 shows a subdivision into five equal parts) and the curves connecting these points show the relative humidity (RH) in percentage, i.e. as a percentage of the SH. In this case the 20%, 40%, 60% and 80% RH curves are shown. For example (with reference to Fig. 1.6, the full psychrometric chart) at 25°C the saturation AH is 20 g/kg. Halving the ordinate we get 10 g/kg, which is half of the SH or 50% RH.

Another expression of humidity is the vapour pressure (pv), i.e. the partial pressure of water vapour in the given atmosphere. The saturation vapour pressure is pv_s.

Thus RH = (AH/SH) × 100 or (pv/pv_s) × 100 (in %).

Vapour pressure is linearly related to AH and the two scales are parallel:

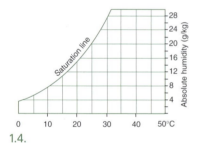

1.4.
Structure of the psychrometric chart.

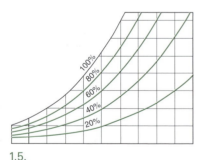

1.5.
Relative humidity curves.

$$AH - \frac{622 \times pv}{pt - pv} \qquad \text{conversely} \qquad pv = \frac{AH \times pt}{622 + AH} \qquad (1.6)$$

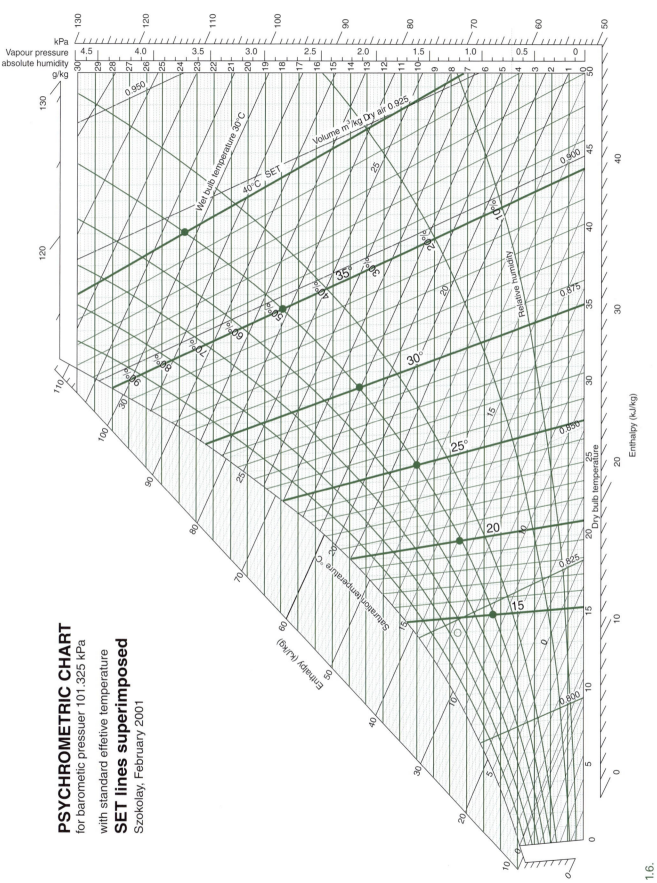

PSYCHROMETRIC CHART
for barometic pressuer 101.325 kPa

with standard effetive temperature

SET lines superimposed

Szokolay, February 2001

kPa
Vapour pressure
absolute humidity
g/kg

1.6.

Psychrometric chart, with SET lines superimposed (after Szokolay, 1980).

Wet bulb temperature 30°C

Volume m³/kg Dry air 0.925

40°C SET

Relative humidity

Saturation temperature °C

Enthalpy (kJ/kg)

Dry bulb temperature

Enthalpy (kJ/kg)

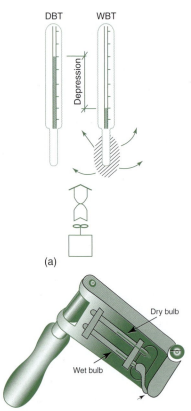

(a)

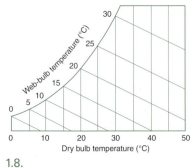

(b) Water container

1.7.

Principles of an aspirated psychrometer (a) and a whirling psychrometer (b).

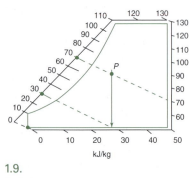

1.8.

Web-bulb temperature lines.

1.9.

Enthalpy scales externally.

where pt = total barometric pressure, taken as 101.325 kPa (standard atmosphere).

For example if pv = 2 kPa, AH = (622 × 2)/(101.325 − 2) = 12.5 g/kg (see Fig. 1.6)

Humidity is best measured by the wet-and-dry bulb (whirling) *psychrometer* or an aspirated psychrometer (Fig. 1.7). These contain two thermometers. One has its bulb wrapped in a gauze, which is kept moist from a small water container. When whirled around (or the fan is operated) to obtain maximum possible evaporation, this produces a cooling effect, showing the *wet-bulb temperature* (WBT). The other thermometer measures the air- or dry-bulb temperature (DBT). The difference DBT–WBT is referred to as the *wet-bulb depression* and it is indicative of the humidity. Evaporation is inversely proportional to humidity. In saturated air there is no evaporation, no cooling, thus WBT = DBT. With low humidity there is strong evaporation, strong cooling and a large wet-bulb depression.

Figure 1.8 shows the sloping WBT lines on the psychrometric chart. These coincide with the DBT at the saturation curve. When a measurement is made, the intersection of the DBT and WBT lines can be marked on the psychrometric chart; it will be referred to as the *status point*, which indicates both the RH (interpolated between the RH curves) and the AH values (read on the right-hand vertical scale).

For example (from Fig. 1.6) if DBT = 29°C and WBT = 23°C has been measured and plotted, the two lines intersect at the 60% RH curve and on the vertical scale the AH is read as just over 15 g/kg.

For any point *P* of a wet-bulb line the *X*-axis intercept will be

$$T = T_p + AH_P \times (2501 - 1.805 \times 24) / 1000)°C$$

For example if $T_p = 25$, $AH_p = 10$ g/kg   (1.7)

$$T = 25 + 10 \times (2501 - 1.805 \times 24) / 1000$$
$$= 49.6°C \text{ (verifiable from Fig.1.6)}$$

Enthalpy (*H*) is the heat content of the air relative to 0°C and 0 humidity. It is measured in kJ/kg, i.e. the heat content of 1 kg air. It has two components: *sensible heat* (H_S) taken up to increase the DBT (approximately 1.005 kJ/kg K) and *latent heat* (H_L) i.e. the heat that was necessary to evaporate liquid water to form the moisture content of the air. As the constant enthalpy lines almost coincide with the WBT lines (but not quite), to avoid confusion, it is indicated by duplicate scales on either side, outside of the body of the psychrometric chart, which are used with a straight edge (Fig. 1.9).

If enthalpy is the diagonal distance of the status point from the 0°C and 0 RH point, then the horizontal component is the H_S and the vertical component is the H_L.

Specific volume of air at any condition is also shown on the chart by a set of steeply sloping lines (Fig. 1.10). This is the volume of air occupied by 1 kg of air (at normal pressure), in m³/kg. It is the reciprocal of density, kg/m³.

Psychrometric processes or changes can be traced on the chart.

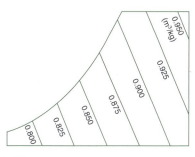

1.10.
Specific volume lines.

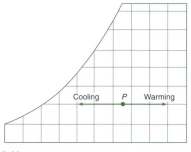

1.11.
Cooling and heating: movement of the status point.

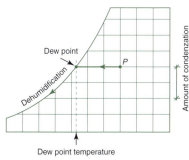

1.12.
Cooling to reduce humidity.

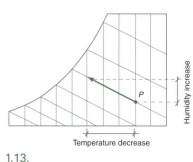

1.13.
Evaporative cooling: humidification.

Heating is represented by the status point moving horizontally to the right. As the DBT increases, with no change in moisture content, the RH is reducing (Fig. 1.11).

Cooling lowers the DBT, the status point moves horizontally to the left. This causes the RH to increase, but the AH is not changed. Where this horizontal line reaches the saturation curve, the *dew-point temperature* (DPT) (corresponding to the given AH) can be read. For the above example this will be at about 20.5°C. At this point the RH will be 100%. If the air is cooled below this point, condensation will start, dew will be formed. Below the dew point the status point moves along the saturation curve and the AH corresponding to the vertical drop will have condensed out.

Continuing the above example, the 29°C air of 15.2 g/kg AH (60% RH) has its dew point at 20.5°C, and if it is cooled to (say) 15°C, at this point its (saturated) AH would be 10.5 g/kg, so the difference of 15.2 − 10.5 = 4.7 g/kg will have condensed out in liquid form (Fig. 1.12).

Humidification, i.e. evaporation of moisture into an air volume is said to be adiabatic, if no heat is added or removed. This causes a reduction of temperature (DBT) but an increase of humidity (both AH and RH). The status point moves up to the left, along a constant WBT line (Fig. 1.13).

Adiabatic *dehumidification* takes place when air is passed through some chemical sorbent (solid, such as silica gel, or liquid, such as glycol spray) which removes some of the moisture content (by absorption or adsorption). This process releases heat, thus the DBT will increase, whilst the humidity (both AH and RH) is reduced (Fig. 1.14).

1.1.4 Air flow

Air flow can be characterized by

- velocity v m/s
- mass flow rate mr kg/s
- volume flow rate v m^3/s or L/s.

Volume flow rate through an opening of A area is **vr = v × A**.

Natural air flow is caused by pressure difference: it will flow from a zone of higher pressure towards a lower pressure. Pressure differences may be due to two effects.

Stack effect occurs when the air inside a vertical stack is warmer than the outside air (provided that there are both inlet and outlet openings). The warmer air will rise and will be replaced at the bottom of the stack by cooler outside air. A good example of this is a chimney flue: when heated, it will cause a considerable 'draught'. Ventilating shafts are often used for internal bathrooms or toilets, which are quite successful in a cool climate.

Stack effect can also occur within a room of significant height, if it has both a high level outlet and a low level inlet. The air flow will be proportional to the height difference between inlet and outlet openings and to the temperature difference between the air within the stack (or room air) and the outdoor air (Fig. 1.15). In low-rise buildings such stack effects are quite small, but – for example – in the staircase of a multistorey building it can develop into a howling gale. In warm climates the outdoor air may be just as warm

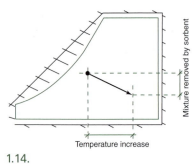

1.14.
Adiabatic dehumidification.

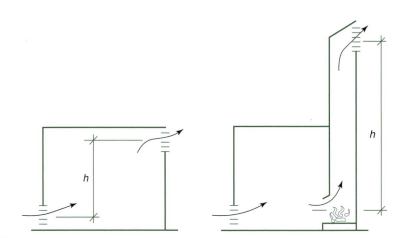

1.15.
Stack effect in a room and in a chimney.

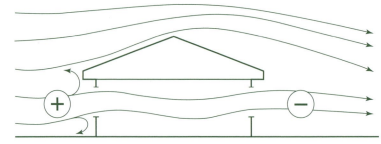

1.16.
Wind effect: cross-ventilation.

as the stack air, so there will be no air flow, or if the stack air is cooler, it can produce a down-draft.

A special case that could be considered as an 'enhanced stack effect' is the *solar chimney*, where at least one side of the stack is exposed to solar radiation and has a high absorptance. This will be heated, it heats the air inside, thus the inside–outside temperature difference is increased, which in turn would increase the air flow.

Wind effects are normally much more powerful. On the windward side of a building a positive pressure field will develop, where the pressure is proportional to the square of the velocity. At the same time a negative (reduced) pressure field may develop on the leeward side and the difference between the two pressures can generate quite a strong cross-ventilation (Fig. 1.16).

Method sheet M.1.2 gives ways of estimating the air flow that would result from stack and wind effects.

1.2 THERMAL COMFORT

1.2.1 Thermal balance and comfort

The human body continuously produces heat by its metabolic processes. The heat output of an average body is often taken as 100 W, but it can vary from about 70 W (in sleep) to over 700 W in heavy work or vigorous activity

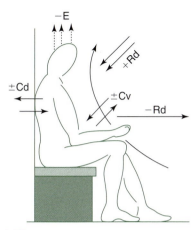

1.17.
Heat exchanges of the human body.

(e.g. playing squash). This heat must be dissipated to the environment, or else the body temperature will increase. This deep-body temperature is normally about 37°C, whilst the skin temperature can vary between 31 and 34°C.

The body's thermal balance can be expressed as (see Fig. 1.17)

$$M \pm Rd \pm Cv \pm Cd - Ev = \Delta S \qquad (1.8)$$

where M = metabolic heat production
  Rd = net radiation exchange
  Cv = convection (including respiration)
  Cd = conduction
  Ev = evaporation (including respiration)
  ΔS = change in stored heat.

A condition of equilibrium is that the sum (i.e. the ΔS) is zero and such an equilibrium is a precondition of thermal comfort. However, comfort is defined as 'the condition of mind that expresses satisfaction with the thermal environment, it requires subjective evaluation'. (ASHRAE, 1997) This clearly embraces factors beyond the physical/physiological.

1.2.2 Factors of comfort

The variables that affect heat dissipation from the body (and thus also thermal comfort) can be grouped into three sets:

Environmental	Personal	Contributing factors
Air temperature	Metabolic rate (activity)	Food and drink
Air movement	Clothing	Body shape
Humidity	State of health	Subcutaneous fat
Radiation	Acclimatization	Age and gender

Air temperature is the dominant environmental factor, as it determines convective heat dissipation. Air movement accelerates convection, but it also changes the skin and clothing surface heat transfer coefficient (reduces surface resistance), as well as increases evaporation from the skin, thus produces a physiological cooling effect. This can be estimated by eq. (1.24), given in Section 1.4.2). Subjective reactions to air movement are:

<0.1 m/s	Stuffy
To 0.2	Unnoticed
To 0.5	Pleasant
To 1	Awareness
To 1.5	Draughty
>1.5	Annoying

but under overheated conditions air velocities up to 2 m/s may be welcome.

Maslow (1984) proposed a 'hierarchy of human needs' and suggested that starting with the dominant item 1, any further needs can (and will) only be satisfied if all lower levels had been satisfied:

1 physical/biological
2 safety/ survival
3 affection/belonging
4 esteem (self- and by others)
5 self-actualization.

Thermal comfort is one of the basic physical/biological needs. For survival our deep-body temperature must stay around 37°C. It is therefore imperative to keep thermal conditions in buildings within acceptable limits, before any of the 'higher level' needs could even be considered.

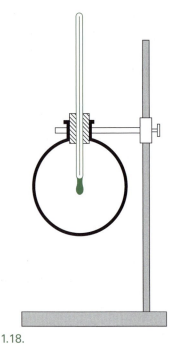

1.18.
Globe thermometer.

Medium humidities (RH 30–65%) do not have much effect, but high humidities restrict evaporation from the skin and in respiration, thus kerb the dissipation mechanism, whilst very low humidities lead to drying out of the mucous membranes (mouth, throat) as well as the skin, thus cause discomfort.

Radiation exchange depends on the temperature of surrounding surfaces, measured by the MRT, or mean radiant temperature. This is the average temperature of the surrounding surface elements, each weighted by the solid angle it subtends at the measurement point.

The unit of solid angle is the steradian (sr), that subtended by unit area (r^2) of the surface at the centre of a sphere of unit radius (r) (see also Fig. 2.5). As the surface area is $4\pi r^2$, the centre point will have a total of 4π sr (per analogiam: the radian is an angular measure, a unit where the arc length is equal to the radius; as the circumference of a circle is $2\pi r$, the complete circle is 2π radians).

The MRT cannot be measured directly, only by a black globe thermometer, which responds to radiant inputs as well as to air temperature. This may be a 150 mm diameter copper ball, painted matt black, with a thermometer at its centre (Fig. 1.18) but recently matt black painted ping pong balls have been used to measure the globe temperature (GT), to the same effect. When the air velocity is zero, MRT = GT but there is a correction for air movement:

$$MRT = GT \times (1 + 2.35\sqrt{v}) - 2.35 \times DBT\sqrt{v}$$

where v = air velocity in m/s.

The effect of this MRT depends on clothing. In warm climates (with light clothing) it is about twice as significant as the DBT, which gave rise to the *environmental temperature*:

$$EnvT = \frac{2}{3}MRT + \frac{1}{3}DBT$$

but in cooler climates (people with heavier clothing) it has about the same influence as the DBT, hence the *dry resultant temperature*:

$$DRT = \frac{1}{2}MRT + \frac{1}{2}DBT$$

At or near comfort levels the difference between DBT and MRT should not be greater than about 3 K.

Metabolic rate is a function of activity level. The unit devised for this is the *met*, which corresponds to 58.2 W/m² of body surface area.

Du Bois (1916) proposed the equation for body surface area (the Du Bois area) as: $A_D = 0.202 \times M^{0.425} \times h^{0.725}$, where M is body mass (kg) and h is height (m). For a man of M = 80 kg, h = 1.8 m, this area is 2 m².

For an average person this would be about 115 W. With higher levels of met a cooler environment will be preferred, to facilitate the heat dissipation.

Clothing is thermal insulation of the body. It is measured in units of *clo*. which means a *U*-value of 6.45 W/m^{2}K (or a resistance of 0.155 m^{2}K/W) over the whole body surface. 1 clo corresponds to a 3-piece business suit, with cotton underwear. Shorts and short-sleeved shirts would give about 0.5 clo, an over-coat may add 1 or 2 clo units to a business suit and the heaviest type of arctic clothing would be some 3.5 clo (see Section 1.2.4 below). If clothing can be freely chosen, it is an important adjustment mechanism, but if it is constrained (e.g. by social conventions or work safety) in a warm environment, it should be compensated for by a cooler air temperature. Acclimatization and habit (being used to …) is a strong influence, both physiologically and psychologically.

Food and drink habits may have an influence on metabolic rates, thus have an indirect effect on thermal preferences. These effects may be changing in time, depending on food and drink intake. Body shape is significant in that heat production is proportional to body mass, but heat dissipation depends on body surface area. A tall and skinny person has a larger surface-to-volume ratio, can dissipate heat more readily, can tolerate warmer temperatures than a person with a more rounded body shape.

This effect is increased by the fact that subcutaneous fat is a very good insulator, will thus lower the preferred temperatures.

At one stage it has been suggested that females prefer about 1 K warmer temperatures than males, but recently this difference has been attributed to differing clothing habits. Age does not make much difference in preferred temperature, but older people have less tolerance for deviations from the optimum, probably because their adjustment mechanisms are impaired.

1.2.3 Adjustment mechanisms

The body is not purely passive, it is *homeothermic*, it has several thermal adjustment mechanisms. The first level is the vasomotor adjustments: *vaso-constriction* (in a cold environment) will reduce the blood flow to the skin, reduce skin temperature, reduce heat dissipation; *vasodilation* (in a warm situation) will increase blood flow to the skin, thus the heat transport, elevate the skin temperature and increase heat dissipation.

If, in spite of the appropriate vasomotor adjustment there remains an imbal-ance, in a warm environment sweat production will start, providing an evap-orative cooling mechanism. The sustainable sweat rate is about 1 L/h, which absorbs about 2.4 MJ/L of body heat (which constitutes a cooling rate of some 660 W). If this is insufficient, *hyperthermia* will set in, which is a circula-tory failure, the body temperature may reach 40°C and heat stroke may occur.

Conversely, in a cold environment shivering will start, which is involuntary muscular work, increasing the heat production by up to a factor of 10. If this cannot restore equilibrium, *hypothermia* would set in, with possible fatal consequences.

There are also longer-term adjustments, after a few days of exposure up to about 6 months. It may involve cardiovascular and endocrine adjustments.

In a hot climate this may consist of increased blood volume, which improves the effectiveness of vasodilation, enhanced performance of the sweat mecha-nism, as well as the readjustment of thermal preferences.

Humphreys (1978) examined a large number of comfort studies, correlated thermal neutrality with the prevailing climate and for free-running buildings suggested the equation

$$Tn = 11.9 + 0.534T_{o.av}$$

(where $T_{o.av}$ is the month's mean outdoor temperature) thus laid the foundation of the adaptability model.

Auliciems (1981) reviewed the above data, supplemented it by others and proposed the equation

$$Tn = 17.6 + 0.31T_{o.av}$$

Since then many other workers found similar correlations, e.g.: Griffiths (1990):

$$Tn = 12.1 + 0.534T_{o.av}$$

Nicol and Roaf (1996):

$$Tn = 17 + 0.38T_{o.av}$$

A very large study by de Dear et al. (1997) produced correlations and suggested eq. (1.9) which is practically the same as the Auliciems expression. This is the one here adopted.

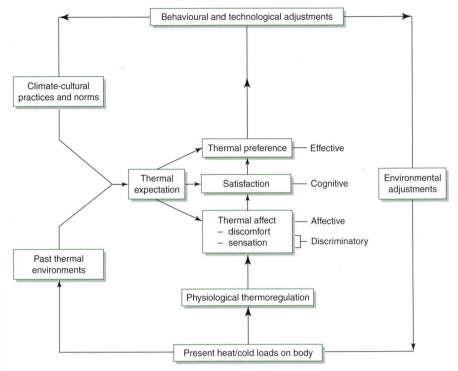

1.19.
The psycho-physiological model of thermal perception.

Under continued underheated conditions the vasoconstriction may become permanent, with reduced blood volume, whilst the body metabolic rate may increase. These adjustments are however not only physiological, there is a strong psychological aspect as well: getting used to the dominant conditions, accepting the prevailing conditions as 'normal'.

The adjustment of seasonal preferences can be quite significant, even over a period of a month. Extensive studies showed that the 'neutrality temperature' (the median of many peoples' votes) changes with the mean temperature of the month, as

$$Tn = 17.8 + 0.31 \times T_{o.av} \qquad (1.9)$$

where $T_{o.av}$ is the mean temperature of the month.

Auliciems (1981) offered a psycho-physiological model of thermal perception, which is the basis of the adaptability model (Fig. 1.19).

1.2.4 Comfort indices, comfort zone

The range of acceptable comfort conditions is generally referred to as the comfort zone. The temperature limits of such a comfort zone can be taken relative to the above Tn (neutrality temperature) for 90% acceptability as from $(Tn - 2.5)°C$ to $(Tn + 2.5)°C$.

As thermal comfort is influenced by another three environmental variables, attempts have been made since the early 1900s to create a single figure comfort index, which would express the combined effect of all four (or at

Yagloglou (1927) devised the ET (effective temperature) scale to recognize the effect of humidity on thermal sensation. ET coincides with DBT at the saturation curve of the psychrometric chart and 'equal comfort lines' are sloping down to the right.

This and the nomogram derived have been widely used, not only in the USA (e.g. by most ASHRAE publications) but also in the UK (e.g. Vernon and Warner, 1932; Bedford, 1936; Givoni, 1969; Koenigsberger *et al.*, 1973).

Gagge *et al.* (1974) in the light of more recent research, created the 'new effective temperature' scale, denoted ET* (ET star). This coincides with DBT at the 50% RH curve. Up to 14°C humidity has no effect on thermal comfort (ET* = DBT) but beyond that the ET* lines have an increasing slope. The slopes were analytically derived, differing for various combinations of activity and clothing.

Recognizing this difficulty, Gagge *et al.* (1986) devised the SET (standard effective temperature) scale, which is here also adopted.

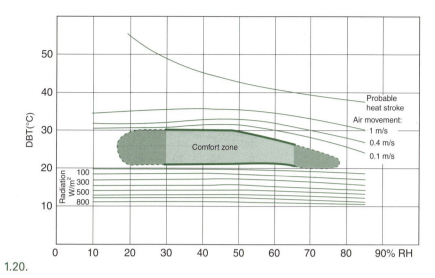

1.20.
Olgyay's bioclimatic chart, converted to metric, modified for warm climates.

least several) of these variables. The first one was proposed by Houghten and Yagloglou in 1927, named 'effective temperature'. At least 30 different such indices have been produced over the years by various research workers, all based on different studies, all with different derivations and names.

Olgyay (1953) introduced the 'bioclimatic chart' (Fig. 1.20) which has the RH on the horizontal and the DBT on the vertical axis, and the aerofoil shape in the middle is the 'comfort zone'. Curves above show how air movement can extend the upper limits and lines below it show the extension by radiation.

The latest comfort index now generally accepted, is the ET* (ET star) or new effective temperature, and its standardized version, the **SET**.

The ET* constructed for 0.57 clo and 1.25 met has been found to be valid for pairs of conditions such as (an increase in met could be compensated for by a decrease in clo):

met	clo
1	0.67
1.25	0.57
2	0.39
3	0.26
4	0.19

so this is now referred to as SET.

The SET isotherms are shown in Fig. 1.6 drawn on the psychrometric chart. The SET coincides with DBT at the 50% RH curve. The slope of the SET lines indicates that at higher humidities the temperature tolerance is reduced, whilst at lower humidities higher temperatures are acceptable. Up to 14°C the SET lines coincide with the DBT. Above that the slope of these isotherm lines is progressively increasing, with the slope coefficient taken as X/Y or DBT/AH = $0.023 \times (T - 14)$ which gives the deviation from the corresponding vertical DBT line for each g/kg AH, positive below the 50% and negative above it.

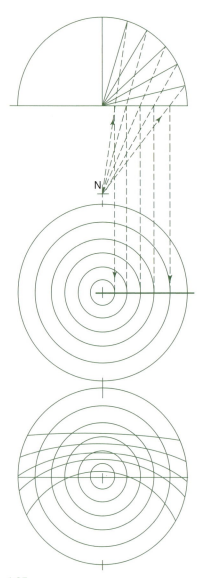

1.25.
Stereographic projection method.

1.3.1.1 Sun-path diagrams

Sun-path diagrams or solar charts are the simplest practical tools for depicting the sun's apparent movement. The sky hemisphere is represented by a circle (the horizon). *Azimuth* angles (i.e. the direction of the sun) are given along the perimeter and *altitude* angles (from the horizon up) are shown by a series of concentric circles, 90° (the zenith) being the centre.

Several methods are in use for the construction of these charts. The orthographic, or parallel projection method is the simplest, but it gives very compressed altitude circles near the horizon. The equidistant method is in general use in the US, but this is not a true geometrical projection. The most widely used are the stereographic charts (developed by Phillips, 1948). These are constructed by a radial projection method (Fig. 1.25), in which the centre of projection is vertically below the observer's point, at a distance equal to the radius of the horizon circle (the nadir point).

The sun-path lines are plotted on this chart for a given latitude for the solstice days, for the equinoxes and for any intermediate dates as described in method sheet M.1.4. For an equatorial location (LAT = 0°) the diagram will be symmetrical about the equinox sun-path, which is a straight line; for higher latitudes the sun-path lines will shift away from the equator. For a polar position the sun paths will be concentric circles (or rather an up and down spiral) for half the year, the equinox path being the horizon circle, and for the other half of the year the sun will be below the horizon. The shifting of sun paths with geographical latitudes is illustrated by Fig. 1.26.

The date-lines (sun-path lines) are intersected by hour lines. The vertical line at the centre is noon. Note that on equinox dates the sun rises at due east at 06:00h and sets at due west at 18:00h. As an example a complete sun-path diagram for latitude 36° is given as Fig. 1.27.

The time used on solar charts is solar time, which coincides with local clock time only at the reference longitude of each time zone. Every 15° longitude band gives 1h difference (360/24 = 15), therefore every degree longitude means a time difference of 60/15 = 4 min.

For example for Brisbane, longitude 153°E the reference longitude is 150° (10h ahead of Greenwich); the 3° difference means that the local clock time is $3 \times 4 = 12$ min behind solar time (i.e. at solar noon the clock shows only 11:48h).

1.3.1.2 Solar radiation

Its quantity can be measured in two ways:

1 Irradiance, in W/m² (in older texts referred to as 'intensity'), i.e. the instantaneous flux- or energy flow density, or 'power density' (see Fig. 1.28)
2 Irradiation, in J/m² or Wh/m², an energy quantity integrated over a specified period of time (hour, day, month or year).

(see also Section 1.4.1)

The sun's surface is at a temperature of some 6000°C, thus the peak of its radiant emission spectrum is around the 550 nm wavelength, extending

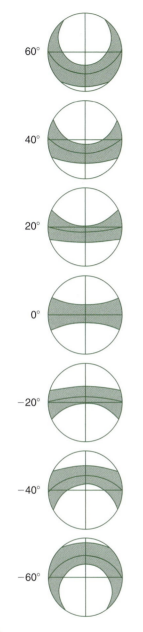

1.26.

The shift of sun-path lines on the solar chart, with latitudes.

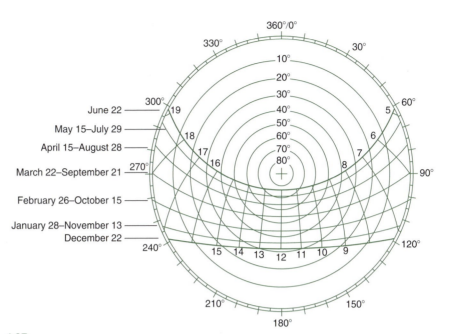

1.27.

A stereographic sun-path diagram for latitude 36° (e.g. Tokyo).

from 20 to 3000 nm. According to human means of perception we can distinguish:

a UV radiation, 20–380 nm (most of the UV below 200 nm is absorbed by the atmosphere, thus some sources give 200 nm as the lower limit), which produces photochemical effects, bleaching, sunburn, etc.

b Light, or visible radiation, from 380 (violet) to 700 nm (red)

c Short infrared radiation, 700–2300 nm, or thermal radiation, with some photochemical effects (for wavelengths see also Fig. 1.2).

If a graph of continuously changing solar radiation is drawn against time (Fig. 1.28), the ordinate represents irradiance and the area under the curve is irradiation (the 10 a.m. irradiance is numerically the same as irradiation for the hour 9:30–10:30).

At the outer limits of the earth's atmosphere the annual mean value of irradiance is 1353 W/m^2, measured at normal incidence, i.e. on a plane perpendicular to the direction of radiation. This is referred to as the 'solar constant', but it varies ±2% due to variations in the sun's emission itself and ±3.5% due to the changing earth–sun distance.

As the earth's radius is 6376 km (6.376 × 10^{6}m), its circular projected area is (6.376 × 10^6)^2 × 3.14 ≈ 127 × 10^{12} m^2, it continuously receives a radiant energy input of 1.353 × 127 × 10^{12} ≈ 170 × 10^{12} kW. Some 50% reaches the earth's surface and enters the terrestrial system. Ultimately all of it is re-radiated, this being a condition of equilibrium (see Fig. 1.36).

There are large variations in irradiation amongst different locations on the earth, for three reasons:

1 angle of incidence: according to the cosine law (Fig. 1.29) the irradiance received by a surface is the normal irradiance times the cosine of the INC

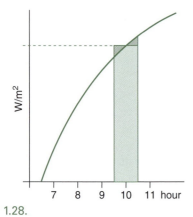

1.28.
Irradiance and irradiation (ordinate: irradiance, area irradiation).

2 atmospheric depletion, a factor varying between 0.2 and 0.7, mainly because at lower altitude angles the radiation has to travel along a much longer path through the atmosphere (especially through the lower, denser and most polluted layer), but also because of variations in cloud cover and atmospheric pollution (Fig. 1.30)

3 duration of sunshine, i.e. the length of daylight period (sunrise to sunset) and to a lesser extent also on local topography.

The maximum irradiance at the earth's surface is around 1000 W/m² and the annual total horizontal irradiation varies from about 400 kWh/m²y near the poles to a value in excess of 2500 kWh/m²y in the Sahara desert or north-western inland Australia.

As Fig. 1.31 shows, some 31% of solar radiation arriving at the earth is reflected, the remaining 69% enters the terrestrial system. Some is absorbed in the atmosphere and a little more than 50% reaches the ground surface.

1.3.2 Global climate, greenhouse effect

At the global level climates are formed by the differential solar heat input and the almost uniform heat emission over the earth's surface. Equatorial regions receive a much greater energy input than areas nearer to the poles. Up to about 30° N and S latitudes the radiation balance is positive (i.e. the solar 'income' is greater than the radiant loss), but at higher latitudes the heat loss far exceeds the solar input. Differential heating causes pressure differences and these differences are the main driving force of atmospheric phenomena (winds, cloud formations and movements), which provide a heat transfer mechanism from the equator towards the poles.

In the absence of such heat transfer the mean temperature at the north pole would be −40°C, rather than the present −17°C and at the equator it would be about 33°C and not 27°C as at present.

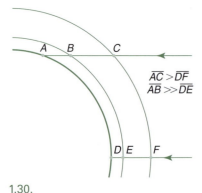

Area C > Area B   irrad C < irrad B INC
C = B/cos INC $G_C = G_B \times \cos INC$

1.29.
Angle of incidence.

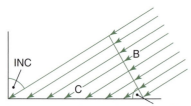

$$\overline{AC} > \overline{DF}$$
$$\overline{AB} \gg \overline{DE}$$

1.30.
Radiation path-lengths through the atmosphere.

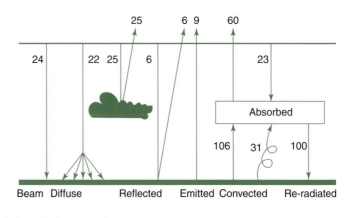

Beam Diffuse   Reflected   Emitted Convected   Re-radiated

1.31.
Radiation balance in the atmosphere.

IN: 24 + 22 + 25 + 6+23 = 100%   Reflected: 25 + 6 = 31%   Emitted: 9 + 60 = 69%
OUT: 25 + 6+9 + 60 = 100%   (31 + 69 = 100%)

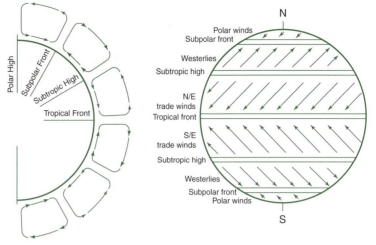

1.32.
The global wind pattern.

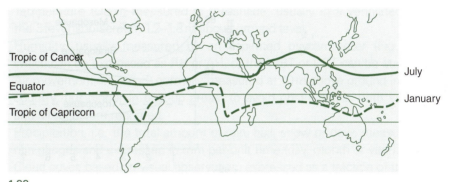

1.33.
North–south shift of the ITCZ.

At points of strong heating the air rises and at a (relatively) cold location it sinks. The movement of air masses and of moisture-bearing clouds is driven by temperature differentials, but strongly influenced by the *Coriolis force*, explained below (Fig. 1.32):

A 'stationary' air mass at the equator in fact moves with the earth's rotation and it has a certain circumferential velocity (some 1600 km/h or 463 m/s), hence it has a moment of inertia. As it moves towards the poles, the circumference of the earth (the latitude circle) is reducing; therefore it will overtake the surface. An air mass at a higher latitude has a lesser velocity and inertia, and when moving towards the equator (a larger circumference), it will lag behind the earth's rotation. This mechanism causes the N/E and S/E trade winds.

The tropical front, or ITCZ (inter-tropical convergence zone) moves seasonally north and south (with a delay of about 1 month behind the solar input, thus extreme north in July and south in January), as shown in Fig. 1.33. Note that the movement is much larger over continents than over the oceans.

The atmosphere is a very unstable three-dimensional system, thus small differences in local heating (which may be due to topography and ground cover) can have significant effects on air movements and influence the swirling patterns of low and high pressure (cyclonic and anticyclonic) zones.

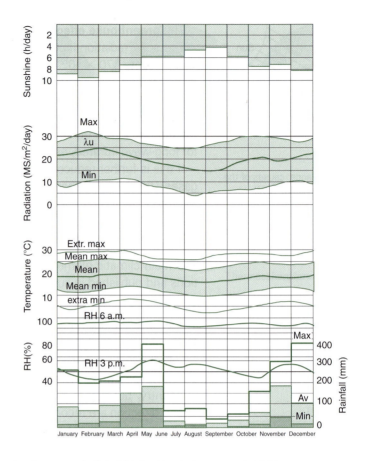

1.38.

A composite climate graph (Nairobi) (after Koenigsberger *et al.*, 1973).

For all but the most detailed thermal performance analysis the following data are adequate, as a minimum requirement (see tabulation, as Fig. 1.39):

- Temperature: monthly means of daily maxima (°C)
  – standard deviation of its distribution (K)
  monthly means of daily minima (°C)
  – standard deviation of its distribution (K)
- Humidity: early morning RH (%)
  early afternoon RH (%)
- Rainfall: monthly totals (mm)
- Irradiation: monthly mean daily total (Wh/m^2)

Such data may also be presented in graphic form, e.g. as Fig. 1.38.

Figure 1.39 is in fact a sample of the climatic database of the program-package ARCHIPAK, that is briefly described in method sheet M.1.8. The inclusion of standard deviations of temperatures allows the calculation of various percentile values of the variable.

Much more detailed data may be required for the purposes of some thermal response simulation programs, such as hourly data for a year, which itself may be a composite construct from many years of actual data. Such data are available for some locations in digital format, referred to as 'weather-tapes or files'.

Much effort has been spent on producing a year of hourly climatic data, variously referred to as TRY (test reference year) or TMY (typical meteorological year) or WYEC (weather year for energy calculations). These are

Climatic data for NAIROBI											Latitude: −1.2°	
	Jan	Feb	Mar	Apr	May	Jun	Jul	Aug	Sep	Oct	Nov	Dec	
T.max	25	26	26	24	23	22	21	22	24	25	23	23	°C
SD. max	1.7	1.7	1.5	1.1	1.7	1.6	1.5	1.5	1.5	1.1	1.1	1.2	K
T.min	11	11	13	14	13	11	9	10	10	12	13	13	°C
SD min	2	1.7	1.2	1.2	2.2	2.5	2.5	2	1.6	1.2	1.7	2	K
RH a.m.	95	94	96	95	97	95	92	93	95	95	93	95	%
RH p.m.	48	42	45	55	61	55	57	53	48	45	56	55	%
Rain	88	70	96	155	189	29	17	20	34	64	189	115	mm
Irrad	6490	6919	6513	5652	4826	4664	3838	4047	5245	5629	5489	6024	Wh/m²

(standard deviations are estimated only)

1.39.
The simplest set of climatic data.

required and used by various computer programs to simulate the thermal performance of buildings and consequent energy use.

The US program DoE-2 includes a large number of 'weather files', hourly data for a sample year of a whole range of variables. TMY2 is derived from the SAMSON database of NREL (National Renewable Energy Laboratories). The primary source is the US NCDC (National Climatic Data Center). Typical Weather Years (TWY) for Canada have been developed by the University of Waterloo. Many TRY sets do not include solar radiation data. In Australia the Bureau of Meteorology provides data (www.bom.gov.au). The most comprehensive database is METEONORM, (www.meteotest.ch/eu/mn) containing data for over 7400 locations world-wide.

There are many levels of simplification, such as using 3-hourly data or representing each month by a typical sequence of 3 days of hourly data. For the purposes of all calculations in this book the above described monthly mean data are adequate.

1.3.3.1 Wind data

Wind data are best presented graphically. Several different types of wind roses can be used for this purpose. One method presents a separate wind rose (Fig. 1.40) for each month (or sometimes one wind rose representing 3 months, i.e. four wind roses representing the four seasons of the year). The length of lines radiating from a small circle is proportionate to the frequency of wind from that direction. Different line thicknesses may indicate wind velocity categories.

For architectural purposes the most useful form of wind rose is an octagon, with 12 lines on each side, corresponding to the 12 months, from January to December in a clockwise direction, where the length of a line is proportionate to the frequency (% of observations) of wind from that direction in that month. If the winds were evenly distributed, all lines would extend to the outer octagon, which indicates a line length of 12.5%. Small dashes on the inside of the base octagon indicate that there is no wind in that month from that direction (Fig. 1.41).

The 12 numbers inside the graph give the % of total calm periods for the 12 months. It is usual to give a wind rose for an early morning and one for a mid-afternoon hour. Often two such graphs are shown, one for 9 a.m. and one for 3 p.m.

These may be supplemented by a tabulated wind frequency analysis, such as that shown in Fig. 1.42 for one month. (Bureau of Meteorology, Australia, 1988).

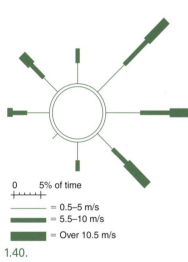

0   5% of time

——— = 0.5–5 m/s
▬▬ = 5.5–10 m/s
▬▬ = Over 10.5 m/s

1.40.
A wind rose for one month.

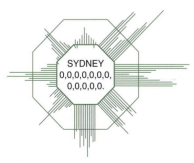

SYDNEY
0,0,0,0,0,0,0,0,
0,0,0,0,0.

1.41.
An annual wind rose.

9 a.m. January calm 25 km/h	N	NE	E	SE	S	1859 observations SW	W	NW	All
1–10	1	1	1	9	22	3	1	1	39
11–20	1	–	–	5	21	2	–	1	30
21–30	–			1	4	–	–	–	6
>30				–	–	–			1
all	2	1	1	15	47	5	1	2	100

3 p.m. January calm 5 km/h	N	NE	E	SE	S	1854 observations SW	W	NW	All
1–10	6	5	3	2	2	2	–	1	20
11–20	12	14	9	8	4	–	–	1	50
21–30	2	3	5	10	3	–	–	–	23
>30	–		–	2	–	–	–		3
all	20	22	17	22	10	1	1	2	100

–	less than 1%		no wind from that direction

1.42.
A wind frequency analysis, for January 9 a.m. and 3 p.m. (Cairns).

1.3.3.2 Derived data

Derived data may be useful to facilitate some quick calculations:

Degree-days (DD or Kd, Kelvin-days) or heating degree-days (HDD) is a climatic concept that can be defined as 'the cumulative temperature deficit below a set base temperature (Tb)'. In other words: the temperature deficit times its duration, summed up for the year. It can be obtained if from January 1 we go through the year day by day and whenever the mean temperature of the day (T_{av}) is less than this Tb, we write down the difference and add these up (negative differences are ignored). Thus for the year, if Tb = 18°C:

$$DD = Kd = \Sigma(18 - T_{av}) \quad \text{(from day 1 to 365)}$$

or generally

$$DD = Kd = \Sigma(Tb - T_{av}) \tag{1.10}$$

Such sums can be produced separately for each month.

Degree-hours can be estimated as Dh = Kh = Kd × 24, but more accurately a summation similar to the above can be carried out on an hourly basis. If T_h = hourly temperature:

$$Kh = \Sigma(18 - T_h) \quad \text{(from hour 1 to 8760)} \tag{1.11}$$

or indeed, separately for each month.

This can also be visualized from a continuous temperature graph (Fig. 1.43) as the area under the curve measured below the Tb level, where the ordinate is in K (degrees temperature difference) and the abscissa in h (hours), therefore the area is Kh, Kelvin-hours or degree-hours[5]. Method sheet M.1.9

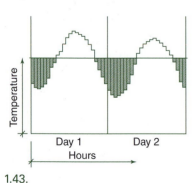

1.43.
Definition of degree-hours (Kh).

[5]Kd and Kh are the preferred terms, to avoid confusion with American DD data given in terms of °F.

Cooling DD:

This is nowhere near as reliable as the heating requirement calculation, as cooling requirements depend also on solar heat gain (which is different for each building surface and also depends on fenestration), internal heat gain and on atmospheric humidity (the determinant of latent heat load). There are methods of making some allowance for these (making assumptions of 'average conditions') but these have no general validity.

shows the calculation for converting degree-days into degree-hours from monthly mean data to any base temperature, which can be used if the standard deviation of the temperature distribution is known.

The concept is useful for estimating the annual (or monthly) heating requirement. Kelvin-hours is the climatic parameter used and the building parameter is the *building conductance* (specific heat loss rate) (q). The heating requirement (Htg) is the product of the two:

$$Htg = Kh \times q \quad (Kh \times W/K = Wh) \tag{1.12}$$

Sometimes the 'cooling degree-days' (or degree-hours) concept is used for the estimation of cooling requirements. This is conceptually similar to the above, but the base temperature is usually taken as 26°C and the temperatures in excess of this base are considered:

$$CDD = \Sigma(T_{av} - 26) \quad \text{(from day 1 to 365)}$$

1.3.4 Classification of climates

Many different (and some very complex) systems of climate classification are in use, for different purposes. Some are based on vegetation, others on evapotranspiration. Some serve the purposes of agriculture, some are used in human health studies. The most generally used system is the Köppen–Geiger classification, which distinguishes some 25 climate types. This is shown in Fig. 1.44, followed by a tabulation of the main types.

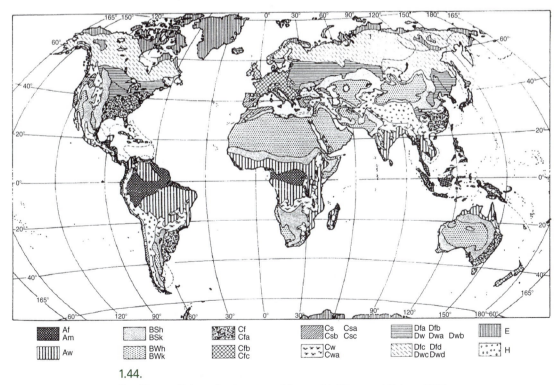

1.44.

The Köppen–Geiger climate zones of the world. (Köppen of Geiger, 1936).

The Köppen–Geiger climate classification (main types)

Type	Main group	Sub-group	Second sub-group
Af	Hot	Rainy all seasons	
Am		Monsoonal rain	
Aw		Dry winter	
As		Dry summer	
Bsh	Dry	Semi-arid steppe	Very hot
Bsk			Cold or cool
Bwh		Arid	Very hot
Bwk			Cold and cool
Cfa	Mild winter	Moist all seasons	Hot summer
Cfb			Warm summer
Cfc			Cool short summer
Cwa		Dry winter	Hot summer
Cwb			Warm summer
Csa		Dry summer	Hot summer
Csb			Warm summer
Dfa	Severe winter	Moist all seasons	Hot summer
Dfb			Warm summer
Dfc			Short cool summer
Dfd			Very cold winter
Dwa		Dry winter	Hot summer
Dwb			Cool summer
Dwc			Short cool summer
Dwd			Very cold winter
ET	Polar climate	Short summer allows tundra vegetation	
EF		Perpetual ice and snow	

For the purposes of building design a simple system (after Atkinson, 1953), distinguishing only four basic types, is adequate. This is based on the nature of the human thermal problem in the particular location (Fig. 1.45):

1 **Cold** climates, where the main problem is the lack of heat (underheating), or an excessive heat dissipation for all or most of the year.
2 **Temperate** (moderate) climates, where there is a seasonal variation between underheating and overheating, but neither is very severe.
3 **Hot-dry** climates, where the main problem is overheating, but the air is dry, so the evaporative cooling mechanism of the body is not restricted. There is usually a large diurnal (day–night) temperature variation.
4 **Warm-humid** climates, where the overheating is not as great as in hot-dry areas, but it is aggravated by high humidities, restricting the evaporation potential. The diurnal temperature variation is small.

Sometimes we consider also the following sub-types:

• island or trade-wind climate
• maritime desert climate
• tropical highland climate.

or indeed 'composite climates', with seasonally changing characteristics.

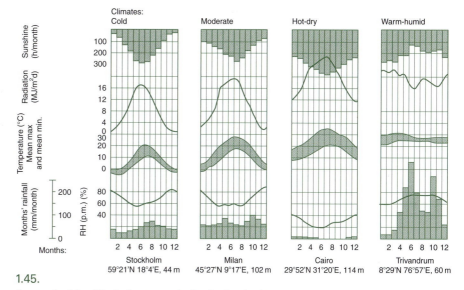

1.45.

Composite (simplified) climate graphs for the four basic types.

Use of the composite climate graphs allows a visual appreciation at a glimpse of the differences of the four basic climates.

There are distinct seasonal variations in the first three. Both the temperature and the solar radiation curves are stepping up, except the last one, which shows very small seasonal variations. Contrast the rainfall histogram and humidity curves of Cairo and Trivandrum.

1.4   THERMAL BEHAVIOUR OF BUILDINGS

A building can be considered as a thermal system, with a series of heat inputs and outputs (analogous to eq. (1.8) for the human body):

Qi – internal heat gain
Qc – conduction heat gain or loss
Qs – solar heat gain
Qv – ventilation heat gain or loss
Qe – evaporative heat loss.

The system can be depicted by the following equation:

$$Qi + Qc + Qs + Qv + Qe = \Delta S \tag{1.13}$$

where ΔS is a change in heat stored in the building.

Thermal balance exists when the sum of all heat flow terms, thus ΔS, is zero:

If the sum is greater than zero, the temperature inside the building is increasing, or if it is less than zero, the building is cooling down.

The system can be analysed assuming *steady-state* conditions, i.e. that both the indoor and the outdoor conditions are steady, non-changing or we can consider the building's dynamic response. The former may be valid when the diurnal changes are small compared with the indoor–outdoor temperature difference, or as the basis of finding the required heating or cooling capacity, under assumed "design" conditions, or – indeed – as a first approach to fabric design.

The most significant energy input into a building is solar radiation. The next section examines the solar heat input and its control, this will be followed by the other components of eq. (1.13).

1.4.1 Solar control

The first task in solar control is to determine when solar radiation would be a welcome input (solar heating for the underheated period) or when it should be excluded (the overheated period). This overheated period can then be outlined on the sun-path diagram (take the sun-path dates as the *Y*-axis and the hours as the *X*-axis, the only difference being that here both axes are curved). The performance of a shading device is depicted by a *shading mask*, which can be constructed with the aid of the shadow-angle protractor (Fig. 1.46). This is then superimposed on the diagram, corresponding to the window's orientation. A device is to be found, the shading mask of which covers the overheated period.

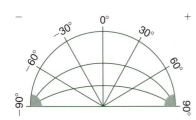

1.46.

The shadow-angle protractor.

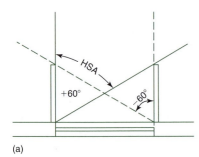

(a)

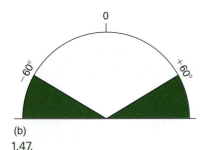

(b)

1.47.

Plan of a pair of vertical devices (fins) and their shading mask.

1.4.1.1 Shading design

Shading design for the exclusion of solar input is a geometrical task. External shading devices are the most effective tools to control sun penetration. Three basic categories of shading devices can be distinguished:

1 **Vertical devices**, e.g. vertical louvres or projecting fins. These are characterized by *horizontal shadow angles* (HSA) and their shading mask will be of a sectoral shape (Fig. 1.47). By convention HSA is measured from the direction of orientation (i.e. from the surface normal), positive in clockwise and negative in the anticlockwise direction. The HSA cannot be greater than 90° or less than −90°, as that would indicate that the sun is behind the building. These devices may be symmetrical, with identical performance from left and right, or asymmetrical. They are most effective when the sun is towards one side of the direction the window is facing. We may distinguish the 'device HSA' (as above) and the 'solar HSA', which is the required performance at a given time.

2 **Horizontal devices**, e.g. projecting eaves, a horizontal canopy or awning, or horizontal louvres (Fig. 1.48). These are characterized by a *vertical shadow angle* (VSA). One large or several small elements may give the same performance, the same VSA. Their shading mask, constructed by using the shadow-angle protractor (see method sheet M.1.4), will be of a segmental shape. They are most effective when the sun is near-opposite to the window considered.

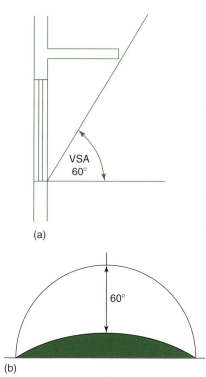

(a)

(b)

1.48.

A horizontal device (a canopy) and its shading mask.

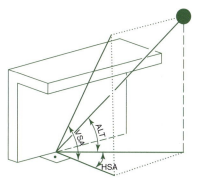

1.49.

Relationship of ALT and VSA.

3 The "solar VSA" is the same as the ALT (altitude) only when the sun is directly opposite the window (when AZI = ORI, or solar HSA = 0). When the sun is to one side of the surface normal, its altitude must be projected onto a vertical plane perpendicular to the window (Fig. 1.49). For the calculation of these angles see method sheet M.1.3.

4 *Egg-crate devices*, e.g. concrete grille blocks, metal grilles. These produce complex shading masks, combinations of the above two and cannot be characterized by a single angle. An example of this is shown in Fig. 1.50.

A window facing the equator (south in the northern hemisphere and due north in the southern hemisphere) is the easiest to handle, it can give an automatic seasonal adjustment: full shading in summer but allowing solar heat gain in winter (Fig. 1.51). For complete summer 6 months sun exclusion (for an equinox cut-off) the VSA will have to be VSA = 90° − LAT; e.g. for LAT = 36° it will be VSA = 90 − 36 = 54°.

This shading mask exactly matches the equinox sun-path line. For other dates the match is not so exact, but still quite similar to the sun-path line. For orientations other than due north the situation is not so simple. A combination of vertical and horizontal devices may be the most appropriate answer.

The suggested procedure is the following (refer to Fig. 1.52):

1 Draw a line across the centre of the sun-path diagram, representing the plan of the wall face considered (i.e. the surface normal being the orientation). During any period when the sun is behind this line, its radiation would not reach that wall, thus it is of no interest. The illustration shows a north-east orientation (LAT = − 36°, ORI = 45°).

2 Mark on the sun-path diagram the period when shading is desirable. In the illustration this shading period is taken as the summer 6 months, i.e. its boundary is the equinox sun-path line (heavy outline).

3 Select a shading mask, or a combination of shading masks which would cover this shading period, with the closest possible match.

4 Several combinations of vertical and horizontal shadow angles may give satisfactory results:
– a combination of VSA = 30° and HSA = + 20° would give the required shading, but would also exclude the winter sun from about 10:00 h, which is undesirable
– a combination of VSA = 47° and HSA = + 0° would also provide complete shading for 6 months, but still exclude the mid-winter sun after 12:00 h (noon)
– a combination of VSA = 60° and HSA = + 20° may be an acceptable compromise: on February 28 the sun would enter from 09:20 to 11:00 h (a little longer in early March).

1.4.1.2 Radiation calculations

At any location and with respect to a surface of any orientation (ORI) and any tilt angle (TIL) the INC is continuously changing. For any desired point in time it can be calculated by the expressions given in method sheet M.1.3.

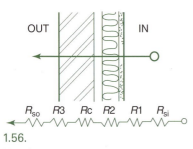

1.56.
Heat flow through a wall through the three material layers and a cavity: in series, thus the **resistances** must be added.

Any cavity or air gap may also offer a resistance (Rc), thus the air-to-air resistance of an element will be (Fig. 1.56)

$$R_{a-a} = R_{si} + R1 + R2 + Rc + R3 + R_{so}$$

where $R1$, $R2$ = resistance of material layers
Rc = the resistance of any cavity.
Data sheet D.1.4 also gives cavity resistance values.
The U-value is the reciprocal of this R_{a-a}.
U-values of many elements are given in data sheets D.1.2 and D.1.3, but it can also be calculated from its component resistances.
The actual total conduction heat flow rate of the building will be

$$Qc = qc \times \Delta T \qquad (1.26)$$

or $Qc = \Sigma(A \times U) \times \Delta T$

where $\Delta T = T_o - T_i$, the difference between outside and inside air temperature. ΔT and Qc are negative for heat loss, positive for heat gain.

1.4.3.2 Insulation
Insulation means the control of heat flow, for which three different mechanisms can be distinguished: reflective, resistive and capacitive.

Reflective insulation: where the heat transfer is primarily radiant, such as across a cavity or through an attic space, the emittance of the warmer surface and the absorptance of the receiving surface determine the heat flow. A shiny aluminium foil has both a low emittance and a low absorptance, it is therefore a good reflective insulator. It will be effective only if it is facing a cavity, so it does not itself have an R-value, but it modifies the R-value of the cavity. For example, a cavity at least 25 mm wide, in a wall would have the following resistances:

– with ordinary building materials 0.18 m²K/W
– if one surface is lined with foil 0.35
– if both surfaces are lined with foil 0.6 (see data sheet D.1.4 for further data).

A reflective surface in contact with another material would have no effect, as heat flow would take place by conduction.

An often asked question (in hot climates) is: what would be more effective to reduce downward heat flow in an attic space, to have a foil (a) on top of the ceiling, with its face upwards (relying on its low absorptance) or (b) under the roof skin, with face down (relying on its low emittance). The two would be equally effective, when new. However, in less than a year the foil over the ceiling would be covered in dust, so its low absorptance destroyed, therefore solution (b) would be better on the long run.

In a hot climate, where the downward heat flow is to be reduced, this solution (b) could be very effective, but almost useless in a cold climate, in reducing upward heat flow. Here the top of the ceiling (of a heated room) is warm, will heat the air adjacent to it, which will then rise and transmit its

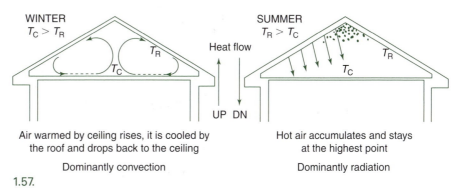

WINTER
$T_C > T_R$

SUMMER
$T_R > T_C$

Heat flow

UP   DN

Air warmed by ceiling rises, it is cooled by
the roof and drops back to the ceiling

Hot air accumulates and stays
at the highest point

Dominantly convection

Dominantly radiation

1.57.
Heat flow through an attic space: foil is very effective when $T_{roof} > T_{ceiling}$.

heat to the underside of the roof. So the upward heat transfer is dominantly convective, unaffected by the foil. Figure 1.57 shows that the downward heat transfer is primarily radiant (strongly affected by the foil): the heated air will remain adjacent to the roof skin, as it is lighter than the rest of the attic air, so there will be practically no convective transfer.

On this basis some authors suggest that in a hot climate such a foil insulation under the roof skin is preferable to resistive insulation. It will reduce downward heat flow, but will allow the escape of heat at night, thus permit the building to cool down; act practically as a 'thermal diode'. A resistive insulation would affect the up and down heat flow almost equally.

Resistive insulation of all common materials, air has the lowest thermal conductivity: 0.025 W/m K (other values are given in data sheet D.1.1), as long as it is still. However, in a cavity, convection currents will effectively transfer heat from the warmer to the cooler face. The purpose of resistive insulation is just to keep the air still, dividing it into small cells, with the minimum amount of actual material. Such materials are often referred to as 'bulk insulation'. The best ones have a fine foam structure, consisting of small closed air cells separated by very thin membranes or bubbles, or consist of fibrous materials with entrapped air between the fibres.

The most often used insulating materials are expanded or extruded plastic foams, such as polystyrene or polyurethane or fibrous materials in the form of batts or blankets, such as mineral wool, glass fibres or even natural wool. Loose cellulose fibres or loose exfoliated vermiculite can be used as cavity fills or as poured over a ceiling. Second class insulators include strawboard, wood wool slabs (wood shavings loosely bonded by cement), wood fibre softboards and various types of lightweight concrete (either using lightweight aggregate or autoclaved aerated concrete).

Heat flow into (and out of) buildings is driven by two external (climatic) forces: air temperature and solar radiation. The expressions used for calculating these heat flows are summarized in Table 1.3.

1.4.3.3 Thermal bridges
Thermal bridges usually cause multidimensional (steady-state) heat flow. In the above discussion the assumption was made that heat flows through an envelope element with the flow path being perpendicular to the plane of that element, i.e. the phenomenon is analysed as a *one-dimensional heat*

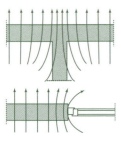

1.58.
Thermal bridge due to geometry.

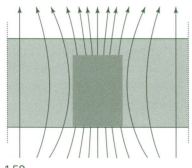

1.59.
Thermal bridge in mixed construction.

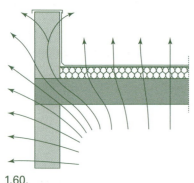

1.60.
The above two effects combined.

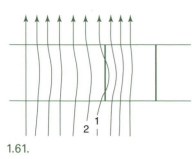

1.61.
A concrete column in a brick wall.

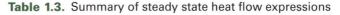

Table 1.3. Summary of steady state heat flow expressions

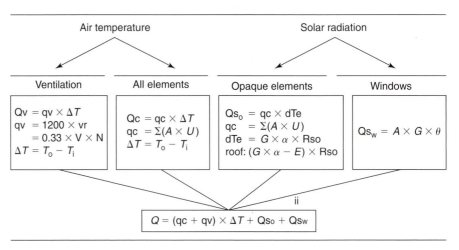

	Air temperature		Solar radiation	
Ventilation	All elements	Opaque elements	Windows
$Q_v = q_v \times \Delta T$ $q_v = 1200 \times v_r$ $\quad = 0.33 \times V \times N$ $\Delta T = T_o - T_i$	$Q_c = q_c \times \Delta T$ $q_c = \Sigma(A \times U)$ $\Delta T = T_o - T_i$	$Q_{s_o} = q_c \times dT_e$ $q_c = \Sigma(A \times U)$ $dT_e = G \times \alpha \times R_{so}$ roof: $(G \times \alpha - E) \times R_{so}$	$Q_{s_w} = A \times G \times \theta$

$$Q = (q_c + q_v) \times \Delta T + Q_{s_o} + Q_{s_w}$$

flow. This is true only for infinitely large elements with parallel plane surfaces and uniform cross-section. The results obtained with calculation techniques presented above are therefore approximate only.

In real building elements the criteria of one-dimensional heat flow are often not fulfilled. Where the boundaries are other than plane parallel surfaces, or the material is not homogeneous, two- or three-dimensional heat flows develop. Areas where increased, multidimensional heat flow occurs are called *thermal bridges*. These may be consequences of the geometric form (Fig. 1.58), including corner effects, the combination of materials of different conductivities (Fig. 1.59) or both (Fig. 1.60).

Temperature distribution around thermal bridges

Heat flow will be greater along the shortest path, the path of least resistance. In Fig. 1.61 the resistance along flow path 1 is less than it would be along a line perpendicular to the surface, due to the higher conductivity of the column. Along flow path 2 the resistance is less, due to the bigger 'cross-section', not 'occupied' by other flows. In a heat loss situation the heat flow density will be greater at thermal bridges, therefore the surface temperature outside increased and inside reduced.

Heat flows in the direction of the steepest temperature gradient, as water flows in the direction of the steepest slope (Fig. 1.62). Thus the heat flow paths are at right angles to the isotherms (an isotherm is the locus of points of equal temperature). In Fig. 1.63 the density of heat flow paths indicates an increased heat flow, whilst the isotherms show an increased outside surface temperature at the column and a reduced inner surface temperature.

If, as in Fig. 1.64 an insulating element is inserted (here: on the outside face of the concrete column), which blocks the heat flow, the temperature in the highly conductive column will be higher than in the adjoining wall, therefore a sideways heat flow will occur, increasing the flow density near the column. The outside surface temperature over the insulating insert will be lower and next to this insert higher than of the plain wall.

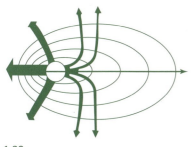

1.62.
Heat flows 'downhill'.

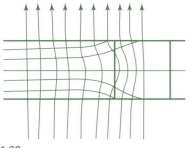

1.63.
Temperature distribution near a thermal bridge (explaining Fig. 1.61).

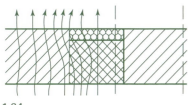

1.64.
Flow paths when column is insulated.

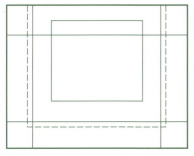

1.65.
The whole area of a wall module is affected by thermal bridges.

As a rule of thumb, the effect of thermal bridges diminishes to negligible levels beyond a strip of a width of twice the wall thickness. If the wall thickness is 300 mm, the width of this strip is approximately 600 mm, in both directions from the edge. Viewing a usual room size facade element and marking these strips along the joints it can be seen that there is no area on this element that would be free of thermal bridge effects and of multidimensional temperature distribution (Fig. 1.65). For further discussion of thermal bridges see Section 1.5.1 and data sheet D.1.5.

Capacitive insulation will be considered in the following section.

1.4.4 Dynamic response of buildings

Capacitive insulation, i.e. material layers of a high thermal capacity (massive construction) affect not only the magnitude of heat flow, but also its timing. Both reflective and resistive insulation respond to temperature changes instantaneously. As soon as there is a heat input at one face, a heat output on the other side will appear, albeit at a controlled rate. Not so with capacitive insulation. This relies on the thermal capacity of materials and their delaying action on the heat flow.

In a non-steady, randomly varying thermal environment the tracing of heat flows requires sophisticated and lengthy calculation methods, which are feasible only if included in computer programs. There is a sub-set of non-steady heat flow regimes, the *periodic heat flow*, the analysis of which is relatively easy. Fortunately, most meteorological variables (temperature, solar radiation) show a regular variation, a repetitive 24-h cycle. The following discussion relates to such a periodic heat flow analysis.

Periodic heat flow is illustrated in Fig. 1.66 over a 24-h period. The solid line is the heat flow through an actual masonry wall and the dashed line is the heat flow through a "zero-mass" wall of the same *U*-value. This curve would be the result if we calculated the heat flow by a steady-state method for each hour and connected the points.

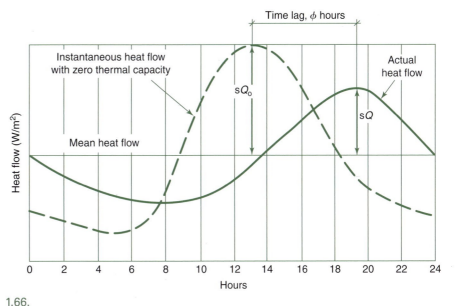

1.66.
Heat flow through a real wall, compared with a wall of zero mass.

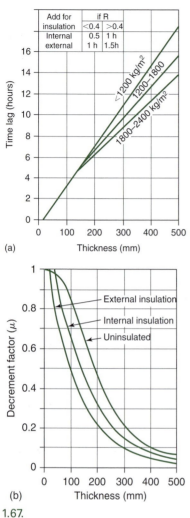

(a)

(b)

1.67.

Time lag and decrement factors for solid homogeneous walls.

Both curves show a 24-h cycle, but they differ in two ways:

1 The actual heat flow curve is delayed behind the zero-mass curve by some time. This delay of the peak of the solid curve behind the peak of the dashed-line curve is referred to as the **time lag** (or phase-shift, denoted ϕ) measured in hours.

2 The amplitude or swing of the peak from the daily average heat flow is smaller for the solid line (sQ), than for the dashed line showing the wall of zero mass (sQ$_0$). The ratio of the two amplitudes is referred to as the **decrement factor**, or amplitude decrement, denoted μ:

$$\mu = \frac{sQ}{sQ_0}$$

A similar diagram could be drawn with temperature on the vertical scale. The dashed line would then show temperatures of the outer surface and the solid line indicating temperatures at the inside surface. From this the same two properties could be derived.

The calculation of these two properties is fairly involved, particularly for multi-layer elements, but data sheets D.1.2 and D.1.3 give these values for numerous everyday constructions, alongside their U-values. Figure 1.67 shows graphs for the time lag and decrement factor properties of solid, homogeneous massive walls (brick, masonry, concrete or earth) and the effect of insulation applied to the inside or the outside of the massive wall. These are based on the work of Danter (1960) at the BRE (Building Research Establishment), also given in Petherbridge (1974), often quoted in many publications, but seem to be superseded by Milbank and Harrington-Lynn (1974) and for a more accurate and reliable calculation of these factors see method sheet M.1.11. This method was used to find the ϕ and μ values in D.1.2 and D.1.3.

If we take a 220 mm brick wall with a U-value of 2.26 W/m²K and take a polystyrene slab of about 10 mm thickness, which would have about the same U-value, under steady-state conditions the heat flow through these two would be identical and calculations based on steady-state assumptions would give the same results. In real life their behaviour will be quite different. The difference is that the brick wall has a surface density of about 375 kg/m² and the polystyrene slab only some 5 kg/m². The respective thermal capacities would be 300 and 7 kJ/m². In the brick wall each small layer of the material will absorb some heat to increase its temperature before it can transmit any heat to the next layer. The stored heat would then be emitted with a considerable time delay.

A time sequence of temperature profiles through this wall is shown in Fig. 1.68. It can be observed that from evening hours onwards the middle of the wall is the warmest and the stored heat will also start flowing backwards. So (assuming inward heat flow) only a part of the heat that had entered the outside surface will reach the inside surface. In the polystyrene slab the temperature profile would be a sloping straight line moving up and down as the temperature changes on the input side.

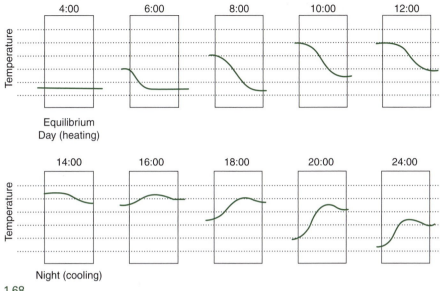

Temperature

4:00 6:00 8:00 10:00 12:00

Equilibrium
Day (heating)

Temperature

14:00 16:00 18:00 20:00 24:00

Night (cooling)

1.68.
Time sequence of temperature profiles in a massive wall (in a warm climate).

The procedure to calculate periodic heat flow consists of two parts, e.g. for a solid element:

1 find the daily mean heat flow, $\overline{Qc}$
2 find the deviation from (or swing about) this mean flow for time (hour) 't' of the day: sQc_t.

First find the mean sol–air temperature of the outside surface: $\overline{T}_{sa}$, then find the mean temperature difference $\Delta \overline{T}$ then

$$\overline{Qc} = qc \times \Delta \overline{T} \tag{1.27}$$

Then calculate the swing in heat flow at time t due to the deviation of conditions ϕ hours earlier (at time $t - \phi$) from the day's average

$$sQc_t = qc \times \mu \times (T_{sa(t-\phi)} - \overline{T}_{sa}) \tag{1.28}$$

For example if the calculation is done for 14:00 h and $\phi = 5$ h, then take the sol–air temperature at $14 - 5 = 9$ o'clock ($T_{sa9:00}$).

The heat flow at time t will then be the sum of the mean and the swing:

$$Qc_t = \overline{Qc} + sQc_t \text{ substituting:}$$

$$Qc_t = A \times U \times [(\overline{T}_{sa} - T_i) + \mu \times (T_{sa(t-\phi)} - \overline{T}_{sa})] \tag{1.29}$$

The deviation from the mean heat flow rate (sQc_t) at time t can be calculated on the basis of eq. (1.28) (included in eq. (1.29)) for a single element. The following Table 1.4 summarizes the six components of such flow swing. Items 3, 4 and 5 will have to be repeated for each envelope element of a different orientation.

Table 1.4. Expressions for the swing in heat flow

		Building parameter	Environmental parameter
1	Ventilation	$sQv = qv$	$\times (T_{o.t} - T_{o.av})$
2	Conduction, glass	$sQc_g = A \times U$	$\times (T_{o.t} - T_{o.av})$
3	Conduction, opaque	$sQc_o = A \times U \times \mu$	$\times (T_{o(t-\phi)} - T_{o.av})$
4	Solar, glass	$Qs_g = A \times \theta_a$	$\times (G_t - G_{av})$
5	Solar, opaque	$sQs_o = A \times U \times \mu \times \alpha \times Rso$	$\times (G_{t-\phi} - G_{av})$
6	Internal gain	$sQi = Qi_t - Qi_{av}$	

where μ = decrement factor, ϕ = time lag, θ_a = alternating solar gain factor,
$qv = 0.33 \times N \times V$ or $1200 \times vr$ (N = number of air changes, vr = volume rate).

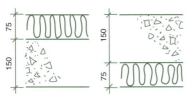

1.69.

Sequence of layers in an insulated concrete roof slab.

The benefits of capacitive insulation (or mass effect) will be greatest in hot-dry climates, which show large diurnal temperature variations. Some sources suggest that a mean range (the range between monthly mean maximum and minimum, averaged for the 12 months) of 10 K would warrant heavy construction, others put this limit at 8 K. Capacitive insulation has a dampening, stabilizing effect, it can improve comfort or, if the building is conditioned, produce energy savings.

The dynamic properties (time lag, decrement factor and admittance) of multilayer elements depend not only on the material and thickness of layers, but also on the sequence of these layers with respect to the direction of heat flow. This is best illustrated by an example (Fig. 1.69).

EXAMPLE 1.3

Take a roof slab of 150 mm reinforced concrete, with 75 mm of EPS insulation (the waterproof membrane is thermally negligible) and consider a summer (heat gain) situation.

The air-to-air resistance will be

$$R_{a-a} = R_{so} + R_{EPS} + R_{concr} + R_{si}$$

$$= 0.04 + \frac{0.075}{0.035} + \frac{0.150}{1.4} + 0.14 = 2.43$$

$$U = 1 / R_{a-a} = 1 / 2.43 = 0.41 \, W/m^2 K$$

This is the same, regardless of the sequence of layers, but for dynamic properties:

	ϕ (hour)	μ	Y_{inside} (W/m²K)
EPS externally	6.28	0.3	5.41
EPS internally	5.03	0.56	0.44
Difference	1.25	0.26	4.97

The last column (Y) is the *admittance* of the element, which is the measure of its ability to pick up (and release) heat from the indoors, as the temperature changes (swings). Y has a strong influence when indoor temperatures are to be calculated which result from the heat flows.

The total admittance of a building (or of a room) is

$$qa = \Sigma(A \times Y) \quad \text{in W/K} \tag{1.30}$$

The EPS externally produces a time lag some 1.25-h longer, reduces the decrement factor from 0.56 to a little over half (to 0.3) and gives an inside surface admittance some 4.97W/m²K more than the reverse order of layers. So, the mass inside of a resistive insulation will reduce the heat gain, delay it more and result in a more stable indoor temperature.

For a summary of dynamic thermal properties see method sheet M.1.10.

1.4.4.1 Thermal response simulation

Thermal response simulation of buildings became an everyday design tool with the rapid development of computers, since the 1970s. PCs are now more powerful than the early mainframe computers and can run the most sophisticated simulation programs.

Relatively simple programs have been produced, which use basically steady-state type calculations adding some 'fudge factor' to approximate dynamic behaviour, e.g. QUICK or BREDEM (BRE domestic energy model). A number of programs are based on the time lag and decrement factor concepts introduced above (a harmonic analysis), and using the 'admittance procedure' of the UK BRE (e.g. ADMIT and ARCHIPAK) to find the temperatures resulting from such heat flows. These analyse the dynamic thermal response, but in a strict sense, do not 'simulate' the various heat flows.

There are numerous programs which trace the heat flow hour-by-hour through all components of the building, using an annual hourly climatic data base (such as those mentioned in Section 1.3.3). These can predict hourly indoor temperatures or the heating/cooling load if set indoor conditions are to be maintained. Some go further and simulate the mechanical (HVAC (heating, ventilation or air conditioning)) systems, thus predict the energy consumption for the hour, the day, the month or the year.

CHEETAH (of the CSIRO) became the basis of the Australian NatHERS (National House Energy Rating Scheme) and AccuRate (accurate rating). ENERGY10 of ENREL (National Renewable Energy Laboratory, Colorado) is a design tool especially for passive solar, but generally for low energy buildings. The most sophisticated of these is ESPr, of the University of Strathclyde (said to solve up to 10 000 simultaneous differential equations), and it is now the European reference simulation program. The most widely used one is the US DoE-2. This is now available to run under Windows, whilst ESPr can now be run on PCs under the LINUX operating system.

The package called TAS of EDSL (Environmental Design Solutions Ltd of Milton Keynes) has a full-fledged 3-D CAD module, as a front end for simulations, down to a CFD (computerized fluid dynamics) module for air flow studies.

Hong *et al.* (2000) reviewed more than a dozen such programs.

COMBINE (of the EU Joule program) integrates a number of CAD and simulation programs, including ESPr, SUPERLITE and VENT. In a similar manner, in America EnergyPlus combines DOE2, BLAST (Building Loads and System Thermodynamics) and COMIS, a multi-zone air flow program.

More detailed discussion of this topic is outside the scope of this work.

1.4.5 Application

The whole is more than the sum of its parts – a statement as true for the thermal behaviour of buildings as in perception psychology.

In perception psychology there are two main schools of thought: the behaviourists analyse simple stimulus-reaction relationships and try to build up an overall picture from such building blocks, whilst followers of the Gestalt school profess that the 'configuration', the totality of experience, the interaction of all sensory channels is important. In a similar way one can discuss the thermal effect of individual building components, but the thermal behaviour of any building will be the result of the interaction of all its elements, of the climate-building-services-user relationship. In this sense we can speak of the 'thermal Gestalt' of a building.

A simple example of this interdependence is the question of roof insulation in a warm climate. There is no doubt that increased roof insulation would reduce daytime (solar) heat gain, but it will also prevent night-time dissipation of heat. Only a careful analysis will give the right answer, the best for both situations. One can quote the example of equator-facing windows, which are desirable in winter, but if the building is lightweight, without adequate thermal storage mass, the resulting heat gain may produce overheating during the day; the user will get rid of this by opening the windows, so there will be no heat left to soften the coldness of the night.

In some texts the use of skylights is advocated as an effective energy conservation measure. It is undoubtedly useful for daylighting, but it produces more solar heat gain in the summer (with high angle sun) than in winter, and in winter in most cases it will be a net loser of energy. It depends how it is done.

Over the last 10 years – or so – there was a battle raging over the usefulness of courtyards in hot-dry climates. Both the protagonists and adversaries produced measured results. The resolution is that it depends on how the courtyard is treated. It can be both good and bad.

The answer to any simple question is usually quite complicated, and most of it is of the 'if ... then ...' type. When the designer asks what the width of eaves of a house should be, the answer can only be: 'It depends ...' and a long sequence of counter-questions, such as where is the house? in what climate? what is the overheated period? what is the orientation? is it single or double storey? is a window considered or a door with glass down to floor level?

The architect must make thousands of (larger or smaller) decisions during the design of even the simplest building. There is no time to analyse every single question in detail. However, the analytical attitude is important. The designer working in a given climate, given culture and the given building industry, will probably examine such questions once and remember the answer. Many such answers derived from serious analysis will enrich his/her experience. Accumulated experience (including experience of failures or the experience of others) may make quick decisions possible but would also suggest what factors, what conditions would have a bearing on a given question. And this is what constitutes professional know-how.

1.5   THERMAL DESIGN: PASSIVE CONTROLS

The first step in any bioclimatic design approach is to examine the given climate and establish the nature of the climatic problem: relate the climate to human requirements. A good way of doing this is to use the psychrometric chart as the base.

Once the comfort zone for winter and summer has been plotted (as in Section 1.2.4, Fig. 1.21), the climate can be plotted on the same diagram.

Mark on the chart two points for each of the 12 months: one using the mean maximum temperature with the afternoon RH and one using the mean minimum temperature with the morning RH. Connect the two points by a line. The 12 lines thus produced would indicate the median zone of climatic conditions. The relationship of these lines to the comfort zone indicates the nature of the climatic problem. Lines to the right of the comfort zone indicate overheating, to the left underheating. Lines above the 12 g/kg limit indicate that humidity may be a problem. Long lines indicate large diurnal variations, short ones are characteristic of humid climates with small diurnal variations.

Figure 1.70 (printouts of the ARCHIPAK program) shows psychrometric plots for each of the four basic climate types.

The next step would then be the choice of passive control strategy. Four basic strategies can be distinguished, with some subdivisions in each.

1 passive solar heating (with efficiency or *utilizability* of 0.5 and 0.7)
2 mass effect (summer and winter + for summer with night ventilation)
3 air movement (physiological cooling) effect, for 1 and 1.5 m/s
4 evaporative cooling (direct and indirect).

The range of outdoor conditions, for which each of these strategies has the potential to ensure indoor comfort (referred to as the CPZ or control potential zone) can be outlined on the psychrometric chart. The method is described in method sheet M.1.7 but introduced here for each of these strategies.

1.5.1   Passive control of heat flows

In climates where there is a large temperature difference between the inside and the outside (the climate lines extend far from the comfort zone), where some form of heating or cooling will be necessary, thermal insulation of the

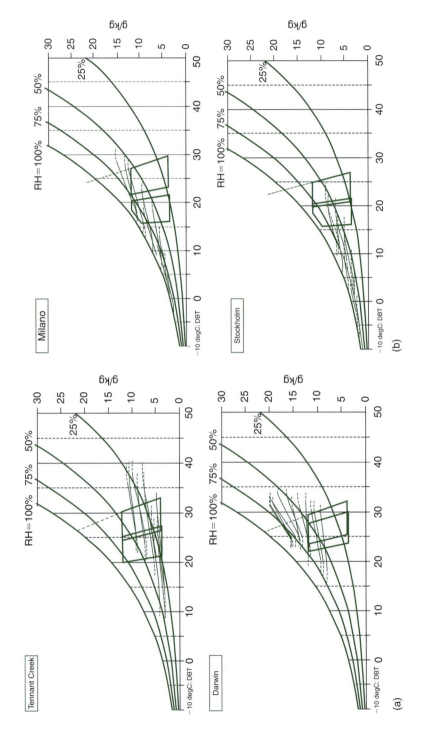

1.70.

Four basic climate types vs. the local comfort zones

Tennant Creek: *Hot-dry* a dry climate with large diurnal ranges (long lines), hot summer and cool winter nights

Darwin: *Warm-humid* little variation in comfort between summer and winter, mostly over-humid

Milano: *Temperate* comfortable summer, cool but not too severe winter

Stockholm: *Cold* large seasonal difference in comfort conditions, rarely reaches comfort.

envelope is the most important means of control. In most countries there are regulatory requirements for the insulation of envelope elements, walls, roofs and windows. These may stipulate a maximum U-value (which must not be exceeded) or a minimum R-value (R_{a-a}) which must be achieved by the construction.

EXAMPLE 1.4

Assume that we propose to have a 260 mm cavity brick wall (105 + 50 + 105), with 10 mm plastering on the inside. Conductivities are:

Facing brick (outer skin): $\lambda = 0.84$ W/m K
Inner skin of brick: $\lambda = 0.62$
Plastering $\lambda = 0.5$

Inside R_{si}	= 0.12 m²K/W
10 mm plastering 0.010/0.5	= 0.02
105 mm inner brick 0.105/0.62	= 0.17
Cavity Rc	= 0.18
105 mm outer brick 0.105/0.84	= 0.12
Outside surface R_{so}	= 0.06
R_{a-a}	= 0.67 $U = 1/0.67 = 1.49$ W/m²K

The regulations require (say)
$U \leq 0.8$ W/m²K $R_{a-a} > 1/0.8 =$ **1.25**

Additional R required: $1.25 - 0.67 = 0.58$

Consider using EPS boards inside the cavity, held against the inner skin of brick, which has a conductivity of $\lambda = 0.033$ W/m K.
The required thickness (b for 'breadth') will be:
as $R = b/\lambda$,
we need 0.58 m²K/W $= b/0.033$ $b = 0.58 \times 0.033 = 0.019$ mm
that is we must install a 20 mm EPS board.

This method can be generalized, to say that take the resistance of the construction selected for reasons other than thermal and find the additional resistance required. From that the necessary thickness of added insulation can be found.

Thermal bridge effects (discussed in Section 1.4.3.3) can be allowed for by using linear heat loss coefficients, k (see data sheet D.1.5) in addition to the U-value-based calculation. Dimensionally these coefficients are W/m K and are to be multiplied by the length, to give W/K.

This is illustrated by an example.

EXAMPLE 1.5

Assume that a wall element of 5 m length and 3 m height is at the corner of a building and it incorporates a window of 2.5×1.5 m dimensions. There is an internal partition joining at the other end. The wall is of the construction examined above ($U = 0.8$ W/m²K) and the window is double glazed, with a U-value of 3.6 W/m²K (Fig. 1.71).

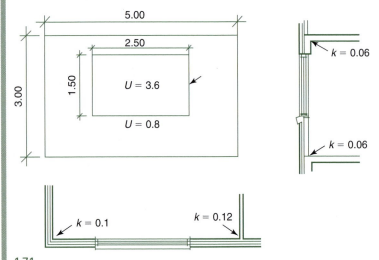

1.71.

Locations of thermal bridges: linear heat loss coefficients (k).

The wall is $5 \times 3 = 15$ m² less the window: $2.5 \times 1.5 = 3.75$ m² net wall area $= 11.25$ m².

The $A \times U$ products are:

$$
\begin{array}{l}
\text{wall } 11.25 \times 0.8 = 9 \text{ W/K} \\
\underline{\text{window } 3.75 \times 3.6 = 13.5} \\
\qquad\qquad\qquad\quad 22.5 \text{ W / K}
\end{array}
$$

The following linear losses must be added (values from data sheet D.1.5):

$$
\begin{array}{r}
\text{for the window perimeter } 8\,\text{m} \times 0.15 = 1.2 \\
\text{for the outer corner } 3\,\text{m} \times 0.1 = 0.3 \\
\text{for the wall/partition junction } 3\,\text{m} \times 0.12 = 0.36 \\
\underline{\text{for the wall/floor slab joints } 2 \times 5\,\text{m} \times 0.06 = 0.6 \text{ W/K}} \\
2.46 \text{ W/K}
\end{array}
$$

so the average U-value will be

$$
U_{av} = \frac{22.5 + 2.46}{15} = 1.66 \text{ W/m}^2\text{K}
$$

in a generalized form:

$$
U_{av} = \frac{\Sigma(A \times U) + \Sigma(L \times k)}{\Sigma A}
$$

where L is the length of each linear component.

A quick look at any table of U-values would show that the weakest point of any building envelope is the window. Whilst even an uninsulated brick wall (as in Example 1.4) would have a U-value around 1.5 W/m²K, an ordinary single glazed window would be about four times as much, 5.5–6.5 W/m²K.

The U-value of a window depends on

1 the glazing: single, double, low-e, etc.
2 the frame : wood, metal, discontinuous metal
3 frame thickness: 10–30% of the elevational area of the window
4 exposure: sheltered, normal, exposed.

A window with a sealed double glazing unit would have a U-value of 2.7–4.3 W/m²K, depending on the frame. A wood frame has a lower U-value than a metal one, but the latter can be improved by a built-in discontinuity (which would break the thermal bridge effect of the frame).

A low emittance coating inside a sealed double glazing unit would reduce the radiant heat transfer and a low pressure inert gas (krypton or argon) fill (partial vacuum) would reduce the conductive transfer. Such glazing, with a discontinuous 10% metal frame (where the frame takes up 10% of the overall window area) would have a U-value as low as 2.0W/m²K.

A good window must perform five functions:

1 provide a view
2 admit daylight
3 reduce heat loss
4 admit solar heat (in a cold situation)
5 allow a controllable ventilation.

In a cold situation a large window may be a liability. It would cause a large heat loss, but it could also produce a significant solar heat gain. A comparison can be made between heat loss and gain in a very simple way, based on a unit area of window.

EXAMPLE 1.6

Taking Canberra as an example, calculate the gains and losses over a day of the coldest month (July). Comparison can be made for a unit area:

$T_{o.av}$ = 5.8°C. Take T_i as 23°C, thus the ΔT is 17.2 K
Take a single glazed window: U = 5.3 W/m²K and solar gain factor: θ = 0.76
Orientation: North, daily vertical irradiation $D_{v.360}$ = 2801 Wh/m²

Assume a solar 'efficiency' (utilizability) of 0.7
Gain: 2801 × 0.76 × 0.7 = 1490 Wh/m²
Loss: 5.3 × 17.2 × 24 = 2188
Loss > Gain, thus the window is not beneficial.

However, if double glazing is used, U = 3 W/m²K, θ = 0.64.
Gain: 2801 × 0.64 × 0.7 = 1255 Wh/m²
Loss: 3 × 17.2 × 24 = 1238
Loss < Gain, thus it is beneficial (marginally).

If we look at the same window, facing east: $D_{v.90}$ = 1460 Wh/m²
Gain: 1460 × 0.64 × 0.7 = 654 Wh/m²
Loss: same as above = 1238
Loss >>Gain.∴ the window would be a liability.

The situation changes if we use an insulating shutter overnight.

Assume one that would reduce the *U*-value with single glazing to 1.5 and with double glazing to 1.3 W/m²K and that it would be closed for 14 h. The (daytime) gain is the same as above. The loss will be

single glazing: $(1.5 \times 14 + 5.3 \times 10) = 1272$ Wh/m²   1490 > 1272 ∴ OK
double glazing: $(1.3 \times 14 + 3 \times 10) = 829$ 1255 > 829 ∴ OK

1.5.1.1 Passive solar heating

Passive solar heating in its simplest form requires no more than a good window facing the equator. An appropriate horizontal shading device could provide shading in the summer but allow the entry of solar radiation in the winter (see Fig. 1.51). Adjustable shading could also be considered. The performance of such a system would also depend on the available thermal storage mass. In a lightweight building the solar heat input would overheat the interior, which may lead to discomfort, but also to a large heat loss.

Heavy walls and floor (especially where it is reached by the solar beam) would absorb much heat, reduce the overheating and the stored heat would be released at night. The mass need not be very much. For the 24-h cycle the depth of heat penetration (the effective storage, where the heat input and release surface is the same, so there would be a cyclic reversal of heat flow) may not be more than 100–120 mm.

A massive wall exposed to solar radiation would also act as a heat collector and storage device, but much heat would be lost through the outside surface, both whilst it is heated by the sun and after sunset. Such loss could be reduced by a glazing or a transparent insulation cover on the outside. This would be recognized as a passive solar 'mass wall' heating system. However, as the wall surface behind the glass is heated, it will heat the air in the gap and cause a large heat loss, backwards, through the glazing.

This can be reduced by the 'Trombe–Michel'[6] system (Fig. 1.72), which incorporates vent openings near the floor and near the ceiling. As the heated air rises, it would enter the room through the top vent, drawing in cooler air from the room near the floor level, forming a thermosiphon circulation.

Another passive solar heating system is the 'attached greenhouse'. This can be considered as an enlargement of the air gap of the above system (of about 100 mm) to perhaps 2 m or more. The thermal function is the same as for the Trombe–Michel wall, but whilst it heats the room behind it, it also provides a useable space for plants and even for sitting, as a 'winter garden' or conservatory. At night such a greenhouse can lose much heat, so it is essential to provide for closing off the room it serves, or else it becomes a net loser of heat.

The CPZ (see above in Section 1.5.1) for passive solar heating (by whatever system) can be estimated on the following basis. The critical parameter is solar radiation on the equator-facing vertical surface, for the average day of

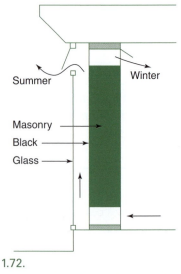

1.72.
Principles of the Trombe–Michel wall.

Summer
Winter

Masonry
Black
Glass

---

[6] Named after Jacques Michel (architect) and Felix Trombe (physicist).

the coldest month (D_v). Find the lowest temperature at which the solar gain can match the heat losses. The limiting condition will be

$$D_v \times A \times \eta = q \times (T_i - T_o) \times 24$$

where D_v = vertical irradiation (Wh/m^2 day)
  A = area of solar aperture
  η = efficiency (utilizability), taken as 0.5 or 0.7
  q = qc + qv, building conductance (W/K)
  T_i = indoor temperature limit, taken as Tn − 2.5
  T_o = the limiting temperature to be found

Assume a simple house of 100 m^2 floor area and 20% (=20 m^2) solar window and a building conductance of 115 W/K. Substituting:

$$D_v \times 20 \times 0.5 = 115 \times (T_i - T_o) \times 24$$

rearranging for T_o

$$T_i - T_o = D_v \times 20 \times 0.5 \, /(115 \times 24) = D_v \times 0.0036$$
$$T_o = T_i - 0.0036 \times D_V$$

EXAMPLE 1.7

If in Los Angeles in January

  $D_{V.180} = 3774$ Wh/m^2 and $T_{o.av} = 13°C$, Tn = 21.6°C
thus the lower limit of $T_i = 19.1°C$ then with $\eta = 0.5$, the lowest T_o that the solar gain can compensate for

  $T_o = 19.1 - 0.0036 \times 3774 = 5.5°C$

or with $\eta = 0.7$
  $T_o = T_i - 0.005 \times D_V$
  $T_o = 19.1 - 0.005 \times 3774 = 0.2°C$

which means that down to 5.5°C (or even 0.2°C) outdoor temperature the passive solar heating system has the *potential* of keeping the indoors comfortable.

This example is illustrated by Fig. 1.73 showing the CPZ for passive solar heating.

1.5.1.2 The mass effect

The mass effect provided by a heavy construction is beneficial in many situations, even without any such special devices.

In a cold climate, for a continuously occupied building (e.g. a house or a hospital), where it would allow the use of intermittent heating and still keep a stable temperature. In an intermittently used and heated building (an office or a school) lightweight (insulated) construction may be better. Massive construction would have a longer heating-up period in the morning and the stored heat would be dissipated overnight, thus wasted.

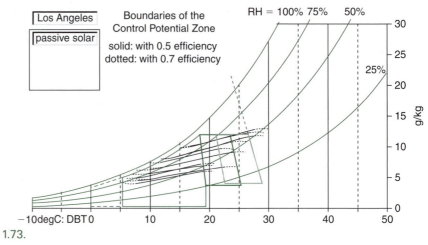

1.73.
CPZ for passive solar heating.

The same argument is valid for an air-conditioned building in a hot-humid climate, where even the nights are too warm.

The 'mass effect' is one of the most important passive control strategies. If there is a storage mass, it can be manipulated according to the climatic needs. In a typical hot-dry climate, with a large diurnal variation, where the temperature varies over the daily cycle between too high and too cold (where the day's mean is within the comfort zone) massive construction may provide the full solution, it may ensure comfortable indoor conditions without any mechanical cooling (or night heating).

What is the definition of a 'massive, heavyweight' and a 'lightweight' building? The criterion may be the *specific mass* of the building:

$$sM = \frac{\text{Total mass of the building}}{\text{Floor area of the building}} \, \frac{kg}{m^2}$$

or the CIBSE 'response factor' (f), which is defined as

$$f = \frac{qa + qv}{qc + qv} \tag{1.31}$$

where qa = total admittance (see Section 1.4.4, eq. (1.30)), qv and qc have been defined in Sections 1.4.2 and 1.4.3.1.

The boundaries for two or three divisions are

Light	<150 kg/m²	f < 3
Medium	150–400	3–5
Heavy	>400	>5
Light	≤250 kg/m²	f ≤ 4
Heavy	>250	>4

Night ventilation can be used to modify the mass effect, where the day's average is higher than the comfort limit, to assist the heat dissipation process.

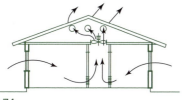

1.74.
An attic fan (or 'whole-house' fan).

This may rely on natural ventilation through windows and other openings, but can also be assisted by a 'whole-house fan' (or attic fan), operated when $T_o < T_i$. (Fig. 1.74). This is a large diameter, slow moving fan, built into the ceiling around the centre of the house. The arrangement should be such that it draws air through all rooms (fresh air inlets in the rooms served) and pushes the air out through the attic, expelling the hot air of that space. This will not provide any sensible air movement, but would help in dissipating any heat stored in the building fabric.

The potential of such a mass effect (the extent of the CPZ) can be estimated by the following reasoning: in a very massive building the indoor temperature would be practically constant at about the level of the outdoor mean.

The outdoor mean can be taken as $(T_{o.max} + T_{o.min}) \times 0.5$.

The amplitude (mean-to-maximum) would be $(T_{o.max} - T_{o.min}) \times 0.5$ but as the building will not quite cool down to the minimum, it is taken as

$$(T_{o.max} - T_{o.min}) \times 0.3$$

If the mean is to be within the comfort zone, the outdoor maximum must be less than the comfort limit plus the amplitude. So the limit of the CPZ will be the upper comfort limit + the amplitude.

EXAMPLE 1.8

If in Phoenix (Arizona) in the hottest month (August)
$T_{o.max} = 38°C$, $T_{o.min} = 25°C$, $T_{o.a} = 31.5°C$,
Tn = 27.3°C, thus upper comfort limit = 29.8°C
Amplitude = $(38 - 25) \times 0.3 = 3.9\,K$
Limit of the CPZ = 29.8 + 3.9 = 33.7°C

If the mass effect is assisted by night ventilation, the fabric will be cooled down more effectively, the amplitude will be taken as $(T_{o.max} - T_{o.min}) \times 0.6$, thus
Amplitude = $(38 - 25) \times 0.6 = 6.5\,K$
Limit of the CPZ = 29.8 + 6.5 = 36.3°C

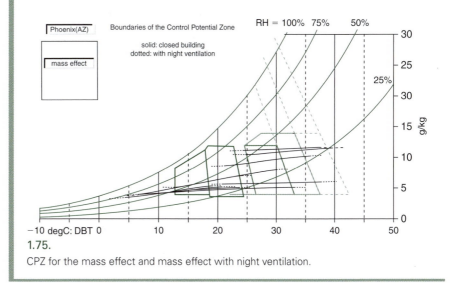

1.75.
CPZ for the mass effect and mass effect with night ventilation.

All these temperatures are taken at the 50% RH curve and the corresponding SET lines are the boundaries of the CPZ. Figure 1.75 illustrates the above example.

In a climate, where air temperatures are below comfort, solar radiation can be relied on to supplement the mass effect, to improve the indoor conditions, possibly ensuring comfort, but certainly reducing any heating requirement.

1.5.1.3 Air movement

Air movement, i.e. a sensible air velocity (as discussed in Section 1.4.2) can be relied on to provide physiological cooling. As such, it is an important tool of passive thermal control. Its apparent cooling effect can be estimated using eq. (1.24). The critical point is to ensure an air velocity at the body surface of the occupants. This may be provided by cross-ventilation, relying on the wind effect, or by electric fans, most often by low-power ceiling fans. A stack effect, relying on the rise of warm air cannot be relied on for this purpose. Firstly, it would only occur when $T_i > T_o$, and that T_i would be too high if T_o is too high. Secondly, even if it works, it may generate a significant air exchange, but not a noticeable air velocity through the occupied space. (Method sheet M.1.2 gives an estimation method for both wind and stack effects.)

Cross-ventilation demands that there should be both an inlet and an outlet opening. The difference between positive pressure on the windward side and negative pressure on the leeward side provides the driving force. The inlet opening should face within 45° of the wind direction dominant during the most overheated periods.

To produce the maximum total air flow through a space, both inlet and outlet openings should be as large as possible. The inlet opening will define the direction of the air stream entering. To get the maximum localized air velocity, the inlet opening should be much smaller than the outlet. Positioning the inlet opening, its accessories (e.g. louvres or other shading devices) as well as the aerodynamic effects outside (before the air enters) will determine the direction of the indoor air stream.

The potential of air movement effect can be estimated as follows:

The cooling effect is found using eq. (1.24) thus it will be
for 1 m/s air velocity: $dT = 6 \times 0.8 - 1.6 \times 0.8^2 = 3.8\,K$
for 1.5 m/s: $dT = 6 \times 1.3 - 1.6 \times 1.3^2 = 5.1\,K$

To define the CPZ for air movement effect these dT values are added to the upper comfort limit along the 50% RH curve. Above that the boundary will be the corresponding SET line, but below 50% there is a cooling effect even without air movement, as the air is dry, so the additional effect of the air movement is taken as only half of the above: the boundary line will be nearer to the vertical. These boundaries define the range of outdoor conditions under which air movement has the potential to render indoor conditions comfortable.

EXAMPLE 1.9

In Mombasa (lat $= -4°$) the warmest month is March, with $T_{o.av} = 29°C$ thus
Tn $= 17.6 + 0.31 \times 29 = 26.6°C$ and
upper comfort limit $= 29.1°C$
Limits of the air movement CPZs will thus be
for 1 m/s: $29.1 + 3.8 = 32.9°C$
for 1.5 m/s: $29.1 + 5.1 = 34.2°C$ as illustrated by Fig. 1.76.

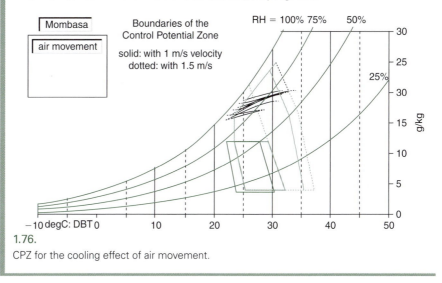

1.76.
CPZ for the cooling effect of air movement.

1.5.1.4   Evaporative cooling

Evaporative cooling can be provided as part of a passive system, for eample, by a roof pool or a courtyard pond, or by a spray over the roof or some other building surface. If evaporation occurs within an enclosed space, it may lower the DBT, but it increases the humidity, therefore the latent heat content, in effect it converts sensible heat to latent heat.

The total heat content of the system does not change, i.e. it is said to be *adiabatic*.

Indirectly, evaporation loss occurs if there is some evaporation within the space or room, which is adiabatic, but the moist air is then removed by ventilation. This process is referred to as 'mass transfer' and must be considered in air conditioning load calculations.

If the evaporation rate (er, in kg/h) is known, the corresponding heat loss will be

$$Qe = (2400/3000) \times er = 666 \times er \ (W) \tag{1.32}$$

where 2400 kJ/kg is the latent heat of evaporation of water.

A *direct evaporative cooler* (Fig. 1.77) would draw air in through fibrous pads, which are kept moist by a perforated pipe and feed it into the space to be cooled. In the process the latent heat of evaporation is taken from the air, so it is cooled, but the humidity (thus also the latent heat content) of the supply air is increased. The status point on the psychrometric chart will move up and to the left along a constant WBT line (see Fig. 1.13).

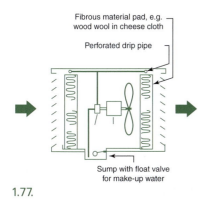

Fibrous material pad, e.g. wood wool in cheese cloth

Perforated drip pipe

Sump with float valve for make-up water

1.77.
Principles of a direct evaporative cooler.

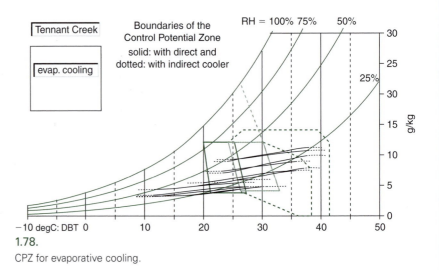

1.78.

CPZ for evaporative cooling.

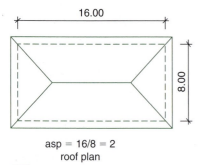

asp = 16/8 = 2
roof plan

1.79.

Definition of 'aspect ratio' (a roof plan).

For this reason, the CPZ for evaporative cooling can be defined by the WBT line tangential to the upper and lower corner of the comfort zone. It is impractical to achieve more than about 11 K cooling effect (from the Tn temperature) thus the CPZ is delimited by a vertical line at the Tn + 11°C temperature (Fig. 1.78).

The indirect evaporative cooler (shown in Fig. 1.119 on p. 91) uses two fans and a plate heat exchanger. It can still be considered as a 'passive' system, as the cooling is done by evaporation. The return air stream is evaporatively cooled and passed through the heat exchanger, to cool the fresh air intake to be supplied to the space, without the addition of any moisture. The exhaust air is then discharged. A slight increase in humidity tolerance (to 14 g/kg) can be accepted if the air is cooled, hence the upper boundary of the CPZ is a horizontal line at this level, whilst the temperature limit would be at Tn + 14 (Fig. 1.78).

The effectiveness of this system is limited by the evaporation potential of the humid air and by the performance of the heat exchanger.

1.5.2   Control functions of design variables

In this section, as a summary of previous discussions, answers to two questions will be attempted:

1 What factors influence the magnitude of each of the components of eq. (1.9)?
2 What attributes of major design variables affect the building's thermal behaviour?

1.5.2.1   Component heat flows

By what building variables are these determined or affected?

1 Qi – internal heat gain can be influenced only in a minor way, by planning: by separating any heat emitting functions from occupied spaces, or attempting to dissipate the generated heat at or near the source. The condensing coil of a refrigerator may be placed outside, or at least ventilated separately, or the control gear of fluorescent lighting could be outside the habitable space. A local exhaust could be used next to a heat generating appliance, such as a kitchen stove.

2 **Qs – solar heat gain** on opaque surfaces is influenced not only by surface properties (reflectance), but also by the shape and orientation of the building. If it is to be reduced, the solar geometry should determine the shape: larger surfaces should face the least solar exposure. Solar heat gain through windows provides the most powerful passive control. It is affected by window size, orientation, glazing material and shading devices. Adjustable shading can provide flexibility in variable climatic situations. The sun's apparent seasonal movement can provide an automatic summer/winter adjustment.

Vegetation and surrounding objects can have a strong influence on sun penetration. Deciduous plants are often used to give summer shade but allow the entry of winter sun. Whilst fenestration determines the admission of solar radiation, the thermal mass of the building affects its retention and release.

3 **Qc – conduction heat flow** is affected by the shape of the building, by the surface-to-volume ratio and by the thermal insulating qualities of the envelope. Reflective and resistive insulation affect the magnitude of the heat flow, whilst capacitive insulation also affects the timing of heat input. In a multilayer element the sequence of resistive and capacitive layers is an important factor. More stable internal conditions are achieved if the thermal mass is located inside the resistive insulation.

4 **Qv – ventilation heat flow** is influenced by the fenestration and other openings, their orientation with respect to the wind direction, their closing mechanisms and generally the air-tightness or wind permeability of the envelope. The building shape can have a strong influence on the creation of positive and negative pressure zones, which in turn influence air entry. External objects, such as fences, wing walls or even vegetation can also have an effect.

5 **Qe – evaporative cooling** is a useful technique, especially under hot-dry conditions. It can be provided by mechanical equipment, but also by purely passive systems, such as a pond or a spray. It cannot be considered in isolation: the cooled air must be retained, if it is not indoors, then, for example, by a courtyard or some other outdoor space enclosed by a solid fence. The designer must ensure that the cooling effect occurs where it is needed and that it is not counteracted by wind or solar heating.

1.5.2.2 Design variables

Design variables that have the greatest influence on thermal performance are: shape, fabric, fenestration and ventilation. These will now be briefly considered as a summary of previous discussions.

i Shape

a *Surface-to-volume ratio*: as the heat loss or gain depends on the envelope area, particularly in severe climates it is advisable to present the least surface area for a given volume. From this point of view the hemisphere is the most efficient shape, but a compact plan is always better than a broken-up and spread-out arrangement.

b *Orientation:* if the plan is other than a circle, orientation in relation to solar gain will have a strong effect. The term 'aspect ratio' (Fig. 1.79) is often used to denote the ratio of the longer dimension of an oblong plan to the shorter. In most instances the N and S walls should be longer than the E and W and the ratio would be around 1.3–2.0, depen-ding on temperature and radiation conditions. It can be optimized in terms of solar incidence and wanted or unwanted solar heat gain or heat dissipation.

ii Fabric

    a *Shading* of wall and roof surfaces can control the solar heat input. In extreme situations a 'parasol roof' can be used over the roof itself to provide shading, or a west-facing wall may be shaded to eliminate the late afternoon solar input. If the plan shape is complex, then the shading of one surface by another wing should be considered.

    b *Surface qualities*: absorptance/reflectance will strongly influence the solar heat input; if it is to be reduced, reflective surfaces are preferred. A white and a shiny metal surface may have the same reflectance, but the white would have an emittance similar to a black body at terrestrial temperatures whilst the emittance of the shiny metal is practically negligible. Thus if heat dissipation is the aim, a white surface would be preferred.

    c *Resistive insulation* controls the heat flow in both directions, it is particularly important in very cold climates (heated buildings) or in very hot climates (air-conditioned buildings).

    d *Reflective insulation*: the best effect is achieved if the (double-sided) foil is suspended in the middle of a cavity, so that both the high reflectance and low emittance are utilized. This is rarely achievable. There is no difference in magnitude between the low emittance and high reflectance effects. Deterioration in time, e.g. dust deposit should be considered, hence a foil under the roof skin, face down is better than one on top of the ceiling, face up. It affects downward heat flow more than the upward flow.

    e *Capacitive insulation* provides a very powerful control of the timing of heat input especially in climates with a large diurnal temperature swing, as it can store the surplus heat at one time, for release at another time, when it is needed.

iii Fenestration

    a *Size, position and orientation of windows* affect sun penetration, thus solar heat input, but also affect ventilation, especially where cross-ventilation (physiological cooling) is desirable.

    b *Glass*: single, double, multiple and *glass quality*: special glasses (heat absorbing or heat reflecting glasses) may be used to ameliorate an otherwise bad situation, by reducing the solar heat input. Their qualities are constant, they would reduce solar heating even when it would be desirable and would reduce daylighting. They should be considered as a last resort.

    c *Closing mechanism*: fixed glass, louvres, opening sashes, type of sashes used (Fig. 1.80).

    d *Internal blinds and curtains* can slightly reduce the solar heat input, by reducing the beam (direct) radiation, but they become heated and will re-emit that heat, thus causing convective gains.

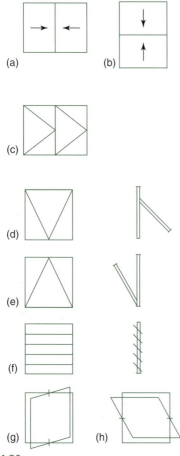

1.80.
Window types by closing mechanism: (a) horizontal sliding, (b) vertical sliding (double hung), (c) casements, (d) top hung (friction stays), (e) bottom hung ('drop-in' hopper), (f) glass louvres, (g) vertical pivot and (h) horizontal pivot.

e *External shading devices* are the most positive way of controlling solar heat input. The effect of such devices on wind (thus ventilation) and on daylighting and views must be kept in mind.

f *Insect screens* (part of fenestration) may be a necessity in hot-humid climates, but their effect on air flow and on daylighting must be recognized. Air flow may be reduced by 30% even by the best, smooth nylon screen and daylighting may also be reduced by 25%. To keep the same effect, the window size may have to be increased.

iv Ventilation

a Air-tight construction to reduce air infiltration is important both in a cold climate and in a hot climate in air-conditioned buildings.

b Beyond the provision of fresh air, ventilation can be relied on to dissipate unwanted heat, when $T_o < T_i$.

c Physiological cooling can be provided even when $T_o > T_i$ (slightly, i.e. $T_o < T_i + 4$) and for this not the volume flow but the air velocity is important. This can only be achieved by full cross-ventilation (or mechanical means, e.g. by fans) and it may be the main determinant of not only fenestration and orientation but also of internal layout (e.g. single row of rooms) or partitions not extending to the ceiling.

1.5.3 Climatic design archetypes

1.5.3.1 In cold climates

In cold climates where the dominant problem is underheating, where even the best building will need some active heating, the main concern is to minimize any heat loss. The surface-to-volume ratio is important and, although we cannot always build Eskimo igloos (Fig. 1.81) (which have the best surface-to-volume ratio), but the idea should be kept in mind. In any case, a compact building form is desirable. **Insulation** of the envelope is of prime concern. U-values of less than $0.5\,\text{W/m}^2\text{K}$ are usual in most locations in this climate. Windows should be small, at least double glazed, but preferably triple glazed, or double glazed with low-e treatment and partially evacuated with inert gas fill.

Where heating is necessary, capacitive insulation (massive construction) can be beneficial in continuously occupied buildings as it may allow intermittent heating (keeping the building reasonably warm during non-heating periods). For intermittent occupancy a lightweight, well-insulated building is preferable, as it has a shorter heating up period. Night temperatures in such a building can be very low, and if equipment protection or freezing (e.g. of water in pipes) is a risk, then a massive construction could save overnight heating.

Winter sunshine for an equator-facing vertical window, at low altitude sun angles may be significant. All other windows should be kept as small as possible. A check should be made whether a well-oriented window could be beneficial, but it is very likely that solar heating would only work if there is some form of night insulation. Any such passive solar heating would work only if there is an adequate thermal storage mass available. An externally insulated massive wall may be a good choice.

Attention should be paid to the air-tightness of the envelope, to ensure that air infiltration is not greater than about 0.5 air changes per hour. If it is

1.81.
Eskimo igloos (minimum surface).

In many countries insulation is specified in terms of its *R*-value, rather than its reciprocal, the *U*-value. In cold climates *R*3 or *R*4 are not uncommon (*U*-values of 0.33–0.25) and 'superinsulated houses' have been built with up to *R*8 (or *U*-values down to 0.125).

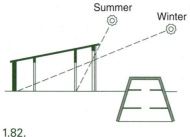

1.82.

A house proposed by Socrates (cca. 400BC) for temperature climates.

very well done, and it is reduced to less than this value, ventilation should be provided to bring it up to 0.5 ach. Inadequate ventilation may lead to the accumulation of undesirable gases (formaldehydes or even radon) emitted by building materials. Entrances should be fitted with an air-lock and should be protected externally from cold winds.

1.5.3.2 In temperate climates

In temperate climates the winter requirements would be similar to those mentioned above for cold climates, but may be somewhat less strict, depending on the severity of the winter. U-values in the order of 0.7 are usual. The building solutions would be different, to allow for the summer requirements. Any large (equator-facing) windows used for winter solar heating may cause summer overheating.

Overhanging eaves or other horizontal shading devices may ensure summer shading but allow winter entry of solar radiation (Figs 1.51 and 1.82). A full cut-off at equinox would be provided with a VSA of 90° minus latitude, but this should be adjusted according to temperatures. For a cool-temperate climate a higher VSA would allow increased solar radiation entry, which may be welcome for the winter half-year, but not for the summer. If overheating occurs in the summer, ventilation could be relied on to dissipate the unwanted heat, as air temperatures are unlikely to be too high. No special provisions are necessary for ventilation beyond facilities for fresh air supply.

In most temperate climates the night-time temperatures are too low even in the summer. For this reason a heavy construction (capacitive insulation) may be preferable. The time lag of a solar heated massive wall can be set to equal the time difference between the maximum of solar input and the time when heating would be welcome.

In most temperate climate countries there are now regulatory requirements for insulation. In the UK there were no such requirements up to 1965. Then an upper limit of acceptable U-value was introduced, 1.7 W/m²K for walls and 1.42 for roofs. Since then this requirement has been tightened several times and at present it is 0.45 W/m²K ($= R2.2$) for walls and 0.25 ($= R4$) for roofs. This development is approximately in line with most EU countries. An interesting point is that some countries require resistive insulation up to twice as good for lightweight elements than for heavyweight construction.

In the USA there are local variations, but most states follow the ASHRAE Standard 90.1 (1999), which for residential buildings prescribes $U = 0.412$ W/m²K ($= R2.4$) for heavy walls and $U = 0.232$ ($= R4.3$) for lightweight ones. For roofs $U = 0.278$ W/m²K ($= R3.6$) is the requirement, if the insulation is on top of the deck, but down to $U = 0.1$ W/m²K ($= R10$) for attic roofs. The requirements are stated as a function of climate characteristics (e.g. degree-days).

The BCA (Building Code of Australia) (2003 amendment) divides the country into eight climatic zones and requires insulation for walls between $R1.4$ ($U = 0.71$ W/m²K) for the warm northern parts, $R1.7$ ($U = 0.59$) for the southern states, and up to $R2.8$ ($U = 0.36$ for the Alpine regions. For roofs the corresponding requirements are $R2.2$ ($U = 0.45$) for the north, $R3$ ($U = 0.33$) for the south and $R4.3$ ($U = 0.23$) for the Alpine regions. For the northern regions roof solar heat gain necessitates the insulation.

In all cases the option is to comply with such elemental prescriptions or to produce energy calculations (by an authorized person or accredited software) to show that the proposed building will be as good as one complying with the elemental prescriptions. This is also discussed in Section 4.3.2.3)

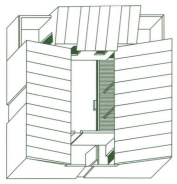

(a)

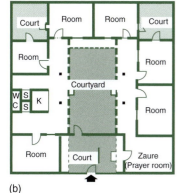

(b)

1.83.

A modern courtyard house: isometric view and plan (by Max Lock; after Saini, 1973).

1.5.3.3 In hot-dry climates

In hot-dry climates the daytime temperatures can be very high but the diurnal range is large, often more than 20 K. Night temperatures may be too cold. Consequently the single most important characteristic should be a large thermal mass: massive walls but also a roof with high thermal capacity.

Building surfaces should be white, which would act as a selective surface. This is most important for roofs exposed to the night sky. The radiant cooling effect can help to dissipate the heat stored during the day. White paint has a high emittance, unlike a shiny metallic surface, as discussed in Section 1.1.2.3.

The outdoor environment is often hostile, hot and dusty, so the best solution may be an inward-looking, courtyard-type building. The air mass enclosed by the building, by solid walls or fences is likely to be cooler than the environment, heavier, thus it would settle as if in a basin. This air can be evaporatively cooled by a pond or a water spray. The reservoir of cool air thus created can then be used for fresh air supply to habitable spaces. With adequate vegetation such a courtyard can become quite a pleasant outdoor living space (Fig. 1.83).

Much depends, however, on how the courtyard is treated. An unshaded courtyard, without water, can be a liability, warmer than external environment, not only in 'winter' but also during the hottest periods. Such unwanted heating up to 5 K above the ambient has been recorded. The traditional courtyards with shading, trees and some water element can be substantially cooler than the ambient at the height of summer.

Ventilation, beyond the small fresh air supply from the courtyard is undesirable as the outdoor air is hot and dusty.

1.5.3.4 Warm-humid climates

Warm-humid climates are the most difficult ones to design for. The temperature maxima may not be as high as in the hot-dry climates, but the diurnal variation is very small (often less than 5 K), thus the 'mass effect' cannot be relied on. As the humidity is high, evaporation from the skin is restricted and evaporative cooling will be neither effective, nor desirable, as it would increase the humidity. Indirect evaporative cooling may be used, as it does not add moisture to the supply air and produces some sensible cooling.

Typical of these climates is the elevated house (to 'catch the breeze' above local obstructions) of lightweight construction. The best the designer can do is to ensure that the interior does not become (much) warmer than the outside (it cannot be any cooler), which can be achieved by adequate ventilation removing any excess heat input. Warm-humid climates are located around the equator, where the sun's path is near the zenith, so the roof receives very strong irradiation. Keeping down the indoor air temperature is not enough. The ceiling temperature may be elevated due to solar heat input on the roof, thus the MRT would be increased. When people wear light clothing, the MRT has double the effect of the DBT.

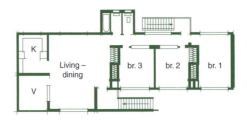

(a)

(b)

1.84.
A typical house for warm-humid climates.

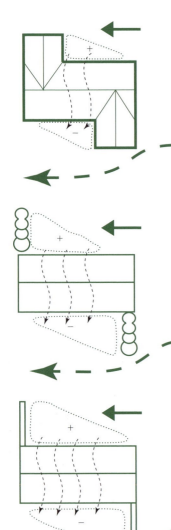

Undue increase of ceiling temperature can be prevented by

1 using a reflective roof surface
2 having a separate ceiling, forming an attic space
3 ensuring adequate ventilation of the attic space
4 using a reflective surface for the underside of the roof skin
5 using some resistive insulation on the ceiling.

East and west walls should have no windows, to avoid heat input from a low-angle sun, and should be reflective and insulated. The sol–air temperature of these walls could be much higher than the air temperature.

Beyond the prevention (or reduction) of heat gains the only passive cooling strategy possible is the physiological cooling effect of air movement. In order to ensure maximum cross-ventilation, the major openings should face within 45° of the prevailing wind direction. It should however be remembered that there are possibilities to influence the wind, but not the solar incidence.

Therefore solar orientation should be dominant. North and south walls could have large openings. The rooms could be arranged in one row, to allow both inlet and outlet openings for each room. Figure 1.84 shows such a typical tropical house.

With a north-facing wall, if the wind comes from the east or near-east a wing wall placed at the western end of a window would help creating a positive pressure zone (Fig. 1.85). At the same time, a wing wall placed at the eastern edge of a south-facing window could help creating a negative pressure zone. The difference between the positive and negative pressure would drive an adequate cross-ventilation, probably better than with a normal wind incidence. It can work even if the wind direction is due east or west. A projecting wing of the building or even vegetation (e.g. a hedge) may achieve the same result.

The above discussion applies to a reasonably free-standing house. With urban developments and increasing densities in warm-humid tropical areas the ventilation effect disappears. The solution then is to use a low-power,

1.85.
Projecting building wings, vegetation screens or wing walls can be used to generate cross-ventilation.

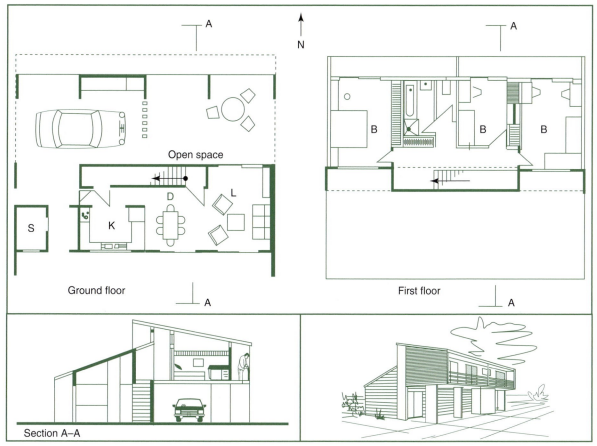

1.86.
A hybrid house for warm-humid climates.

low-velocity slow moving ceiling fan, which can generate the required velocity for physiological cooling. This is a useful standby in any case, for times when there is no breeze available.

In such a dense situation (when all other houses are also elevated) the benefit of the elevated house may also disappear. A concrete slab-on-ground floor may provide a desirable heat sink. For daytime rooms (living, dining, kitchen) a heavy construction may ensure indoor temperatures close to the day's minimum. Bedrooms should cool down quickly after sunset, therefore a lightweight construction and cross-ventilation would be desirable. On this basis a house form of hybrid construction has been suggested to get the best of both worlds (Fig. 1.86).

1.5.4 Condensation and moisture control

Condensation occurs whenever moist air is cooled to, or comes into contact with a surface below its DPT. The process can be followed on the psychrometric chart and is best illustrated by an example.

EXAMPLE 1.10

Mark the status point on the chart corresponding to (say) 26°C and 60% RH (Fig. 1.87). The AH is 12.6 g/kg and the vapour pressure is just over 2 kPa. If this horizontal line is extended to the saturation curve, the DPT is obtained as 17.5°C. This means that if this air comes into contact with a surface of 17.5°C or less, condensation will occur.

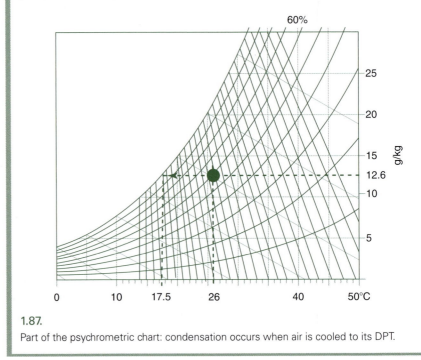

1.87.
Part of the psychrometric chart: condensation occurs when air is cooled to its DPT.

This can often be observed on the bathroom mirror or the inside of windows in winter. Surface condensation can be allowed, e.g. a 'condensation trough' may be included on the bottom rail of a window, which is drained to the outside. More difficult to handle and potentially damaging is the interstitial condensation, which may occur within the materials of envelope elements, especially in winter.

Vapour will permeate the envelope fabric, driven by the indoor–outdoor vapour pressure difference. The cross-section of an envelope element, such as a wall has a temperature gradient between the warm inside and the cold outside. When the vapour reaches a layer of temperature at or below the DPT, condensation will occur within the pores of the material. This liquid water may fill the pores, thus reducing the insulating qualities of the material; the fabric will become colder, which will further increase the condensation. In many cases in cold winters a roof leak was suspected, which subsequently proved to be 'only' condensation.

It may lead to mould growth over such damp surfaces and may damage the construction (e.g. the plastering may fall off). In cold situations the risk is greatest at the outer edge of roof/wall junction, where the fabric is cold (due to the thermal bridge effect), especially in low-income housing, where bedrooms may not be heated at all, any vents may be sealed 'to preserve the heat', but the kitchen door is left open to allow the warm (moisture-laden) air to go up to the bedrooms.

The causes of condensation are

1 Moisture input, increased humidity of the room air. An average person would exhale some 50 g of water vapour in an hour. A shower may contribute 200 g and cooking or indoor drying of clothes are large producers of vapour (see data sheet D.1.6 for moisture production rates).
2 Lack of ventilation, which means that the vapour generated stays in the room.
3 Inadequate heating and poor insulation can produce very cold inside surface temperatures.

Vapour flow quantities are analogous to heat flow quantities:

Heat	J		Vapour quantity	g	(usually $\mu g = 10^{-6}$ g)
Temperature	T	°C	Vapour pressure	pv	Pa
Conductivity	λ	W/m K	Permeability	δ	μg/m s Pa
Transmittance	U	W/m^{2}K	Permeance	π	μg/m^2 s Pa
Resistance	R	m^{2}K/W	Vapour resistance	vR	MPa s m^2/g

See method sheet M.1.1 for the process of calculation.[7]

In a space with large vapour production (e.g. a place of assembly), which in winter could lead to uncontrollable condensation, a simple passive method of dehumidification is the use of a 'condenser window'. If all windows are double glazed, install one (or several) narrow, single glazed windows, fitted with a condensation trough on the inside, which is drained to waste. As this window will be the coldest surface in the space, this is where condensation will start and if it works properly, it will precipitate much of the vapour content of the indoor atmosphere, thus reduce humidity and condensation risk elsewhere. It is clearly a simple form of passive dehumidification.

1.5.5 Microclimatic controls

Most published climatic data had been collected from meteorological stations, usually located on an open site, often at airports. The climate of a given site may differ from that indicated by the available data, quite significantly. On-site measurements are impractical, as nothing less than a year would suffice, and such time is rarely available for a project. The best one can do is to obtain data from the nearest meteorological station and exercise a qualitative judgement how and in what way would the site climate differ.

Local factors that will influence the site climate may be the following:

- *topography*, slope, orientation, exposure, elevation, hills or valleys at or near the site

---

[7]Note that in the SI the denominator is usually kept as the basic unit and the prefix is applied to the numerator, thus the reciprocal of μ (g/m^2 s Pa) is M (Pa s m^2/g).

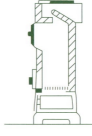

1.94.
A typical cast iron stove.

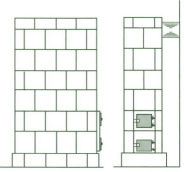

1.95.
A ceramic stove built *in situ*.

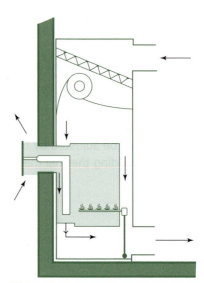

Figure 1.96.
A gas convector heater with a balanced flue.

Table 1.6. Correction factors for heating requirement

For length of working week:	7 days		1
	5 days massive buildings		0.85
	lightweight buildings		0.75
For building and plant response:	continuous heating		1

Intermittent heating (night shut-down)		If plant response	
		Quick	Slow
If building mass	Light	0.55	0.70
	Medium	0.70	0.85
	Heavy	0.85	0.95

For intermittent heating only, length of heating day		If building mass	
		Light	Heavy
	4 h	0.68	0.96
	8 h	1	1
	2 h	1.25	1.02
	16 h	1.4	1.03

3 liquid fuel – (oil, kerosene) piped from an external tank or in batch (cans, bottles)

4 solid fuel – (coal, coke, firewood) in batch (cans, bins, baskets).

In all these (except electrical appliances) heat is produced by the combustion of some fuel. This uses oxygen, thus air supply must be ensured and the combustion products must be removed. This requires that they should be connected to a flue.

Oil heaters are available in small portable form. These use the room air and discharge their combustion products into the room. One point, often forgotten is that the combustion of 1 L of oil produces about 1 kg of water vapour, which increases vapour pressure in the room and thus the risk of condensation. Adequate ventilation is therefore essential.

Solid fuel appliances (or stoves) may be industrial products made of metal (e.g. cast iron, Fig. 1.94) or may be built *in situ* of ceramic blocks (these have a large thermal inertia, Fig. 1.95). Both are connected to a flue. Such flues can remove a significant quantity of air and will operate well only if the room air can be replenished through appropriate vents. Open fireplaces are often used as decorative elements (many people love to look at the fire) but cannot be considered as serious heating devices because of their very low efficiency.

Gas heaters may have a 'balanced flue' (Fig. 1.96) where fresh air supply and the discharge of combustion products is a circuit separated from the room air. In large spaces (a church or industrial buildings) flueless gas-fired radiators may be used, usually mounted overhead, in a tilted position. The burners heat a refractory plate (of shaped, perforated ceramic elements) to 800–900°C, which thus becomes incandescent and emits heat primarily by radiation.

Electric heaters have the greatest variety in terms of heat output (radiant/convective) and form, although all of them are based on resistance heater elements. Table 1.7 lists the basic types of electric heaters, but a wide variety of products exists within each type.

Table 1.7. Types of electric heaters

Type	Heat emission (%)	
	Radiant	Convective
Infrared lamps	100	–
Incandescent radiators	80	20
Medium temperature (tube or panel) radiators	60	40
Low temperature panels (oil filled)	40	60
Convectors	20	80
Fan convectors	–	100
Storage (block) heaters	10	90
Floor warming	20	80
Ceiling warming	70	30

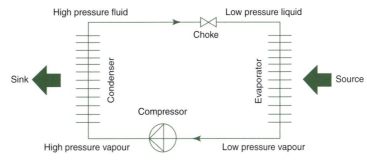

1.97.
Principles of a heat pump (or cooling machine).

Electricity is often referred to as the most convenient 'fuel', because of its ease of transport, as it can be readily controlled (at the flick of a switch), as it has no combustion products at the point of heat delivery and as its efficiency at conversion to heat is practically 100%. It is rather seductive, but this view is deceptive. Its adverse characteristics are only shifted to the generating stations, with their emissions polluting the atmosphere and contributing to the greenhouse effect as well as the low efficiency of conversion from heating fuel to electricity of around 33% (on average). So 1 kWh of electricity used means the use of fuel of some 3 kWh energy content and the release of some 3 kg of CO_2 into the atmosphere.

A special form of electric heating is based on the *heat pump*, where the input of electricity at the rate of 1 kW can produce heating of up to 4 kW. This appears to contravene the first law of thermodynamics, but the heat is not actually produced by the heat pump. The input of 1 kW to drive the compressor facilitates the delivery of heat from a low grade (low temperature) source, upgrading and delivering it at a useful temperature at the rate of 4 kW. Figure 1.97 shows the principles of such a heat pump.

A working fluid or refrigerant (such as an organic fluoride or a hydrocarbon) is circulated in a closed loop by the compressor. A pressure release valve (choke) keeps the condenser side under high pressure and the evaporator

Organic fluorides (freons, CFCs) were largely responsible for ozone depletion in the upper atmosphere (the ozone holes) and consequent increase in UV radiation at ground level. These are now almost completely phased out, as a result of the 'Montreal protocol' of 1987, and replaced by hydrocarbons.

side under low pressure and low temperature. When the fluid is compressed, it becomes hot and liquefies, whilst it will emit heat to the *sink,* in this case the room air. Passing through the choke it evaporates and its temperature drops, so that it can pick up heat from a *source.* This heat source may be the atmosphere (with the evaporator shaped as an air-to-liquid heat exchanger), may be warm 'grey' water discharged into a sump or a natural body of water (a river or the sea), where the evaporator is shaped as a liquid-to-liquid heat exchanger.

If the purpose of using this machine is to gain heat, then the coefficient of performance (CoP) is defined as

$$\text{CoP} = \frac{Q}{W} = \frac{\text{Heat delivered to sink}}{\text{Compressor work input}} \tag{1.33a}$$

This CoP is higher for a small temperature increment (or step-up) but it reduces if the necessary step-up is large. In the ideal (Carnot) cycle the CoP is inversely proportionate to the temperature increment:

$$\text{CoP} = \frac{T'}{T' - T''}$$

where T' = sink temperature
    T'' = source temperature (in °K).
but a real cycle will give 0.82–0.93 (average 0.85) of the Carnot performance. This will be further reduced by the actual component efficiencies, such as

electric motor 0.95
compressor 0.8
heat exchangers 0.9

EXAMPLE 1.11

If there is a source of 10°C (=283°K) and the heat is to be delivered at 55°C (=328°K)

$$\text{CoP} = 0.85 \times 0.95 \times 0.8 \times 0.9 \times \frac{328}{328 - 283} = 4.24$$

but if the source is 0°C (=273°K) and 60°C (333°K) is wanted then

$$\text{CoP} = 0.85 \times 0.95 \times 0.8 \times 0.9 \times \frac{333}{333 - 283} = 3.23$$

If the same machine is used for cooling, i.e. to remove heat, then the definition of CoP is slightly different:

$$\text{CoP} = \frac{Q}{W} = \frac{\text{Heat removed from source}}{\text{Compressor work input}} \tag{1.33b}$$

The difference is that in a heat pump application the compressor input is added to the heat gained, it is included in the value of Q, but in a cooling application it is not.

1.6.1.2 Central heating

Heat may be produced centrally in a building (or group of buildings), distributed to the occupied spaces by a heat transport fluid and emitted to provide the required heating. Schematically:

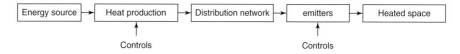

The energy source may be fossil fuels: coal, oil or gas, electricity, produced from fossil fuels, nuclear or hydropower, or renewable sources, such as solar-, wind-, tidal-, wave-, ocean-, thermal- or geothermal energy or biogas. At one stage coal was the most often used source, but today oil or gas is most frequently relied on. The transport fluid may be water or air. Heat is produced in boilers, for a water system and in a furnace for an air system.

Architectural implications are the accommodation of any fuel storage, the heat production plant and its flue, the routing and accommodation of the distribution network: pipes for a water system and ducts for an air system, as well as the choice and placement of emitters.

Figure 1.98 shows an outdoor storage arrangement for a bank of gas cylinders. Gas leaks indoors mixed with air can produce a highly explosive mixture, which can be ignited by the smallest spark. Figure 1.99 is the section of an oil storage tank chamber. Here fire precautions are dominant: note the foam inlet valve and the high threshold, which must be high enough for the chamber to contain the full tank volume of oil in case of leakage. Storage for heavier oils may have to be heated to at least the following temperatures:

class E − 7°C
class F − 20°C
class G − 32°C

The emitter for a warm air system may be a grille or a diffuser (on rare occasions a directional jet). This system has the disadvantage that the room surface temperatures are below the air temperature, whereas human preference is fort an MRT slightly (1–2 K) warmer than the air temperature.

Figure 1.100 shows the ducting arrangement for a domestic warm air system. The volume flow rate (m^3/s) in a duct is

$$vr = A \times v$$

where A = duct cross-sectional area (m^2)
     v = air velocity (m/s).

Air velocities in ducts may be 2.5–7.5 m/s for low-velocity systems, but up to 25 m/s for high-velocity (high pressure) systems. The latter would require smaller ducts, but would result in a much larger flow resistance, would need a greater fan power and would tend to be more noisy. In habitable rooms an outlet velocity of not more than 2.5 m/s is preferred and in no case should it exceed 4 m/s.

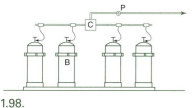

1.98.
Gas storage bottles. B: buckles and straps; C: changeover valve and P: pressure regulator.

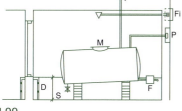

1.99.
Oil storage tank room. V: vent; P: filling pipe; S: sludge valve; D: depth to contain full volume; Fi: foam inlet; M: manhole and F: fire shut-off.

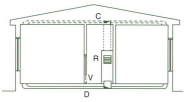

1.100.
A domestic warm air system: D: radial under-floor ducts; C: alternative ceiling ducts; V: vents in doors and R = return air grill.

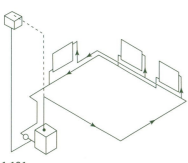

1.101.
Central heating ring-main system.

4 Electrostatic filters: Up to 12 kV static charges on metal plates. These are effective down to 0.01 μm particle size, and normally used with a coarser pre-filter. These are the best filters for particularly clean areas, such as laboratories or operating theatres.

Ducts are used to convey and distribute the air. Usually made of sheet metal of rectangular cross-section, but in recent times plastic materials are often used in circular or oval sections. For larger sizes 'builder's work' ducts may be used, formed in brick or concrete, or framed and sheeted. These may have a greater surface friction (suitable for lower flow velocities) and it is difficult to prevent air leakages.

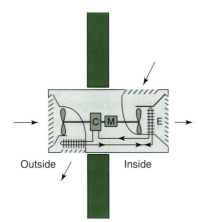

1.112.
Schematic diagram of a packaged air conditioner unit. C: compressor, M: motor and E: evaporator.

1.6.3.2 Air conditioning systems

Air conditioning systems control the temperature and humidity as well as the purity of the air. The simplest system is the room conditioner: a packaged unit which can be installed in a window or an external wall. Its capacity may be up to 10 kW. It has a direct expansion evaporator cooling coil and a condenser cooled by the outdoor air.

Such a unit is shown in Fig. 1.112 in diagrammatic terms and Fig. 1.113 is a similar unit in console form. The split units have the cooling coil (evaporator, E) and fan inside the room, whilst the more noisy compressor and condenser (C) are included in the outdoor unit (Fig. 1.114). Some models have a reverse-cycle facility, to act as (air-source) heat pumps for heating in winter. These constitute to the most effective way of using electricity for heating, even if the CoP is not more than 2.

In larger systems the air is treated in an air-handling unit, which includes the fan and is distributed by a ductwork. The heating coil of the air-handling unit is served by a boiler, which delivers hot water. The cooling coil can be of a direct expansion type, i.e. the evaporator of the cooling machine itself, or the cooling machine can become a chiller (the evaporator shaped as a refrigerant-to-water heat exchanger) supplying chilled water to the cooling coil.

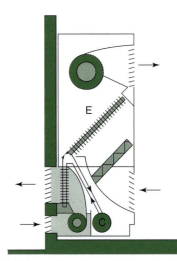

1.113.
A console type air conditioner unit.

Figure 1.115 shows a central air-handling unit and Fig. 1.116 presents the four basic system types in diagrammatic form.

The chiller machine of an air conditioner may be a compressor type, such as that shown in Fig. 1.97 or an absorption chiller. Fig. 1.117 is a schematic diagram of such a chiller, using ammonia as the refrigerant and water as the absorbent. A heat input (e.g. a gas flame) expels the ammonia from the solution. The hot ammonia gas is cooled to the atmosphere. This high pressure gas is released to the evaporator, where it expands and cools, ready to pick up heat from its environment. It is then re-absorbed in the water.

Both chillers can be used to produce chilled water, which is then circulated to the air conditioner unit cooling coil, or in a direct expansion coil, where the evaporator becomes the cooling coil.

In an *all-air system* (Fig. 1.117a) the plant is centralized and the treated air is distributed by a network of ducts. A rather inflexible system, using quite large ducts for both supply and return. The air volume flow rate to each room is constant and the required condition is set at the central plant. It may include a terminal re-heat facility, to provide some flexibility, but at a cost in energy.

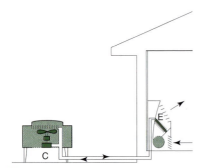

Figure 1.114.
An air conditioner 'split unit'.

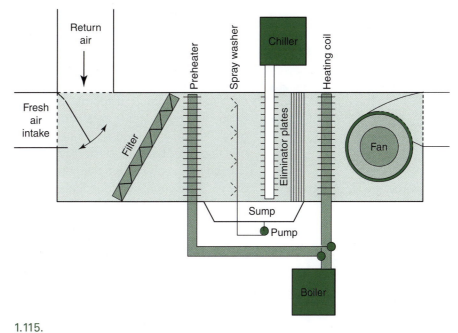

1.115.

A typical central air-handling unit (arrangement diagram).

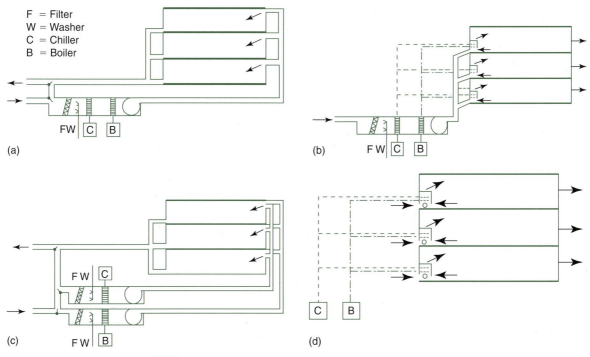

F = Filter
W = Washer
C = Chiller
B = Boiler

(a)

(b)

(c)

(d)

1.116.

Four basic air conditioning systems: (a) an all-air system, (b) an induction system, (c) a dual duct system and (d) local air-handling system.

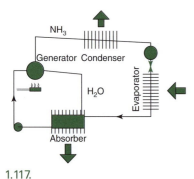

1.117.

An ammonia/water absorption chiller.

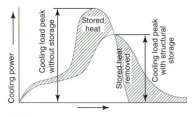

1.118.

The effect of structural storage on air conditioning load and required plant capacity.

A significant improvement is the variable air volume (VAV) system, where the supply air condition is constant and the cooling requirement of each room can be matched by reducing or increasing the air flow at the diffuser. This is the most energy efficient system.

At the other extreme is the local air-handling system (Fig. 1.117d), where each room or group of rooms would have its own fan-coil unit, supplied by chilled and hot water from a central plant. Each room may have its own controls. The decentralized air handling is similar to the above, but a whole zone or a floor may have its air-handling unit.

In an induction system the central plant may produce over-cooled and very dry air and supply this to induction units in each room, where the supply air jet induces a flow and mixing with room air, thus creating a recirculation. Heating and cooling coils may or may not be included in these units, which may be supplied from a central chiller and boiler (Fig. 1.117b).

In a dual duct system there may be two central air-handling units, supplying cooled or heated air respectively, which are ducted to each room and can be mixed at the outlet to the desired condition. A very flexible but in energy terms very wasteful system (Fig. 1.117c).

These are only the basic types: a very large number of variations and permutations are available, both in terms of system arrangement and in size. In large systems the air-handling units would be room size and may provide conditioned air supply to a number of separate zones. A building of any size could (and should) be divided into zones, according to exposure to external load, to occupancy variations and the timing of such loads.

Significant energy savings can be achieved by the control of air conditioning systems. All systems must provide a fresh air supply, at least as much as required for ventilation purposes. However, internal loads can be removed, if the outdoor air is cooler than the indoors, with an increased outdoor air supply, without running the chiller plant. This is often referred to as an *economy cycle*.

In many instances it is advisable to provide a *night flush* of (cool) outdoor air to remove the heat stored in the building fabric, thus reduce the following day's cooling requirement. Storage of heat in the fabric of the building can also be relied on to reduce the peak cooling requirement, as indicated by Fig. 1.118. Another possibility is to provide individual work-station controls: providing a minimum of general conditioning (e.g. in a large office) with individually controllable supplementary air supply to each work station.

Such controls may become parts of a BEMS (building energy management system) which would coordinate all the building's energy using equipment in a responsive manner, to minimize energy use. Ultimately such systems can produce what has been referred to as *intelligent buildings*.

1.6.4 Open-cycle cooling systems

In conventional cooling machines (such as Fig. 1.97) the refrigerant (or coolant) fluid circulates in a closed loop. Its evaporation provides cooling and it is then 'reactivated' (condensed) by the action of a compressor. As opposed to this, in the open-cycle systems water is the coolant, its evaporation provides cooling and it is then discharged. The whole system is open to the atmosphere.

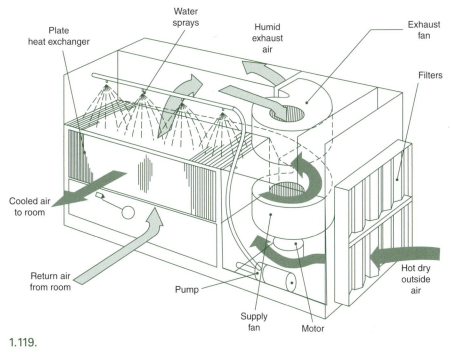

1.119.
An indirect evaporative cooler.

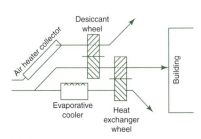

1.120.
An open-cycle cooling system using solid sorbents.

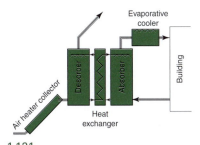

1.121.
An open-cycle system using a liquid desiccant.

The simplest open-cycle system is the *direct evaporative cooler* (Fig. 1.77), which has been discussed in Section 1.5.1.4. It was considered as a 'passive system', although it may use a small pump and a fan, but the cooling is provided by natural evaporation. Its disbenefit is that it increases the humidity of the supply air (see Fig. 1.13).

This is avoided by the indirect evaporative cooler, where the exhaust air is cooled and in turn it cools the intake air through a heat exchanger, without adding moisture to the supply air. The crucial element is the plate heat exchanger, shown in Fig. 1.119 (see explanation in Section 1.5.1.4).

A more sophisticated system is shown in Fig. 1.120. This uses a 'desiccant' or moisture transfer wheel, which is packed with silica gel (or some other absorbent or adsorbent) between two wire meshes. In its upper position it is dried out (reconditioned) by solar heated air. Slowly turning, this dry sorbent will come into the path of the supply air and will pick up much of its moisture content. Sorption is an exothermic process (see Fig. 1.14), thus both the wheel and the air becomes warm. This air will be passed through and cooled by a rotary heat exchanger (heat transfer wheel). This, in its lower half, is cooled by the evaporatively cooled air stream, which is then discharged. Besides the supply air passage, the system has two auxiliary passages open to the atmosphere: one to remove moisture, the other to provide cooling.

Another open-cycle system is shown in Fig. 1.121. This is using a liquid sorbent (such as a glycol) in aqueous solution. This is sprayed downwards in the 'desorber', against an upward moving solar heated air stream, which 'dries out' the solution, evaporating much of the water. The warm enriched solution passes through a heat exchanger and is sprayed downwards in a second column (the absorber) against an upward air stream (return air from the house, possibly mixed with fresh air) where much of its moisture content is absorbed by the rich solution (which becomes diluted and returns to the desorber). The air is then supplied to the house through an evaporative cooler.

These two and several other open-cycle systems have been produced and a few have reached the commercial development stage. Their electricity consumption for a given cooling capacity is only 15–20% of that of a conventional air conditioner. Unfortunately they tend to be bulky and the performance of sorbent materials tends to be reduced in time, over thousands of cycles.

1.6.5   Integration/discussion

HVAC services must be integrated with the architectural design in two ways:

1 in performance
2 in hardware.

Examples of performance integration occur throughout this chapter. The last of these was in conjunction with Fig. 1.118, which showed that building mass can reduce the necessary installed capacity of the AC system. Table 1.6 and the associated discussion showed the interdependence of occupancy pattern, building mass and plant response. Table 1.7 implies that even electric heaters should be matched to occupancy pattern and building fabric. Floor warming is appropriate for continuously and uniformly occupied buildings. Convectors can be used where the air should be heated up quickly, but with heavy construction this would leave the room surfaces colder. Panel radiators are good where quick response is not required, but steady warmth is welcome. Infrared lamps and incandescent radiators are the choice where there is no chance of heating up the fabric, or the room air, but instantaneous heating effect on the body surface of people can ameliorate the situation (e.g. in a church).

The need for 'hardware' integration includes the provision of adequate space, where it is best situated, for fuel storage, plant rooms, cooling towers (or dry condensers) and last but not least the required ductwork. These are most often under the floor slab and covered by a suspended ceiling, but can also be located on top of a floor slab, with an elevated raised floor. In both cases such a service space would add to the building height.

Such ducts could be quite bulky. The volume flow rate is the product of air velocity and cross-sectional area, thus the two are inversely related. Velocities may be between 10 and 20 m/s. Higher velocities require smaller ducts (easier to accommodate) but produce greater friction and need larger fan power; they may also be noisy. Often two sets of ducts are required: for supply air and return/exhaust air. The two should never cross each other, as that would set the depth of ceiling space necessary. Ducts should also be coordinated with the structural system, for example, to avoid crossing deep beams. Structural elements themselves may be used as ducts, e.g. hollow beams. Sometimes, for example, when a long row of offices is served by a central corridor, the corridor could serve as the return air duct (large cross-section, low velocity) and the return air picked up by a riser duct near the lift lobby.

These are just examples, by no means treating the subject systematically, but indicating the kind of thinking required.

At the early stages of design one can get a rough idea of the necessary duct size. This is best illustrated by an example.

EXAMPLE 1.12

In an office building there will be 6000 m^2 space per floor. Data sheet D.1.8 shows that one person should be counted for every 10 m^2, thus there will be 600 persons on this floor. The ventilation (fresh air) requirement is 10 L/s per person, i.e. 6000 L/s or 6 m^3/s. To remove or deliver heat at least twice that flow would be required, say 12 m^3/s.

Assuming a medium velocity of 15 m/s, the duct cross-section required would be 12/15 = 0.8 m^2, which could be a 1 m × 0.8 m size. To minimize the ceiling space depth, an oblong shape would be used, but the ratio of the two side should not exceed 2. Something like 1.25 m wide and 0.64 high would be the limit. From the aerodynamic viewpoint a circular duct would be preferable (air flows in a spiral motion), as this gives the least resistance, needs the least fan power. The area of a circle is $r^2\pi$, which gives an r of some 0.5 m, i.e. a diameter of 1 m (!). However, in a circular duct (lesser resistance) a higher velocity may be acceptable.

There are also economic implications. It is not unusual, even with a good design that the ceiling spaces required for ductwork would add up over 10 floors to the height of an extra floor. This would imply extra cost of structure and envelope, which will not produce any returns.

At an early stage of the design strategic decisions should be reached in consultation with the services engineer, such as where to put the plant room(s) the outline of the distribution system, any need for major riser ducts, etc. A good start would save many problems later and avoid having a patched-up job.

DATA SHEETS AND METHOD SHEETS (THERMAL)

DATA SHEET D.1.2

Thermal properties of walls

Note: EPS = expanded polystyrene fc = fibrous cement sheet			U-value (W/m²K)	Admittance (W/m²K)	Time lag (hours)	Decrement factor
Brick and block						
Brick	Single skin	105 mm	3.28	4.2	2.6	0.87
		220 mm	2.26	4.7	6.1	0.54
		335 mm	1.73	4.7	9.4	0.29
	Single skin	105 mm plastered	3.02	4.1	2.9	0.83
		220 mm plastered	2.14	4.5	6.5	0.49
		335 mm plastered	1.79	4.5	9.9	0.26
	Single skin	105 + 13 mm LW plaster	2.59	3.3	3.0	0.82
		220 + 13 mm LW plaster	1.91	3.6	6.6	0.46
		335 + 13 mm LW plaster	1.50	3.6	10.0	0.24
	Single skin	105 + 10 mm plasterboard	2.70	3.5	3.0	0.83
		220 + 10 mm plasterboard	1.98	3.8	6.5	0.47
		335 + 10 mm plasterboard	1.60	3.8	10.0	0.25
	Cavity	270 mm	1.53	4.2	6.9	0.52
		270 mm plastered	1.47	4.4	7.4	0.47
		– same, + 25 mm EPS in cavity	0.72	4.6	8.9	0.34
		– same, + 40 mm EPS in cavity	0.55	4.7	9.1	0.32
		– same, + 50 mm EPS in cavity	0.47	4.7	9.2	0.31
		270 mm + 13 mm LW plaster	1.36	3.4	7.5	0.44
		+ 10 mm plasterboard	1.12	2.3	8.1	0.36
		+ UF foam cavity fill	0.57	4.6	8.7	0.35
Brick 105, cavity, 100 Lw concrete Block, Lw plaster			0.92	2.2	7.0	0.55
– same + 25 mm EPS			0.55	2.3	8.0	0.43
– same but 50 mm EPS			0.40	2.4	9.0	0.41
Concrete block, solid 200, plasterboard			1.83	2.5	6.8	0.35
– same, but foil-backed plasterboard			1.40	1.82	7.0	0.32
– same, but 25 cavity, 25 EPS, plasterboard			0.70	1.0	7.3	0.29
– same, but lightweight concrete			0.69	1.8	7.4	0.46
– same, but foil-backed plasterboard			0.61	1.5	7.7	0.42
– same, but 25 cavity, 25 EPS, plasterboard			0.46	1.0	8.3	0.34
Concrete block, LW 200, 25 cavity + 10 plasterboard			0.69	1.8	7.0	0.47
– same but foil-back plasterboard			0.64	1.6	8.0	0.44
– same but 20 mm EPS			0.55	1.2	8.0	0.39
– same but 25 mm EPS			0.51	1.1	8.0	0.37
– same but 25 polyurethare			0.45	1.0	8.0	0.34
Concrete block, hollow 100 mm + plasterboard			2.76	3.4	1.8	0.93
200 mm, insulated plasterboard			2.42	4.1	3.0	0.83
Concrete, dense, cast, 150 mm			3.48	5.3	4.0	0.70
– same + 50 mm wood wool slab, plastered			1.23	1.7	6.0	0.50
– same, but lightweight plaster			1.15	1.7	6.3	0.49
Concrete, dense, cast, 200 mm			3.10	5.5	5.4	0.56
– same + 50 mm wood wool slab, plastered			1.18	2.2	7.7	0.36
– same, but lightweight plaster			1.11	1.7	6.2	0.35

(Continued)

DATA SHEET D.1.2 (Continued)

Note: EPS = expanded polystyrene fc = fibrous cement sheet	U-value (W/m²K)	Admittance (W/m²K)	Time lag (hours)	Decrement factor
Concrete, precast panel, 75 mm	4.28	4.9	1.9	0.91
– same + 25 cavity + 25 EPS + plasterboard	0.84	1.0	3.0	0.82
Concrete, precast, 75 + 25 EPS + 150 Lw concrete	0.58	3.8	9.5	0.41
– same, but 50 mm EPS	0.49	3.8	9.2	0.26
Brick/block veneers				
Brick 105 + cavity (frame) + plasterboard	1.46	2.4	3.6	0.99
– same, but foil-backed plasterboard	1.35	1.7	3.7	0.75
– same with 25 mm EPS or glass fibre	0.72	1.1	4.0	0.77
– same with 50 mm EPS or glass fibre	0.47	0.8	4.2	0.72
– same, 25 EPS + foil-backed plasterboard	0.64	1.0	4.1	0.81
Block 100 + cavity (frame) + plasterboard	1.57	2.1	4.1	0.72
– same, but foil-backed plasterboard	1.24	1.7	4.3	0.69
– same with 25 mm EPS or glass fibre	0.74	1.1	4.7	0.65
– same with 50 mm EPS or glass fibre	0.48	0.9	4.9	0.62
– same, 25 EPS + foil-backed plasterboard	0.66	1.0	4.7	0.64
Framed				
Framed, single fc or galvanized steel	5.23	5.2	0	1
– same + cavity + plasterboard	2.20	2.2	0.3	1
– same with 25 mm EPS or glass fibre	0.86	1.1	0.5	0.99
– same with 50 mm EPS or glass fibre	0.53	0.9	0.7	0.99
Framed, 20 mm timber boarding	3.19	3.2	0.4	1
– same + cavity + plasterboard	1.68	1.8	0.8	0.99
– same with 25 mm EPS or glass fibre	0.68	1.0	0.9	0.99
– same with 50 mm EPS or glass fibre	0.46	0.8	1.0	0.98
Framed, tile hanging + paper + cavity + 50 EPS + plasterboard	0.54	0.78	1.0	0.99
– same, but 100 EPS or glass fibre	0.32	0.71	1.0	0.99
Reverse brick veneer: 5 mm fc + cavity + 105 brick	1.39	4.13	3.70	0.97
– same + 25 mm EPS in cavity	0.70	4.53	4.50	0.68
– same but 50 mm EPS	0.47	4.62	4.80	0.61
– same but only aluminium foil in cavity	1.14	4.22	3.90	0.99
– same but both foil and 25 mm EPS	0.63	4.54	4.50	0.70
Reverse block veneer: 5 fc + cavity + 100 hollow block	1.41	3.14	2.20	1.00
– same but 100 mm solid concrete block	1.63	6.05	4.40	0.79
– same but 50 EPS in cavity + 100 hollow block	0.47	3.59	3.20	0.85
– same but 50 EPS in cavity + 100 solid block	0.49	6.45	5.20	0.46
– same but 50 EPS in cavity + 200 solid block	0.48	6.16	7.70	0.21
Sandwich panels				
6 mm fibrous cement + 25 EPS + 6 mm fc	1.20	1.1	0.5	1
6 mm fibrous cement + 50 polyurethane + 6 fc	0.45	0.9	0.7	1
Doors				
Timber 35 mm 10 mm inset panels	3.24	3.24	0.6	1
45 mm hollow core, flish	2.44	2.44	0.4	1
45 mm solid core, flush	2.20	2.10	1.0	0.97
Metal (roller shutter, tilt-a-door)	5.54	5.00	0	1

DATA SHEET D.1.3

Thermal properties of windows, roofs and floors

				U-value (W/m²K)	Admittance (W/m²K)	sgf (θ)	asg1 light	asg2 heavy
Windows								
Wood frame,	10%	Single	6 mm clear glass	5.3	5.3	0.76	0.64	0.47
			surface tinted glass	5.3	5.3	0.60	0.53	0.41
			body tinted glass	5.3	5.3	0.52	0.47	0.38
			reflective glass	5.3	5.3	0.18	0.17	0.15
		Double	Clear glazing	3.0	3.0	0.64	0.56	0.42
			surface tinted + clear	3.0	3.0	0.48	0.43	0.34
			body tinted + clear	3.0	3.0	0.40	0.37	0.30
			reflective + clear	3.0	3.0	0.28	0.25	0.21
			sealed, reflective + clear	3.0	3.0	0.15	0.14	0.11
	20%	Single	6 mm clear glass	5.0	5.0	0.76	0.64	0.42
			surface tinted glass	5.0	5.0	0.60	0.53	0.41
			body tinted glass	5.0	5.0	0.52	0.47	0.38
			reflective glass	5.0	5.0	0.18	0.17	0.15
		Double	Clear glazing	2.9	2.9	0.64	0.56	0.42
			surface tinted + clear	2.9	2.9	0.48	0.43	0.34
			body tinted + clear	2.9	2.9	0.40	0.37	0.30
			reflective + clear	2.9	2.9	0.28	0.25	0.21
			sealed, reflective + clear	2.9	2.9	0.15	0.14	0.11
	30%	Single	6 mm clear glass	4.7	4.7	0.76	0.64	0.47
			surface tinted glass	4.7	4.7	0.60	0.53	0.41
			body tinted glass	4.7	4.7	0.52	0.47	0.38
			reflective glass	4.7	4.7	0.18	0.17	0.15
		Double	Clear glazing	2.8	2.8	0.64	0.56	0.42
			surface tinted + clear	2.8	2.8	0.48	0.43	0.34
			body tinted + clear	2.8	2.8	0.40	0.37	0.30
			reflective + clear	2.8	2.8	0.28	0.25	0.21
			sealed, reflective + clear	2.8	2.8	0.15	0.14	0.11
Metal frame	10%	Single	6 mm clear glass	6.0	6.0	0.76	0.64	0.47
			surface tinted glass	6.0	6.0	0.60	0.53	0.41
			body tinted glass	6.0	6.0	0.52	0.47	0.38
			reflective glass	6.0	6.0	0.18	0.17	0.15
		Double	Clear glazing	3.6	3.6	0.64	0.56	0.42
			surface tinted + clear	3.6	3.6	0.48	0.43	0.34
			body tinted + clear	3.6	3.6	0.40	0.37	0.30
			reflective + clear	3.6	3.6	0.28	0.25	0.21
			sealed, reflective + clear	3.6	3.6	0.15	0.14	0.11
	20%	Single	6 mm clear glass	6.4	6.4	0.76	0.64	0.47
		Double	Clear glazing	4.3	4.3	0.64	0.56	0.42
Metal frame	10%	Discontinuous frame, single		5.7	5.7	0.76	0.64	0.47
		same, body tinted		5.7	5.7	0.52	0.47	0.38
		Discontinuous frame, double		3.3	3.3	0.64	0.56	0.42
	20%	Discontinuous frame, single		5.8	5.8	0.76	0.64	0.47
		Discontinuous frame, double		3.7	3.7	0.64	0.56	0.42
Vinyl frame		Double (clear + clear) glazing		2.8	2.8	0.58	0.50	0.39
		Bronze + clear glass		2.8	2.8	0.48	0.43	0.34
		Argon filled clear + clear glazing		1.9	1.9	0.55	0.49	0.39
		Argon filled low-e clear + clear		1.7	1.7	0.32	0.28	0.23

(Continued)

DATA SHEET D.1.3 (Continued)

		U-valuve (W/m²K)	admittance (W/m²K)	sgf (ω)	asg1 light	asg2 heavy
Insulated vinyl frame	Krypton fill, triple clear glass	1.9	1.9	0.5	0.47	0.38
	Krypton fill, triple(2 low-e)glass	0.9	0.9	0.37	0.34	0.27
Roof glazing	Single 6mm glass	6.6	6.6	0.76	0.64	0.47
	body tinted glass	6.6	6.6	0.52	0.47	0.38
	Double clear glazing	4.6	4.6	0.64	0.56	0.42
	body tinted + clear	4.6	4.6	0.40	0.37	0.30
Horizontal	Laylight + skylight, ventilated	3.8	3.8	0.60	0.56	0.42
	same but unventilated	3.0	3.0	0.60	0.56	0.42

Note: fc = fibrous cement

	U-valuve (W/m²K)	admittance (W/m²K)	time lag hours	decrement factor
Flat roofs				
150 concrete slab, plastered, 75 screed + asphalt	1.80	4.50	8	0.33
– same, but lightweight concrete	0.84	2.30	5	0.77
25 timber deck, bituminous felt, plasterboard ceiling	1.81	1.90	0.9	0.99
– same + 50mm EPS	0.51	0.80	1.3	0.98
10 fc deck, 13 fibreboard, asphalt, fc ceiling	1.50	1.90	2	0.96
50 ww, 13 screed, 20 asphalt, plasterboard ceiling	1.00	1.40	3	0.93
13 fibreboard, 20 asph,10 foil-back plasterboard	1.20	1.30	1	0.99
Metal deck, 25 EPS, bituminous felt	1.10	1.20	1	0.99
– same + 13 fibreboard + plasterboard ceiling	0.73	0.91	1	0.99
– same, but 50mm EPS	0.48	0.75	1	0.98
Pitched roofs				
Corrugated fibrous cement sheet	4.9	4.9	0	1
– same + attic + plasterboard ceiling	2.58	2.6	0.3	1
– same + 50mm EPS or glass fibre	0.55	1	0.7	0.99
Tiles, sarking + attic + plasterboard ceiling	2.59	2.6	0.5	1
– same + 50mm EPS or glass fibre	0.54	1.0	1.5	0.97
Tiles, sarking, 25 timber ceiling (sloping)	1.91	2.1	1.0	0.99
– same + 50mm EPS or glass fibre	0.51	1.5	1.4	0.97
Metal sheet (corrugated or profiled)	7.14	7.1	0	1
Metal sheet + attic + plasterboard ceiling	2.54	2.6	0.3	1
– same + 50mm EPS or glass fibre	0.55	1.0	0.7	0.99
Floors				
Suspended timber, bare or lino				
3 × 3m	1.05	2.0	0.7	0.99
7.5 × 7.5m	0.68	2.0	0.8	0.98
15 × 7.5m	0.61	2.0	0.8	0.98
15 × 15m	0.45	2.0	0.9	0.97
30 × 15m	0.39	2.0	0.9	0.97
60 × 15m	0.37	2.0	1.0	0.97

(Continued)

DATA SHEET D.1.3 (Continued)

Note: fc = fibrous cement	U-valuve (W/m²K)	admittance (W/m²K)	time lag hours	decrement factor
Concrete slab on ground, 2 adjacent edges exposed				
3 × 3 m	1.07	6.0	–	0.01
6 × 6 m	0.57	6.0	–	0
7.5 × 7.5 m	0.45	6.0	–	0
15 × 7.5 m	0.36	6.0	–	0
15 × 15 m	0.26	6.0	–	0
30 × 15 m	0.21	6.0	–	0
60 × 15 m	0.18	6.0	–	0
100 × 40 m	0.09	6.0	–	0
Concrete slab on ground, 2 parallel edges exposed				
3 × 3 m	1.17	6.0	–	0.01
6 × 6 m	0.58	6.0	–	0
7.5 × 7.5 m	0.48	6.0	–	0
15 × 7.5 m	0.32	6.0	–	0
15 × 15 m	0.29	6.0	–	0
30 × 15 m	0.25	6.0	–	0
60 × 15 m	0.21	6.0	–	0
100 × 40 m	0.13	6.0	–	0
Concrete slab on ground, 4 edges exposed				
3 × 3 m	1.47	6.0	–	0.02
6 × 6 m	0.96	6.0	–	0.01
7.5 × 7.5 m	0.76	6.0	–	0.01
15 × 7.5 m	0.62	6.0	–	0
15 × 15 m	0.45	6.0	–	0
30 × 15 m	0.36	6.0	–	0
60 × 15 m	0.32	6.0	–	0
100 × 40 m	0.16	6.0	–	0

DATA SHEET D.1.4

Thermal properties of surfaces and cavities

		For 6000°C solar radiation		At 50°C
		Absorptance and emittance	Reflectance	absorptance and emittance
		$\alpha + \varepsilon$	ρ	$\alpha + \varepsilon$
Radiation properties				
Brick	White, glazed	0.25	0.75	0.95
	Light colours	0.40	0.60	0.90
	Dark colours	0.80	0.20	0.90
Roofs	Asphalt or bitumen	0.90	0.10	0.96
	Red tiles	0.65	0.35	0.85
	White tiles	0.40	0.60	0.50
	Aluminium, oxidized	0.30	0.80	0.11
	Bright aluminium, chrome, nickel	0.10	0.90	0.05
	Bright (new) aluminium foil			0.03
Weathered building surfaces	Light	0.50	0.50	0.60
	Medium	0.80	0.20	0.95
Paint	White	0.30	0.70	0.92
	Matt black	0.96	0.04	0.96
Generally:	Reflectance = $(V \times V - 1)/100$ where V = Munsell value of the paint			

Surface resistances ($m^2 K/W$)		Normal surfaces	Low emittance surfaces
Inside,	Walls	0.12	0.30
	Ceiling, floor: heat flow up	0.10	0.22
	heat flow down	0.14	0.55
	45° ceiling		
	heat flow up	0.11	0.24
	heat flow down	0.13	0.39
Outside	Walls, sheltered	0.08	0.11
	normal exposure	0.06	0.07
	Severe exposure	0.03	0.03
Roofs	Sheltered	0.07	0.09
	normal exposure	0.04	0.05
	severe exposure	0.02	0.02

Cavity resistances ($m^2 K/W$)		Normal	Low emittance
Unventilated:			
5 mm cavity	Any position	0.10	0.18
>25 mm cavity,	Heat flow horizontal	0.18	0.35
	Heat flow up	0.17	0.35
	Heat flow down	0.22	1.06
	45°, heat flow up	0.19	0.40
	45°, heat flow down	0.20	0.98
Multiple foil	Heat flow horizontal or up	–	0.62
	Heat flow down	–	1.76
Ventilated:			
Between fibrous cement sheet ceiling and dark metal roof		0.16	0.30
Between fibrous cement sheet ceiling and fibrous cement roof		0.14	0.25
Between fibrous cement sheet ceiling and tiled roof		0.18	0.26
Between tiles and sarking		0.12	–
Air space behind tile hanging (including the tile)		0.12	–
In ordinary cavity walls		0.18	

DATA SHEET D.1.5

Thermal bridges, ground floors and basement walls

Linear heat loss coefficients	k
Window perimeter	0.15 W/m K
Same, but if window is in the plane of insulation and joint sealed	0
Outer corner of homogeneous wall	0.10
Outer corner of wall with external insulation	0.15
External wall with internal insulation	0
Joint of homogeneous external wall and internal wall (both edges counted)	0.12
Joint of external wall with external insulation and internal wall (both edges counted)	0.06
Joint of homogeneous. external wall and floor slab with insulation strip (both edges counted)	0.15
Joint of external wall with external insulation and floor slab (both edges counted)	0.06
Parapet wall, cornice	0.20
Projecting balcony slab	0.3

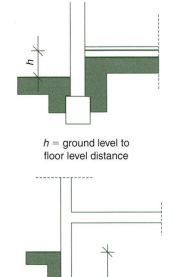

h = ground level to floor level distance

On-ground floor losses linear heat transmission coefficients W/m K

Height (h) relative to ground level (m)	If floor thermal resistance is (m²K/W)							
	No insulation	0.2–0.35	0.4–0.55	0.6–0.75	0.8–1.0	1.05–1.5	1.55–2	2.05–3
>|6.0|	0	0	0	0	0	0	0	0
−6.00 to −4.05	0.20	0.20	0.15	0.15	0.15	0.15	0.15	0.15
−4.00 to −2.55	0.40	0.40	0.35	0.35	0.35	0.35	0.30	0.30
−2.50 to −1.85	0.60	0.55	0.55	0.50	0.50	0.45	0.45	0.40
−1.80 to −0.25	0.80	0.70	0.70	0.65	0.60	0.60	0.55	0.45
−1.20 to −0.75	1.00	0.90	0.85	0.80	0.75	0.70	0.65	0.55
−0.70 to −0.45	1.20	1.05	1.00	0.95	0.90	0.80	0.75	0.65
−0.40 to −0.25	1.40	1.20	1.1 0	1.05	1.00	0.90	0.80	0.70
−0.20 to +0.20	1.75	1.45	1.35	1.25	1.15	1.05	0.95	0.85
+0.25 to +0.40	2.10	1.70	1.55	1.45	1.30	1.20	1.05	0.95
+0.45 to +1.00	2.35	1.90	1.70	1.55	1.45	1.30	1.15	1.00
+1.05 to +1.50	2.55	2.05	1.85	1.70	1.55	1.40	1.25	1.10

Losses through earth sheltered walls

Height (h) relative to ground level (m)	If U-value of wall itself is (W /m²K)							
	0.4–0.49	0.5–0.6	0.85–0.79	0.8–0.99	1–1.19	1.2–1.49	1.5–1.79	1.8–2.2
>6.0	1.40	1.65	1.85	2.05	2.25	2.45	2.65	2.80
6.00 to 5.05	1.30	1.50	1.70	1.90	2.05	2.25	2.45	2.65
5.00 to 4.05	1.15	1.35	1.50	1.65	1.90	2.05	2.24	2.45
4.00 to 3.05	1.00	1.15	1.30	1.45	1.65	1.85	2.00	2.20
3.00 to 2.55	0.85	1.00	1.15	1.30	1.45	1.65	1.80	2.00
2.50 to 2.05	0.70	0.85	1.00	1.15	1.30	1.45	1.65	1.80
2.00 to 1.55	0.60	0.70	0.85	1.00	1.10	1.25	1.40	1.55
1.50 to 1.05	0.45	0.55	0.65	0.75	0.90	1.00	1.15	1.30
1.00 to 0.75	0.35	0.40	0.50	0.60	0.65	0.80	0.90	1.05
0.70 to 0.45	0.20	0.30	0.35	0.40	0.50	0.55	0.65	0.75
0.40 to 0.25	0.10	0.15	0.20	0.25	0.30	0.35	0.40	0.45

DATA SHEET D.1.6

Moisture movement data

A *Indoor moisture production*

One person	At rest	40 g/h	
	Sedentary activity	50 g/h	
	Active	200 g/h	
Cooking (gas)	Breakfast	400 g	
	Lunch	500 g	} 3000 g/day
	Dinner	1200 g	
Dishwashing	Breakfast	100 g	
	Lunch	100 g	
	Dinner	300 g	
Floor mopping		1100 g	
Clothes washing		2000 g	
Clothes drying (indoors)		12 000 g	
Shower		200 g	
Bath		100 g	
Oil (kerosene, paraffin)	heater (flueless)	1 kg	per kg oil burnt
Animal houses:			
dairy cows	per kg body mass	1–1.5 µg/s	

B Permeability (δ) of some materials

	mg/s m kPa or µg/s m Pa
Brickwork	0.006–0.042
Cement render	0.010
Concrete	0.005–0.035
Cork board	0.003–0.004
Expanded ebonite (Onozote)	<0.0001
Expanded polystyrene	0.002–0.007
Fibreboard (softboard)	0.020–0.070
Hardboard (Masonite)	0.001–0.002
Mineral wool	0.168
Plastering	0.017–0.025
Plasterboard	0.017–0.023
Plywood	0.002–0.007
Polyurethane foam Open cell	0.035
Closed cell	0.001
Strawboard	0.014–0.022
Timber Air dry	0.014–0.022
Wet	0.001–0.008
Urea formaldehyde foam	0.031–0.053
Wood wool slab	0.024–0.070

Surface coefficients (permeance)		µg/s m² Pa
With still air	if $h = 4.5$ W/m²K	25.5
With moving air	if $h = 11.4$ W/m²K	62.3
	if $h = 17$ W/m²K	96.3

(Continued)

DATA SHEET D.1.6 (continued)

C Permeance (π) of some elements and surfaces

		mg/s m²kPa or µg/s m²Pa
Acrylic sheet	1.5 mm	0.007
Aluminium foil		<0.006
Bituminous paper		0.090
Brickwork	105 mm	0.04–0.060
Concrete blocks	200 mm hollow	0.140
Cellulose acetate	0.25 mm	0.260
	3 mm	0.018
Cement render, or screed		
	25 mm, 4:1	0.670
	25 mm, 1:1	0.400
Corkboard	25 mm	0.40–0.540
Fibreglass sheet	1.2 mm	0.003
Fibrous cement sheet	3 mm	0.20–0.500
same with oil paint		0.02–0.030
Glazed brick	105 mm	0.007
Hardboard (Masonite)	3 mm	0.630
same, tempered		0.290
Kraft paper	Single	4.540
	3-ply	2.000
	5-ply	1.600
Oil paint, 2 coats	On plaster	0.09–0.170
3 coats	On wood	0.02–0.060
Plaster on lath	25 mm	0.630
	20 mm	0.830
	12 mm	0.930
Plasterboard	10 mm	1.70–2.800
Plywood		
external quality	6 mm	0.026–0.041
internal quality	6 mm	0.106–0.370
Polyethylene film	0.06 mm	0.009
	0.1 mm	0.005
	0.2 mm	0.002
PVC sheet	0.05 mm	0.040
Same, plasticized	0.1 mm	0.050–0.080
Softwood (pine)	25 mm	0.080
	12 mm	0.10–0.170
Strawboard	50 mm	0.13–0.260
Wood wool slab	25 mm	3.08–4.140
Surface	Internal	25
	External	100

nb: any layer of less than 0.067 mg/s m²kPa (µg/s m²Pa) permeance is taken as a vapour barrier

vapour resistance is the reciprocal of permeance: $vR = 1/\pi$ or $vR = b/\delta^{\leftarrow}$.

DATA SHEET D.1.7

Heat emission of humans and appliances

Heat output of human bodies in **W** (watts)	Total	At 20°C Sensible	latent	At 26°C Sensible	latent
Seated at rest	115	90	25	65	50
Sedentary work	140	100	40	70	70
Seated, eating	150	85	65	70	80
Slow walking	160	110	50	75	85
Light bench type work	235	130	105	80	55
Medium work	265	140	125	90	175
Heavy work	440	190	250	105	335
Very heavy work (gymnasium)	585	205	380	175	420

Electric lighting load		W/(m² lux)
Incandescent	Open enamelled reflector	0.125–0.160
	General diffusing	0.160–0.225
Florescent	Whit, Open trough	0.037
	Enclosed, diffusing	0.050
	De luxe warm white, enclosed, diffusing	0.075–0.100
	Louvred, Recessed	0.085–0.110
Mercury MBF	Industrial reflector	0.050–0.075

Electrical appliances		Sensible (**W**)	Latent (**W**)
Hair dryer (blower)		700	100
Hair dryer (helmet type)		600	100
Coffee urn	14–23 L	800–1000	900–1200
	Computer (PC) Main unit		200–300
	VDU (CRT), VGA	150–300	–
	Printer	30–300	–
Food warmer	Per m² top surface	1000	1000
Frying po,	(300 × 350 mm)	1100	1700
Grill, meat	(250 × 300 cooking area)	1200	600
Grill, sandwich	(300 × 300 cooking area)	800	200
Jug or kettle		[1800	500
Microwave oven		[1300	–
Refrigerator	1 door, manual	150–260	–
	2 door, auto defrost	350–400	–
	2 door, frost-free	500–600	–
Sterilizer, bulk	(600 × 600 × 900)	10000	6500
Sterilizer, water	45 L	1200	4800
Sterilizer, water	70 L	1800	7200
Sterilizer, instrument	(150 × 100 × 450)	800	700
Toaster, pop-up	(2 slices)	700	200
Toaster, continuous	(4 slices)	1800	800
Vacuum cleaner		600–1200	–
Waffle iron		400	200
Water heater (domestic)		2400–3600	–
Coffee urn	14 – 23 L	900–1200	900–1200
Food warmer	Per m² top surface	27002700	1600
Frying pot	280 × 410 mm	2100	1400
Grill, top burner	0.13 m² surface	4400	1100
Toaster, continuous	(2 slices)	2200	1000
Stove, short order, closed top, per m² top surface		11 000	11 000
Laboratory burners (bunsen), 10 mm diameter (natural gas)		500	100

DATA SHEET D.1.8

Typical ventilation requirements

Air inhaled	At sedentary activity	$0.5\,m^3/h$
	At heavy work, up to	$5\,m^3/h$
Limitation	CO_2 content, absolute limit	0.5%
	Markedly 'used air' effect	0.15%

| If room volume per person (m^3) | Then fresh air supply rate per person | |
	Minimum	Recommended
3	12	17
6	7	11
9	5	8
12	4	6

Kitchen, other than domestic	20 air changes per hour
Kitchen, domestic	10
Laundry, boiler room, operating theatre	15
Canteen, restaurant, dance hall	10–15
Cinema, theatre, lavatory	6–10
Bathroom, bank hall, parking station	6
Office, laboratory	4–6
Library	3–4
Staircase, corridor (non-domestic)	2
All other domestic rooms	1

Requirement	If area/pers	Room occupancy type (examples only)
4 L/s.pers	Given number	Sauna, steam room
10 L/s.pers	Given number	Dormitory, ticket booth
	$0.6\,m^2$	Transport concourse, platform, funeral chapel
	$1\,m^2$	Rest room, shops fitting room, kiosk, funeral reception room
	$1.5\,m^2$	Medical waiting room, museum exhibition area, broadcast studio
	$2\,m^2$	School classroom >16 year, music room, locker room, waiting area
	$5\,m^2$	Shops sales floor, arcade, office art room, physiotherapy room, drawing office, library, coin-op laundry, pharmacy
	$10\,m^2$	Photo dark room, florist, dry cleaner, hotel bedroom, general office, bank vault, residential buildings
	$20\,m^2$	Warehouse
12 L/s.pers	$2\,m^2$	School classrooms <16 year
15 L/s.pers	$0.6\,m^2$	Theatre, opera, concert hall, foyer, lecture hall
	$1\,m^2$	Cafeteria, fast food, large assembly room, disco, conference room
	$2\,m^2$	Small conference room

(Continued)

DATA SHEET D.1.8 (Continued)

Requirement	If area/pers	Room occupancy type (examples only)
	4 m²	Theatre, concert hall, lecture hall, hairdresser shop, beauty salon
	5 m²	Hotel suite living room, theatre 'green room', prison cell block
20 L/s.pers	1 m²	Bar, cocktail lounge
	1.5 m²	Cabaret
	2 m²	Air traffic control room
	5 m²	Medical buildings: delivery and operating room
25 L/s.pers	1.5 m²	Smoking room
50 L/s.pers	5 m²	Autopsy room
On a floor area basis:		
	1 L/s m²	corridor, foyer, lobby, stairs, pedestrian tunnel, utility room
	3.5 L/s m²	Pool area, deck
	4 L/s m²	Electricity meter or switch room, fire control room
	5 L/s m²	Veterinary kennel, animal room, operating room, pet shop

METHOD SHEET M.1.1

Temperature and vapour pressure gradient

Add the thermal resistances of all layers. Divide the overall temperature difference by this total resistance. This is the 'unit drop', i.e. the temperature drop per unit resistance. Multiplied by the resistance of each layer, this will give the temperature drop for each layer. Starting with the indoor temperature, subtract the temperature drops to get the temperature at each layer junction point. From this the temperature gradient can be plotted.

Repeat the same procedure for vapour resistance, vapour pressure drop and vapour pressure at each layer junction point. The corresponding dew point temperature (DPT) is to be read from the psychrometric chart.

The method is illustrated by an example:

Take a simple cavity wall, which consists of a 110 mm brick outer skin and an inner skin of 100 mm AAC (aerated autoclaved concrete, such as Thermalite or Hebel blocks), with a 12 mm plastering on the inside.

Assume $T_i = 22°C$ and $T_o = 0°C$, $vp_i = 1.34\,kPa$, $vp_o = 0.4\,kPa$

	Temperature gradient				Vapour pressure gradient			
	R	ΔT	T at junction		vR	Δvp	vp	DPT at junction
Outside air								
External surface	0.06	1.42 K	0°C		0.01	0.001 kPa	0.4 kPa	−5.0°C
			1.42				0.401	−4.8
		3.07				0.538		
Brick: $\frac{b}{\lambda} = \frac{0.110}{0.84} = 0.13$				$\frac{b}{\delta} = \frac{0.110}{0.02} = 5.50$				
			4.49				0.939	6.4
Cavity	0.18	4.26			0.02	0.002		
			8.75				0.941	6.5
		9.94				0.326		
ACC	$\frac{0.100}{0.24} = 0.42$			$\frac{0.100}{0.03} = 0.33$				
			18.69				1.267	10.6
		0.47				0.069		
Plaster	$\frac{0.012}{0.5} = 0.02$			$\frac{0.012}{0.017} = 0.71$				
			19.16				1.336	11.5
Internal surface	0.12	2.84			0.04	0.004		
Inside air			22				1.340	11.7
	0.93	22 K			9.61	0.94 kPa		

As $\Delta T = 22\,K$, the 'unit drop is' $\dfrac{22}{0.93} = 23.65$

the T drop in each layer is $R \times 23.65$

As $\Delta vp = 1.34 − 0.4 = 0.94\,kPa$ thus the 'unit drop' is $\dfrac{0.94}{9.61} = 0.098$ thus the drop in vapour pressure in each layer is $vR \times 0.098$

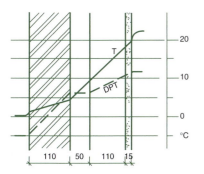

The R, λ, vR and δ values are taken from data sheets D.1.2 and D.1.6.

Where the temperature T drops below the DPT, there is a risk of condensation.

From the plot of the T and DPT profiles on a cross-section of the wall, it will be seen that there is a condensation risk at the inside face of the brick skin.

The gradients can also be determined graphically. This is best introduced by continuing the above example.

The overall vapour resistance is 9.61. Draw the thickness of the wall and its layers to a suitable vapour resistance scale. Here we assume a scale of 5 mm = 1 vR unit, so the total 'thickness' is 48 mm. Draw this section (**A**) alongside a part of the psychrometric chart, so that the vapour pressure scale of that chart (in kPa) can be used for the vertical scale in this section. Mark the level of internal vapour pressure on the inside surface of this section and the outdoor vapour pressure on the outside surface. Connect these two points by a straight line: the intersection with each boundary line will mark the vapour pressure at that plane.

To convert these vapour pressures to DPT values, project all intersection points across to the saturation curve of the psychrometric chart. Project these intersections vertically down to the base line, where the DPT can be read.

It may be convenient to use this (horizontal) temperature scale also in a vertical position, with the physical section of the wall. In the diagram below quadrant arcs have been used to translate the scale into vertical, to an actual

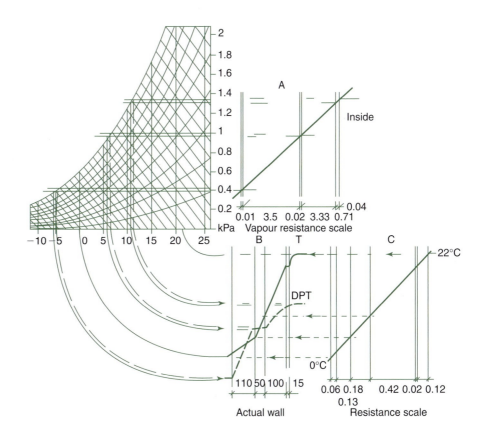

section of the wall (**B**), here drawn to a scale of 1:10. The DPT can be transferred to this section, and will define the DPT gradient.

A third section should be drawn alongside the above, where the thickness is scaled to the thermal resistance of each layer. A scale of 10 mm to 0.1 resistance unit (m^2K/W) is convenient. (**C**) The vertical (temperature) scale should be shared with the actual section. If the indoor and outdoor temperature points are marked on the surfaces and connected by a straight line, the intersection of this with each layer boundary will determine the temperature at that point. The line connecting these points will be the temperature gradient across the wall.

Wherever the dew-point gradient dips below the temperature gradient, there will be a condensation risk (in this case at the inside surface of the outer brick skin).

METHOD SHEET M.1.2

Stack and wind effects

STACK EFFECT

Air flow in a stack is driven by the density difference between inside and outside air.

The density of air at 0°C is $d_o = 1.293 \, kg/m^3$

and at any other temperature T: $\boxed{d_T = 1.293 \times 273 / T}$ (1)
where T is absolute temperature in °K.

The gravitational acceleration is $g = 9.81 \, m/s^2$.

The 'stack pressure' $(p_i - p_o)$ is $\Delta p = h \times g \times (d_o - d_i)$.

Substituting from eq. (1) $\Delta p = h \times 9.81 \times (1.293 \times 273/T_o - 1.293 \times 273/T_i)$

$$\boxed{\Delta p = h \times 3462 \times (1/T_o - 1/T_i)} \quad (2)$$

(as $9.81 \times 1.293 \times 273 = 3462$)

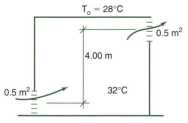

$T_o = 28°C$

0.5 m²

4.00 m

0.5 m²

32°C

where T is in °K,
         height (h) is in m (between centres of inlet and outlet),
then Δp is in Pa (pascal).
A useful rule of thumb is that $\Delta p \approx 0.13 \, Pa/K$ for each storey height.

The volume flow rate will then be $\boxed{vr = 0.827 \times A \times \sqrt{\Delta p}}$ (3)

where A is in m^2 and vr is in m^3/s.
If apertures are in series (e.g. inlet and outlet)

then the effective area will be $A' = \dfrac{A_1 + A_2}{\sqrt{A_1^2 + A_2^2}}$

---

e.g: if $T_o = 28°C = 301°K$, which gives a density of $1.293 \times 273/301 = 1.173 \, kg/m^3$
        $T_i = 32°C = 305°K$, which gives a density of $1.293 \times 273/305 = 1.157 \, kg/m^3$
and if $h = 4 \, m$
Then $\Delta p = 4 \times 3462 \times (1/301 - 1/305) = 0.6 \, Pa$ or $\Delta p = 4 \times 9.81 \times (1.173 - 1.157) = 0.6 \, Pa$ and if inlet = outlet = shaft cross-sectional area: $A = 0.5 \, m^2$
Then $vr = 0.827 \times 0.5 \times \sqrt{0.6} = 0.32 \, m^3/s$ or $320 \, L/s$

WIND EFFECT

The pressure of wind is $p_w = 0.5 \times d \times v^2$
where d = density, as above (often taken as $1.224 \, kg/m^3$ corresponding to 15.5°C)
       v = velocity in m/s
       Thus generally taken as $\boxed{p_w = 0.612 \times v^2}$ (4)

For a building surface this must be multiplied by a pressure coefficient c_p typical values of which are

on windward side $c_{pW} = 0.5$ to 0.8
on leeward side $c_{pL} = -0.3$ to -0.5

Cross-ventilation is driven by the wind pressure difference

$$\Delta p_w = p_w \times (c_{pW} + c_{pL}) \tag{5}$$

and the resulting volume flow rate will be

$$vr = 0.827 \times A \times c_e \times \sqrt{\Delta p_W} \tag{6}$$

where A = effective area of openings (as above)
         c_e = 'effectiveness coefficient'
values of which are
from   0.1 if windows in one wall only (no cross-ventilation)
to   with full cross-ventilation, equal, inlet and outlet, no partitions

e.g.	if v = 3 m/s	$c_{pW} = 0.8$ $c_{pL} = -0.4$
Then		$\Delta_{pW} = 0.612 \times 3^2 \times [0.8 - (-0.4)]$
		$= 0.612 \times 9 \times 1.2 = 6.61$ Pa
and if	$A = 3\,m^2$	$c_e = 1$ (full cross-ventilation)
then		$vr = 0.827 \times 3 \times 1 \times \sqrt{6.61} = 6.38\,m^3/s$

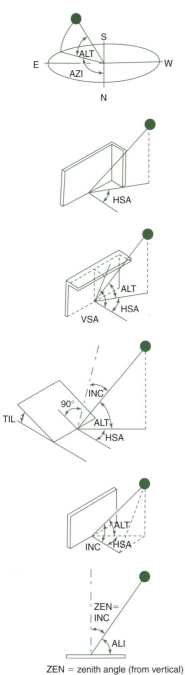

ZEN = zenith angle (from vertical)

METHOD SHEET M.1.3

Solar geometry

Definitions:
AZI = Solar azimuth (0–360°)
ALT = Solar altitude (from horizontal; zenith = 90°)
ZEN = Zenith angle (from the vertical); ZEN = 90 − ALT
ORI = Orientation (azimuth of the surface normal, 0–360°)
HAS = Horizontal shadow angle (azimuth difference)
VSA = Vertical shadow angle (on perpendicular normal plane)
INC = Angle of incidence (from the surface normal)
LAT = Geographical latitude (south negative)
DEC = Declination (between the earth–sun line and the equator plane)
HRA = Hour angle from solar noon, 15° per hour
SRA = Sunrise azimuth, i.e. azimuth at sunrise time
SRT = Sunrise time

Expressions:

DEC = 23.45 × sin[0.9836 × (284 + NDY)]   (result in degrees)
  where NDY = number of day of year
    0.9836 = 360°/365 days
  Or more accurately:

DEC = 0.33281 − 22.984 × cos N + 3.7872 × sin N
    − 0.3499 × cos(2 × N) + 0.03205 × sin(2 × N)
    − 0.1398 × cos(3 × N) + 0.07187 × sin(3 × N)

where N = 2 × π × NDY/366 in radians (if trigonometric functions set for radians)
    N = 0.9836 × NDY in degrees (if trigonometric functions set for degrees)
                        (in any case DEC results in degrees)

HRA = 15 × (hour − 12)

ALT = arcsin(sin DEC × sin LAT + cos DEC × cos LAT × cos HRA)

$$AZI = arcos \frac{\cos LAT \times \sin DEC - \cos DEC \times \sin LAT \times \cos HRA}{\cos ALT}$$

                        gives result 0–180°, i.e. for a.m. only,
        for p.m. take AZI = 360 − AZI (as found from the above expression).

HAS = AZI − ORI
      if 90° < abs|HSA| < 270° then sun is behind the facade, it is in shade
      if HSA > 270° then HSA = HSA − 360°
      if HSA < − 270° then HSA = HSA + 360°

$$VSA = arctan \frac{\tan ALT}{\cos HSA}$$

$$INC = arcos(sin\,ALT \times cos\,TIL + cos\,ALT \times sin\,TIL \times cos\,HSA)$$

where TIL = tilt angle of receiving plane from the horizontal.

For vertical planes, as $TIL = 90$, $cos\,TIL = 0$, $sin\,TIL = 1$:

$$INC = arcos(cos\,ALT \times cos\,HSA)$$

For a horizontal plane:

$$INC = ZEN = 90 - ALT$$

$$SRA = arcos(cos\,LAT \times sin\,DEC + tan\,LAT \times tan\,DEC \times sin\,LAT \times cos\,DEC)$$

$$SRT = 12 - \frac{arcos(-tan\,LAT \times tan\,DEC)}{15}$$

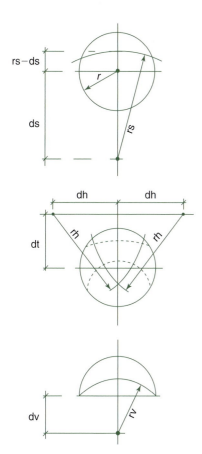

METHOD SHEET M.1.4

Construction of stereographic sun-path diagrams

1 Draw a circle of selected radius (r), most often taken as 75 mm (150 mm diameter). Draw a horizontal and a vertical diameter to indicate the four compass points. Extend the vertical one in the polar direction, to give the locus for the centres of all sun-path arcs.

2 For each sun-path arc (each date) calculate its radius (rs) and the distance of its centre from the centre of the circle (ds)

$$rs = r \times \frac{\cos DEC}{\sin LAT + \sin DEC} \qquad ds = r \times \frac{\cos LAT}{\sin LAT + \sin DEC}$$

where

	LAT = geographical latitude
	DEC = solar declination angle
March 21 and September 23:	DEC = 0
June 22	DEC = 23.45°
December 22	DEC = −23.45°

For intermediate lines the following dates are suggested:

May 12 + August 1	DEC = 18°
April 14 + August 28	DEC = 9°
November 11 + January 30	DEC = −18°
October 14 + February 27	DEC = −9°

3 For the construction of the hour lines calculate the distance of the locus of centres from the centre of the circle (dt) and draw this locus parallel to the east–west axis:

$$dt = r \times \tan LAT$$

For each hour calculate the horizontal displacement of the centre from the vertical centreline (dh) and the radius of the hour-arc (rh):

$$dh = \frac{r}{\cos LAT \times \tan HRA} \qquad rh = \frac{r}{\cos LAT \times \sin HRA}$$

where HRA hour angle from noon, 15° for each hour
　　　e.g. for 8:00 h: HRA = 15 × (8 − 12) = −60°
　　　for 16:00 h: HRA = 15 × (16 − 12) = 60°

Draw the arcs for afternoon hours from a centre on the right-hand side and for the morning hours from the left-hand side. A useful check is that the 6:00 and 18:00 h lines should meet the equinox sun-path at exactly the east and west points respectively.

4 Mark the azimuth angles on the perimeter at any desired increments from 0° to 360° (north) and construct a set of concentric circles to indicate the altitude angle scale.

For any altitude (ALT) the radius will be

$$ra = r \times \frac{\cos ALT}{1 + \sin ALT}$$

5 For a **shadow-angle protractor** draw a semicircle to the same radius as the chart. Extend the vertical axis downwards to give the locus for the centres of all VSA (vertical shadow angle) arcs. For each chosen increment of VSA find the displacement of the centre (dv) and the radius of the arc (rv):

$$dv = r \times \tan VSA \qquad rv = \frac{r}{\cos VSA}$$

6 Mark the HSA (horizontal shadow angle) scale along the perimeter: the centreline is zero, then to 90° to the right (clockwise) and to −90° to the left (anticlockwise). A useful check is that along the centreline of the protractor the VSA arcs should coincide with the corresponding altitude circles of the sun-path diagram.

Comfort limits (Phoenix):

	January	July
$T_U =$	23.5	30.2
Tn $=$	21.0	27.7
$T_L =$	18.5	25.2

METHOD SHEET M.1.5

Determine shading (overheated) period

Solar heat input can be tolerated up to $To = Tn$ (as long as outdoor temperature is less than the neutrality) and it is definitely desirable when To is below the lower comfort limit.

Take Phoenix (AZ) as an example. The printout shows hourly temperatures for an average day of each month, as well as the neutrality (as per eq. (1.9) in section 1.2.3) with the $\pm 2.5\,$K upper and lower comfort limits. Tn varies between 21°C (January) and 27.7°C (July). The lower limit in January is 18.5°C. Below this solar heat input is welcome. Above 27.7°C shading is a must, but the shading limit (a compromise) may be between 21°C and 27.7°C. These three isopleths are plotted on a month × hour chart.

Month\ hour	1	2	3	4	5	6	7	8	9	10	11	12	13	14	15	16	17	18	19	20	21	22	23	24	Average
1	...7.1	6.1	5.2	4.5	4.1	4.0	4.5	6.1	8.3	11.0	13.7	15.9	17.5	18.0	17.9	17.5	16.8	15.9	14.9	13.7	12.4	11.0	9.6	8.3	11.0
2	...9.3	8.2	7.3	6.6	6.1	6.0	6.6	8.2	10.6	13.5	16.4	18.8	20.4	21.0	20.9	20.4	19.7	18.8	17.7	16.4	15.0	13.5	12.0	10.6	13.5
3	...11.6	10.3	9.3	8.6	8.2	8.0	8.6	10.3	12.9	16.0	19.1	21.7	23.4	24.0	23.9	23.4	22.7	21.7	20.4	19.1	17.6	16.0	14.4	12.9	16.0
4	...14.6	13.5	12.7	12.2	12.0	12.5	13.9	16.0	18.6	21.4	24.0	26.1	27.5	28.0	27.8	27.3	26.5	25.4	24.0	22.5	20.8	19.2	17.5	16.0	20.0
5	...18.8	17.6	16.7	16.2	16.0	16.5	18.0	20.2	23.0	26.0	28.8	31.0	32.5	33.0	32.8	32.3	31.4	30.2	28.8	27.1	25.4	23.6	21.9	20.2	24.5
6	...22.9	21.8	21.2	21.0	21.4	22.6	24.5	26.9	29.5	32.1	34.5	36.4	37.6	38.0	37.8	37.2	36.1	34.8	33.2	31.4	29.5	27.6	25.8	24.2	29.5
7	...27.5	26.4	25.6	25.2	25.0	25.5	26.8	28.8	31.2	33.8	36.2	38.2	39.5	40.0	39.8	39.4	38.6	37.5	36.2	34.8	33.3	31.7	39.2	28.8	32.5
8	...26.3	25.3	24.6	24.2	24.0	24.4	25.6	27.5	29.8	32.2	34.5	36.4	37.6	38.0	37.8	37.4	36.7	35.7	34.5	33.2	31.7	30.3	28.8	27.5	31.0
9	...23.5	22.4	21.6	21.2	21.0	21.5	22.8	24.8	27.2	29.8	32.2	34.2	35.5	36.0	35.8	35.4	34.6	33.5	32.2	30.8	29.3	27.7	26.2	24.8	28.5
10	...16.8	15.5	14.4	13.6	13.2	13.0	13.6	15.5	18.2	21.5	24.8	27.5	29.4	30.0	29.8	29.4	28.6	27.5	26.2	24.8	23.2	21.5	19.8	18.2	21.5
11	...10.8	9.5	8.4	7.6	7.2	7.0	7.6	9.5	12.2	15.5	18.8	21.5	23.4	24.0	23.8	23.4	22.6	21.5	20.2	18.8	17.2	15.5	13.8	12.2	15.5
12	...8.2	7.0	6.0	5.1	4.5	4.1	4.0	4.7	6.8	9.8	13.2	16.2	18.3	19.0	18.9	18.5	17.9	17.0	16.0	14.8	13.6	12.2	10.8	9.4	11.5

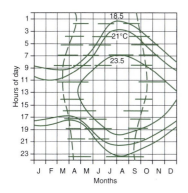

Temperature isopleths for Phoenix, Arizona

On the sun-path diagram the long east–west arcs correspond to the month lines of the above and the short north–south curves are the hour lines. So the above isopleths can be transferred onto this 'twisted' chart base, except that each sun-path curve is valid for two dates, thus two solar charts must be used, one from December to June and the other from July to December.

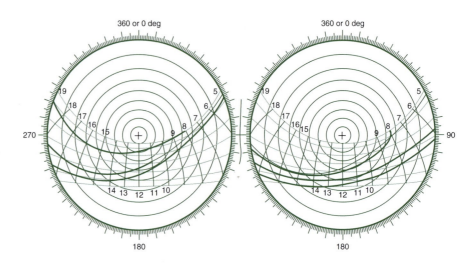

Outside the 18.5°C curve solar input is welcome. Inside the 27.7°C curve solar input must be prevented. The boundary of the shading period will probably be around the 21°C curve, but it could be anywhere between the 18.5°C and 27.7°C isopleths, depending on the particular conditions. It can be noted that the December–June half year requires less shading than the June–December half (temperatures are lagging behind solar heating by 4–6 weeks) thus the solution will have to be a compromise between the spring and autumn limits. The final decision can only be made when building (window) orientation and the form of shading system are considered. Shading design has been discussed in Section 1.4.1.1 and an example was shown in Fig. 1.46, with the protractor laid over the solar chart.

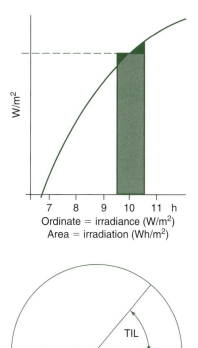

W/m²

7 8 9 10 11 h
Ordinate = irradiance (W/m²)
Area = irradiation (Wh/m²)

TIL

METHOD SHEET M.1.6

Solar radiation calculations

Notation G = irradiance or power density (W/m²)

D = irradiation (Wh/m²) over a specified period, e.g. day or month

First subscript   b = beam (direct)

d = diffuse

r = reflected   if none, then it means Global

Second subscript (surface of incidence)

n = normal to the direction of the beam

p = on a plane (to be defined)

v = vertical (e.g. G_{v270} = irradiance of a west-facing vertical plane)

h = horizontal (may be omitted)

TIL = tilt angle of a plane from the horizontal

ρ = (rho) reflectance

If daily total horizontal irradiation (Dh) is given for an average day of the month

1 estimate beam and diffuse components of the total

a find extraterrestrial irradiance (W/m²) normal to the direction of radiation

$G_{on} = 1353 \times [1 + 0.033 \times \cos(2 \times \pi \times NDY/365.24)$

where NDY = number of day of the year, taken for mid-month

b the daily total irradiation (Wh/m²) on a horizontal plane will be

$D_h = (24/\pi) \times G_{on} \times \cos LAT \times \cos DEC \times (\sin SSH - SSH \times \cos SSH)$

where   LAT = latitude

DEC = solar declination (see method sheet M.1.3)

SSH = sunset hour angle = $\arccos(-\tan LAT \times \tan DEC)$

c the atmospheric clearness index is $k' = Dh/D_{oh}$

d the diffuse fraction will be

if $j = SSH - 0.5 \times \pi$

$df = 0.775 + 0.347 \times j - (0.505 + 0.261 \times j) \times \cos[2 \times (k' - 0.9)]$

e then the diffuse component will be $D_{dh} = Dh \times df$

f and the beam component $D_{bh} = Dh - D_{dh}$

2 estimate hourly values of global radiation and of diffuse component

a pre-calculate five factors

$f1 = \sin(SSH - 1.047)$

$f2 = 0.409 + 0.5016 \times f1$

$f3 = 0.6609 - 0.4767 \times f1$

$f4 = (\pi/24)/[\sin SSH - (SSH \times \cos SSH)]$

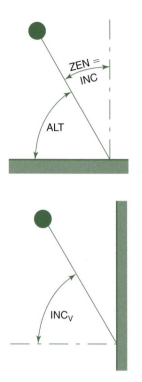

b for each hour from sunrise to sunset the fraction of the day's total for that time $r(_t)$ will be

$f5 = \cos HRA - \cos SSH$

fraction of total:　　　$rt_t = f4 \times f5 \times (f2 + f3 \times \cos HRA)$

fraction of diffuse:　　$rf_t = f4 \times f5$

c total irradiation for the hour　　　$Dh_t = Dh \times rt_t$

diffuse irradiation for the hour　　$Dd_t = Ddh \times rf_t$

the beam component will be the difference between the two

$$Db_t = Dh_t - Dd_t$$

Generally　　　　$G = Gb + Gd\ (+Gr)$

Diffuse　　　　$Gdv = Gdh \times 0.5$
$Gdp = Gdh \times (1 + \cos TIL)/2$
　　　　　when $TIL = 0$, then $\cos TIL = 1$, $(1 + 1)/2 = 1$
　　　　　when $TIL = 90°$ then $\cos TIL = 0$, $(1 + 0)/2 = 0.5$

Reflected　　　$Grv = Gh \times \rho \times 0.5$
$Grp = Gh \times \rho \times (1 - \cos TIL)/2$
　　　　　when $TIL = 0$, then $\cos TIL = 1$, $(1 - 1)/2 = 0$
　　　　　when $TIL = 90°$ then $\cos TIL = 0$, $(1 - 0)/2 = 0.5$

Horizontal/normal　　$Gh = Gn \times \cos ZEN$
$Gn = Gh/\cos ZEN$
$Gh \times \sin ALT$ (as $ALT = 90° - ZEN$)

Beam:
Vertical/normal　　　　　$Gbv = Gn \times \cos INCv$
$Gh \times \cos INCv/\sin ALT$
$Gbp = Gh \times \cos INCp/\sin ALT$

Total:
$Gp = Gh \times \cos INCp/\sin ALT + Gdh \times (1 + \cos TIL)/2$
　　　$+ Gh \times \rho \times (1 - \cos TIL)/2$
$Gv = \cos INCv/\sin ALT + Gdh \times 0.5 \times Gh \times \rho \times 0.5$

METHOD SHEET M.1.7

Construction of comfort zone and CPZs

1 Establish the mean temperature of the warmest and coldest months (Tav).

2 Find the neutrality temperature for both $\qquad$ Tn = 17.6 + 0.31 × Tav°C
and the limits of comfort $\qquad$ lower: T_L = Tn − 2.5°C
upper: T_U = Tn + 2.5 °C.

Mark these on the 50% RH curve.

3 Construct the corresponding sloping SET lines by determining the X-axis intercept from $\qquad T = T_L + 0.023 \times (T_L - 14) \times AH_{50}$
where AH_{50} is the absolute humidity (g/kg) at the RH 50% level at the T_L temperature this can be read from the psychrometric chart (Fig. 1.6) or calculated as half of the SH. The saturation vapour pressure is

$$p_{vs} = 0.133322 \times \exp[18.6686 - 4030.183/T_L + 235)]$$

saturation humidity will be SH = 622 × pvs/(101.325 − pvs)
and $\qquad AH_{50} = 0.5 \times sh$
repeat for T_U and repeat both for the warmest month.

Passive solar heating CPZ

In relation to the July comfort zone (see also Example 1.7 in Section 1.5.1.1)
the extension is if $\qquad \eta = 0.5 \qquad\qquad$ then 0.0036 × Dv.360
$\eta = 0.7 \qquad\qquad$ then 0.005 × Dv.360

Draw vertical lines at these limiting temperatures.
The upper limit will be the 95% RH curve.

Mass effect CPZ

For summer, in relation to the January comfort zone
if 'amplitude' = $(T_{max} - T_{min})$ then for mass: $\qquad$ dT = amplitude × 0.3
with night vent $\quad$ dT = amplitude × 0.6

Limiting temperature = T_U + dT
Draw corresponding SET lines as in (3) above.
The upper boundary of the CPZ is the 14 g/kg.

Repeat for 'winter' in relation to the July comfort zone CPZ to the left.
Mark the limiting temperature on the 50% RH curve.
Find the X-axis intercept as in (3) above; draw the (near vertical) side boundary.
The top boundary cannot be higher than the 95% RH curve

Air movement effect CPZ

For summer, in relation to the January comfort zone for 1 and 1.5 m/s
Effective velocities 0.8 and 1.3 m/s
Apparent cooling effects dT (from eq. (1.24)) limiting temperatures: T_U + dT.
Mark these on the 50% RH curve.
Find the notional X-axis intercept as in (3) above.
Draw the boundary from this intercept upwards from the 50% curve only
For the lower half take half of this increment.
The top limit is the 95% RH curve

Evaporative cooling CPZ

Take lower left corner of January comfort zone (the *S*-point).
Draw the corresponding WBT line to the *X*-axis.

$$X\text{-intercept} = S + AH \times (2501 - 1.805 \times T)/1000.$$

Draw parallel line from top right corner of comfort zone.
The temperature limit is the vertical at $Tn + 11°C$

For indirect this is at $Tn + 14°C$ and the upper boundary is the 14 g/kg horizontal line, e.g. for Brisbane.

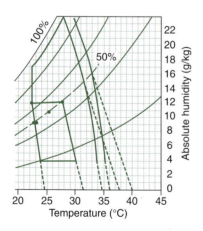

Passive solar

July: mean temperature $\bar{T} = 15.1°C$ north vertical irradiation $D_{v.360} = 3094 \, Wh/m^2$.

$Tn = 17.8 + 0.31 \times 15.1 = 22.5°C$
$TL = 20°C$
$TU = 25$
Limiting outdoor temperatures for passive solar heating:
$20 - 0.005 \times 3094 = 4.5°C$
$20 - 0.0036 \times 3094 = 8.9°C$

Mass effect

July (as above)

			$T_{ampl} = 20.4 - 9.8 = 10.6 \, K$
$T_L = 20$	$p_{vsL} = 2.3 \, kPa$	$sh_L = 14.6 \, g/kg$	$AH_{50: \, L} = 7.3 \, g/kg$
$T_U = 25°C$	$p_{vsU} = 3.15 \, kPa$	$sh_U = 20 \, g/kg$	$AH_{50: \, U} = 10 \, g/kg$

Intercepts: $T1 = 20 + 0.023 \times (20 - 14) \times 7.3 = 21°C$
$T2 = 25 + 0.023 \times (25 - 14) \times 10 = 27.5°C$
Lower limit: $20 - (10.6 \times 0.3) = 16.8°C$

January mean temperature $\bar{T} = 25°C$ $T_{ampl} = 29.1 - 21 = 8.1 \, K$
$Tn = 17.8 + 0.31 \times 25 = 25.5°C$

$T_L = 23°C$	$p_{vsL} = 2.79$	$sh_L = 17.6$	$AH_{50: \, L} = 8.8$
$T_U = 28°C$	$p_{vsU} = 3.75 \, kPa$	$sh_U = 23.9 \, g/kg$	$AH_{50: \, U} = 11.9 \, g/kg$

Intercepts: $T3 = 23 + 0.023 \times (23 - 14) \times 8.8 = 24.4°C$
$T4 = 28 + 0.023 \times (28 - 14) \times 11.9 = 31.8°C$
Upper limit: $28 + (14.5 \times 0.3) = 32.3°C$
With night vent: $28 + (14.5 \times 0.6) = 36.7°C$

Air movement effect

January (as above)
$Tn = 25.5°C$
$TL = 23°C$
$TU = 28°C$
Upper limits: for 1 m/s $T1 = 28 + 6 \times 0.8 - 1.6 \times 0.8^2 = 32.2°C$ $AH1 = 15.2 \, g/kg$
For 1.5 m/s $T2 = 28 + 6 \times 1.3 - 1.6 \times 1.3^2 = 33.1°C$ $AH2 = 16 \, g/kg$
For notional intercept $dT1 = 0.023 \times (32.2 - 14) \times 15.2 = 6.4 \, K$
$dT2 = 0.023 \times (33.1 - 14) \times 16 = 7 \, K$
Notional intercept $T1 = 32.2 + 6.4 = 38.6°C$
$T2 = 33.1 + 7 = 40.1°C$
Actual intercept $T1 = 32.2 + 6.4/2 = 35.4°C$
$T2 = 33.1 + 7/2 = 36.3°C$

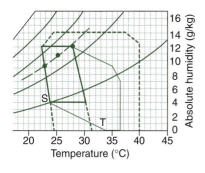

Evaporative cooling

January (as above)

Tn = 25.5 °C

Vertical limits, direct cooler: 25.5 + 11 = 36.5°C

                     indirect cooler: 25.5 + 14 = 39.5°C

T_L = 23°C: AH diff = AH_L − 4 = 9 − 4 = 5 g/kg

S-point: 23 + 0.023 × (23 − 14) × 5 = 24°C

Lower X-axis intercept (as AH dif = 4):

T = 24 + 4 × (2501 − 1.805 × 24)/1000 = 33.8°C

METHOD SHEET M.1.8

Outline of the program 'ARCHIPAK'

A series of small programs have been written by the author over the 1980s, for solar geometry, solar radiation, climate data handling, degree-day, building heat loss calculations, etc. These were put together in the early 1990s to form an architectural package (hence the name ARCHIPAK) and supplemented by a database system. The package has been re-shaped from 1995 on, using VisualBasic, to run under Windows.

Database

This includes almost 200 **climatic data** files, of the form shown in Fig. 1.39 (Section 1.3.3 above). A **materials** file contains data of the kind given here in data sheet D.1.1, with a 2-digit code for each. The **elements** file contains some 500 floor, wall, opening, roof and partition constructions (similar to data sheets D.1.2 and D.1.3 above) with a 3-digit code for each. New items can be created by specifying the thickness and materials code for each and properties (*U*-value, time lag, decrement factor and admittance) are calculated and listed under the code assigned. There are facilities for creating, editing and retrieving any entry.

Climate analysis

The 'Mahoney-table' analysis can be carried out (c.f. Koenigsberger *et al.*, 1973) producing some simple design recommendations. The climatic data can be tabulated or graphically presented. Frequency distributions of temperatures (bell-curves) can be produced. An analysis based on the **CPZ method** can be carried out (e.g. Figs 1.70, 1.73, 1.75, 1.76, 1.78 and method sheet M.1.7) to get strategic guidance. It can calculate degree-hours and estimate the fraction of time overheated, underheated or excessively humid.

Solar design

This section can produce a stereographic **sun-path diagram** for the exact location specified, and has an interactive facility for shading design. (see e.g. Fig. 1.52). It can also calculate solar position and shadow angles as well as calculate daily or hourly values of irradiance for any time of the year and any orientation.

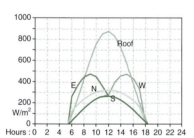
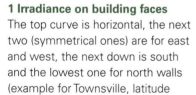

1 Irradiance on building faces
The top curve is horizontal, the next two (symmetrical ones) are for east and west, the next down is south and the lowest one for north walls (example for Townsville, latitude −19°).

Thermal design

This section allows the input of a house (or a similarly simple building), a steady-state and a dynamic thermal analysis. A house is described in a tabular form: one line for each element, inputting sizes, element codes and orientation (horizontal is stated as −1 and all roofs are taken as the horizontal projected area: assuming that if one part the roof gets more solar input, another part will get less, i.e. the total solar input is the same as on the horizontal projected area). The line is then extended by data picked up from the elements file and some attributes calculated (e.g. $A \times U$ or $A \times Y$).

The steady-state analysis (for heating design), 'QBALANCE' calculates the envelope and ventilation conductances and shows the heat loss rate as a function of outdoor temperature. Where this heat loss function has the same value as any heat gain (Qs +i, i.e. solar + internal heat gain), the 'balance-point temperature is obtained. A sequence of alternatives can be tested and the best one selected (see 2 below).

The dynamic analysis, 'HARMON', is based on the BRE method (as in Section 1.4.4 above) and performing the 'admittance procedure'. Here the result is given as a 24-h graph of indoor and outdoor temperature profiles, with the comfort band superimposed, or in tabulated form: 24 columns of the 'driving forces' (outdoor temperatres and solar input on each building face) and the result: the indoor temperature. This can be supplemented by the infoor temperatures resulting from 14th percentile of minima and 86th percentile of maxima. Tabulations can be obtained of the hourly heat flows and of heat flow swings. Alternatively hourly values of air conditioning load can be tabulated or shown in graphic form (3 below), both for controlled mode, in kWh and free-running mode in Kh. An annual summary table can also be produced (4 below).

2 Output of QBALANCE

Dotted sloping line: version 1. Solid line: improved version 2. The heat loss function $q \times dT$. *X*-axis intercept at the 16°C set-point temperature (optional).

Horizontal line Qs + *i*, solar and internal gain, 24 h average.

Intersection of this and the heat loss line gives the balance-point temperature (hence the name of the module: QBALANCE). At any To (*X*-axis) the heat loss line gives the heating requirement from the Qs + *i* line upwards.

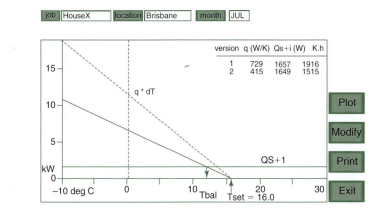

3 Air conditioning load estimate

Lower thin line curve: To, solid curve: Ti.

Dotted curve is what Ti would be (7:30–16:00) if free running.

Histogram: a/c load, lower part: sensible, upper part: latent.

Two parallel horizontal lines: comfort band.

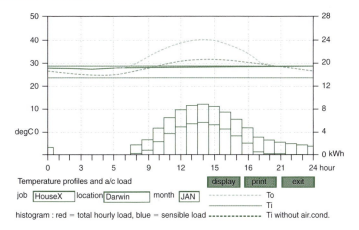

4 Example of an annual summary

SUMMARY for House Y in Brisbane

Month	To_{av}	Ti_{min}	Ti_{max}	Controlled		Free-running	
				Heating (kWh)	Cooling (kWh)	Underheated (Kh)	Overheated (Kh)
January	25.0	22.9	27.9	–	3931	–	400
February	24.8	22.8	27.8	–	2883	01	304
March	23.6	22.4	27.4	–	1592	108	111
April	21.8	21.9	26.9	423	–	445	–
May	18.4	20.8	25.8	843	–	1545	–
June	16.2	20.1	25.1	1130	–	2468	–
July	15.0	19.8	24.8	1378	–	3149	–
August	16.5	20.2	25.2	1158	–	2331	–
September	18.6	20.9	25.9	826	–	1389	–
October	21.1	21.6	26.6	529	–	661	–
November	23.0	22.2	27.2	–	1794	217	101
December	24.1	22.6	27.6	–	2988	66	263

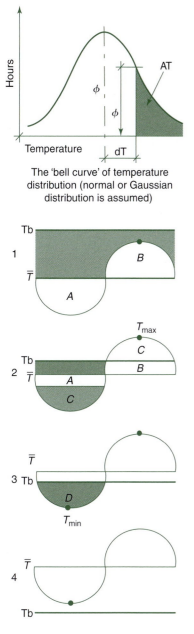

The 'bell curve' of temperature distribution (normal or Gaussian distribution is assumed)

METHOD SHEET M.1.9

Calculation of degree-hours

Heating degree-hours for a month
{Data required: $\bar{T}$ = outdoor mean temperature
Tsd = standard deviation of temperatures
Tb = base temperature (e.g. the lower comfort limit).

Let
dT be Tb − $\bar{T}$
X be dT/Tsd
The probability density function is

$$\phi = \frac{1}{\sqrt{2 \times \pi} \times \exp[-(X^2/2)]} \tag{1}$$

If *t* is taken as

$$t = \frac{1}{1 + 0.33267 \times X} \tag{2}$$

then the 'tail area' will be

$$AT = \phi \times (0.43618 \times X - 0.12016 \times X^2 + 0.93729 \times X^3) \tag{3}$$
(a numerical approximation of the integral)

The fraction below the base temperature will be
if dT > 0 then $\Phi = 1 - AT$
otherwise $\Phi = AT$

Finally
$$Kh = 24 \times N \times (\Phi) \times dT + Tsd \times \phi \tag{4}$$
where *N* = number of days in the month.

For example for Canberra, July
$\bar{T}$ = 5.3°C
Tsd = 2.7 K
Tb = 15.4°C

dT = 15.4 − 5.3 = 10.1

$$X = \frac{10.1}{2.7} = 3.74$$

as $\dfrac{1}{\sqrt{2 \times \pi}} = 0.3989$

$\phi = 0.3989 \times \exp[-(3.74^2/2)] = 0.000365$

$t = \dfrac{1}{1 + 0.33267 \times 3.74} = 0.45$

$AT = 0.000365 \times (0.43618 \times 0.45 - 0.12016 \times 0.45^2 + 0.93729 \times 0.45^3)$
$= 9.25 \times 10^{-5}$

as 10.1 > 0

$P = 1 - AT = 0.9999$
$Kh = 24 \times 31 \times (0.9999 \times 10.1 + 2.7 \times 0.000365) = \mathbf{7514}$

The assumption behind eq. (4) above is that $Kh = 24 \times Kd$ (or $24hN$ $(Tb - \bar{T})$ is not always true. A correction term may have to be added to the Kh value thus obtained. The criteria will be the relative position of Tb, $\bar{T}$, T_{max} and T_{min} and intersections with the diurnal temperature curve (N = number of days in month)

1 if $Tb > T_{max}$ then $Kh = 24 \times Kd$, area A compensates for area B, the assumption is OK

2 $T_{max} > Tb > \bar{T}$ then A compensates for B, but C must be added. Assume semicircle, $r = T_{max} - Tb$, thus $C = r^2\pi/2$. Thus $Kh = 24 \times Kd + N \times C$

3 if $\bar{T} > Tb > T_{min}$ then $Kd = 0$ but area D indicates heating requirement, if semicircle $r = Tb - T_{min}$ thus $Kh = N \times D = N \times r^2\pi/2$

4 if $Tb < T_{min}$ then $Kh = 0$, no heating requirement

in the above example (Canberra, July) $T_{max} = 11.1°C < 15.4$, so this last case is applicable.

METHOD SHEET M.1.10

Dynamic thermal properties

Diffusivity is a composite index of material properties:

$$\alpha = \frac{\lambda}{\rho \times c} \tag{1}$$

dimensionally $\dfrac{W \,/\, mK}{kg/m^3 \times Wh/kgK} = m^2/h$

or if c is in J/kgK then α is in m^2/s.

Decrement factor (non-dimensional) and the **time lag** (hour) are discussed in Section 1.4.4 and method sheet M.1.11.

Specific admittance (or heat penetration coefficient or 'effusivity')

$$\beta = \sqrt{\lambda \times \rho \times c} = \sqrt{\frac{W}{mK} \times \frac{kg}{m^3} \times \frac{Wh}{kgK}} = \frac{W}{m^2K} h^{1/2} \tag{2}$$

Admittance, for a solid homogeneous element
where ω is angular velocity, for 1 cycle per day: $2\pi/24 = 0.2618\,\text{rad/h}$

$$Y = \sqrt{\lambda \times \rho \times c \times \omega} \tag{3}$$

$as \; \sqrt{\omega} = \sqrt{0.2618} = 0.5117\,h^{-1/2}$

$Y = 0.5117 \times \beta \, \text{W/m}^2\text{K}$

Some authors use the concept of **time constant**, the product of resistance and thermal capacity:

$$\gamma = \frac{b}{\lambda} \times b \times \rho \times c = \frac{b^2 \times \rho \times c}{\lambda} \quad \text{and if the } \alpha \text{ term is substituted it becomes}$$

$$\gamma = \frac{b^2}{\alpha}, \text{ and taken for unit area, its dimension will be} \tag{4}$$

s (second) if α is in m^2/s, or in h (hour) if α is in m^2/h.
For the latter

If ρ is density –   kg/m^3
S is surface density –   kg/m^2
H is surface thermal capacity –   Wh/m^{2}K.

Time constant has two derivations:

- capacity/transmittance ratio $\dfrac{H}{U} = \dfrac{\text{Wh} \,/\, m^2K}{W \,/\, m^2K} = h$

- resistance–capacity product $R \times H = m^2K/W \times Wh/m^2K = h.$

The **thermal inertia index** is a non-dimensional index number, the ratio of admittance (Y) to the U-value (both are in units of W/m^{2}K).

METHOD SHEET M.1.11

Calculate time lag and decrement factor

Symbols	(other than earlier or generally used)	
M resultant matrix coefficient	i imaginary number	m matrix coefficient
t temperature	T time period	p (a sub-sum)

The temperature and energy flow cycles can be linked by using matrix algebra

$$\begin{bmatrix} t_1 \\ q_1 \end{bmatrix} = \begin{bmatrix} m_1 & m_2 \\ m_3 & m_1 \end{bmatrix} \times \begin{bmatrix} t_2 \\ q_2 \end{bmatrix}$$

For a homogeneous material the matrix coefficients are given as:

$$m_1 = \cosh(p + ip) \tag{1}$$

$$m_2 = \frac{b \sinh(p + ip)}{\lambda(p + ip)} \tag{2}$$

$$m_3 = \frac{\lambda(p + ip) \sinh(p + ip)}{b} \tag{3}$$

For a multilayer wall the matrices of each layer and the two surface matrices must be multiplied:

$$\begin{bmatrix} t_i \\ q_i \end{bmatrix} = \begin{bmatrix} 1 & R_{si} \\ 0 & 1 \end{bmatrix} \times \begin{bmatrix} m_1 & m_2 \\ m_3 & m_1 \end{bmatrix} \times \begin{bmatrix} n_1 & n_2 \\ n_3 & n_1 \end{bmatrix} \times \cdots \begin{bmatrix} 1 & R_{so} \\ 0 & 1 \end{bmatrix} \tag{4}$$

The hyperbolic trigonometric functions of (1), (2) and (3) above can be solved as

$$\sinh(x) = \tfrac{1}{2}\,[e^x - e^{-x}] \qquad \cosh(x) = \tfrac{1}{2}\,[e^x - e^{-x}]$$

for an imaginary number

$$\sinh(ix) = i \sin(x) \qquad \cosh(ix) = \cos(x)$$

and the exponential function is in trigonometric terms

$$\exp(ix) = e^{ix} = \cos(x) + i \sin(x)$$

but if x is a complex number (here $(p + ip)$, these can be resolved as:

$$\cosh(p + ip) = \frac{1}{2}\Big[(e^p + e^{-p}) \cos p + i(e^p - e^{-p}) \sin p\Big] \tag{5}$$

$$\sinh(p + ip) = \frac{1}{2}\Big[(e^p - e^{-p}) \cos p - i(e^p + e^{-p}) \sin p\Big] \tag{6}$$

$$\text{where } p = b\sqrt{\frac{\pi}{86400}}\sqrt{\frac{\rho c}{\lambda}} \quad \text{(as } 24 \times 3600 = 86\,400) \tag{7}$$

The matrix coefficients will thus be (from (5) and (6)):

$$m_1 = \frac{1}{2} \times \left[(e^p + e^{-p})\cos p + i(e^p - e^{-p})\sin p\right] \tag{8}$$

$$m_2 = \frac{b\left[(e^p - e^{-p})\cos p + (e^p + e^{-p})\sin p - i(e^p - e^{-p})\cos p + i(e^p + e^{-p})\sin p\right]}{4\lambda p}$$

$$m_3 = \frac{\lambda p\left[(e^p - e^{-p})\cos p - (e^p + e^{-p}]\sin p + i(e^p - e^{-p})\cos p + i(e^p + e^{-p})\sin p\right]}{2b} \tag{9}$$

then

$$\mu = \frac{1}{U \times \mu_{\text{imaginary}}} \quad \text{and} \quad \phi = \frac{12}{\pi} \times \text{atn}\,\frac{\mu}{\mu_{\text{real part}}} \tag{10}$$

and for multiplying matrices

$$\begin{bmatrix} a & b \\ c & d \end{bmatrix} \times \begin{bmatrix} A & B \\ C & D \end{bmatrix} = \begin{bmatrix} aA + bC & aB + bD \\ cA + dC & cC + dD \end{bmatrix}$$

Take an example of a single skin brick wall:

$\rho = 1700\,\text{kg/m}^3$ Taking surface resistances as:
$\lambda = 0.84\,\text{W/m K}$ $R_{si} = 0.12\,\text{m}^2\text{K/W}$
$c = 800\,\text{J/kg K}$ $R_{so} = 0.06$
$b = 0.22\,\text{m}\ (220\,\text{mm})$

from (7): $p = \left(0.22\sqrt{\dfrac{\pi}{86400}}\sqrt{\dfrac{1700 \times 800}{0.84}}\right) = (0.22 \times 0.006 \times 1272.418) = 1.688$

from (8): $m_1 = \dfrac{1}{2}\left[\left(e^{1.688} + e^{-1.688}\right)\cos 1.688 + i\left(e^{1.688} - e^{-1.688}\right)\sin 1.688\right]$

$$= \frac{1}{2}\left[(5.4 + 1.849)(-0.1169) + i(5.4 - 0.1849)0.9931\right]$$

$$= \frac{1}{2}(-0.6531 + i\,5.179)$$

$m_1 = -0.3265 + i\,2.5896$

from (9)

$$m_2 = b\left[(e^{1.688} - e^{-1.688})\cos 1.688 + (e^{1.688} + e^{-1.588})\sin 1.688\right.$$
$$\left. -i(e^{1.688} - e^{-1.688})\cos 1.688 + i(e^{1.688} + e^{-1.688})\sin 1.688)\right]/4 \times 0.84 \times 0.8$$

$$m_2 = \frac{b\left[(5.4 - 0.1849)(-0.1169) + (5.4 + 0.1849)0.9931 - i(5.4 - 0.1849)(-0.1169) + i(5.4 + 0.1849)0.9931\right]}{4 \times 0.84 \times 1.688}$$

$$= 0.22\left[5.2151 \times (-0.1169) + 5.5849 \times 0.9931 - i\,5.2151 \times (-0.1169) + i\,5.5849 \times 0.9931\right]/2.69$$

$$= 0.22\left[-0.6096 + 5.5464 - i\,0.6096 + i\,5.5464\right]/5.67$$

$$= 0.22\left[0.8707 + i\,1.0857\right]$$

$$m_2 = 0.1916 + i0.2389$$

from (10)

$$m_3 = \lambda 1.868 \big[(e^{1.688} - e^{-1.688}) \cos 1.688 - (e^{1.688} + e^{-1.688}) \sin 1.688$$
$$+ i(e^{1.688} - e^{-1.688}) \cos 1.688 + i(e^{1.688} + e^{-1.688}) \sin 1.688 \big]/2b$$

$$m_3 = \lambda 1.688 \big[(5.4 - 0.1849)(-0.1169) - (5.4 + 0.1849)0.9931 + i(5.4 - 0.1849)(-0.1169)$$
$$+ i(5.4 + 0.1849)0.9931 \big] 2 \times 0.22$$

$$= 0.84 \times 1.688 \big[5.2151 \times (-0.1169) - 5.5849 \times 0.9931 + i5.2151 \times (-0.1169) + i5.5849 \times 0.9931 \big]/0.44$$

$$= 1.4179 \big[-0.6096 - 5.5464 + i0.6096 + i5.5464 \big]/0.44$$

$$= 1.4179(-13.99 + i11.2199)$$

$$m_3 = -19.8377 + i15.9087$$

Resistance: $\quad R = 0.12 + \dfrac{0.22}{0.84} + 0.06 = 0.4419\,\text{m}^2\text{K/W}$

Transmittance: $\quad U = 1/R = 1/0.4419 = 2.2629\,\text{W/m}^2\text{K}$

The resulting matrix is to be multiplied by the internal surface matrix, in which all four imaginary components will be zero

$$\begin{bmatrix} 1 & R_{si} \\ 0 & 1 \end{bmatrix} \times \begin{bmatrix} 0.3265 + i2.59 & 0.1916 + i0.239 \\ -19.84 + i15.9 & 0.3265 + i2.59 \end{bmatrix} = \begin{bmatrix} -2.72 + i4.5 & 0.15 + i0.551 \\ -19.84 + i15.9 & 0.3265 + i2.59 \end{bmatrix}$$

Finally this is to be multiplied by the external surface matrix (it is sufficient to obtain the products of the second column only (M_2 and M_4). Note that the matrix coefficients are denoted 'm', but the product matrices are 'M'

thus we have $\begin{bmatrix} M_1 & M_2 \\ M_3 & M_4 \end{bmatrix}$

$$\begin{bmatrix} -2.72 + i4.5 & 0.15 + i0.551 \\ -19.84 + i15.9 & -0.3265 + i2.59 \end{bmatrix} \times \begin{bmatrix} 1 & 0.06 \\ 0 & 1 \end{bmatrix} = \begin{bmatrix} * & -0.013 + i0.821 \\ * & -1.52 + i3.54 \end{bmatrix}$$

as $\quad \mu = \dfrac{1}{UM_2} \qquad \mu = \dfrac{1}{2.263(-0.013 + i0.821)}$

To eliminate 'i' from the denominator, to 'rationalize' it), multiply both numerator and denominator by $(-0.013 + i0.821)$:

$$\mu = \text{abs}\,\dfrac{-0.013 + i0.821}{2.263(0.013^2 + 0.821^2)} = \text{abs}\,\dfrac{-0.013 + i0.821}{1.5257} = \text{abs}\,[0.0085 + i0.5381]$$

$$\mu = 0.538$$

$$\phi = 12/\pi \times \text{atn}(\mu/\mu_{(real)}) = 3.82 \times \text{atn}(0.538/0.0085) = 3.82 \times 1.556 = 5.94$$

$$\phi \approx 6\ \textbf{hours}$$

PART 2   LIGHT: THE LUMINOUS ENVIRONMENT

CONTENTS

SYMBOLS AND ABBREVIATIONS IN PART 2

a	acuity (visual)		A	area
asb	apostilb (luminance measure)		ALT	solar altitude angle
c	velocity of light (3×10^8 m/s)		B	bars (framing) factor
cd	candela (source intensity)		BRE	Building Research Establishment (UK)
d	distance		C	contrast
f	frequency (or a 'factor')		CCT	correlated colour temperature
G	glare constant		CIE	commission International d'Éclairage
lm	lumen (light flux)		CRI	colour rendering index
lx	lux (illuminance)		CT	colour temperature
p	position index		DF	daylight factor

DFF	downward flux fraction		UF	utilization factor
DLOR	downward light output ratio		UFF	upward flux fraction
DUF	daylight utilization factor		UGR	unified glare rating
E	illuminance (éclairage), lux		ULOR	upward light output ratio
ERC	externally reflected component (of DF)		V	value (Munsell-)
F	luminous efficacy			
FFR	flux fraction ratio			
G	glass factor		α	absorptance
GI	glare index		β	angle of incidence
H_m	mounting height		γ	altitude angle on sky
I	intensity (of light source), cd		η	efficiency
INC	angle of incidence		θ	viewing (source-) angle, (or vertical displacement angle)
IRC	internally reflected component (of DF)			
L	luminance (cd/m^2)		λ	wavelength
LED	light emitting diode		ρ	reflectance
LOR	light output ratio		σ	visual angle
LT	lighting and thermal (pre-design) analysis		τ	transmittance
M	maintenance factor (glass cleaning)		φ	phase delay angle, (or horizontal displacement angle)
MF	maintenance factor (lumen method)			
PSALI	permanent supplementary lighting of the interior		ω	solid angle
RI	room index		Δ	difference
SC	sky component (of DF)		Φ	light flux (lm)

LIST OF FIGURES

LIST OF TABLES

LIST OF WORKED EXAMPLES

LIST OF EQUATIONS

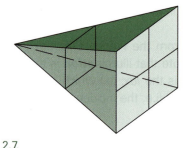

2.7.

Interpretation of the inverse square law.

2.1.4 Transmission of light

In vacuum or in a transparent homogeneous medium (air) light travels in a straight line. The *inverse square law* states that illuminance reduces in proportion to the square of the distance from the source. Fig. 2.7 shows that the flux which at a given distance goes through a unit area, at double that distance will go through four times that area, so the flux density (= illuminance) reduces to one quarter.

A source of 1 candela intensity (I) emits 1 lumen within a steradian and produces an illuminance of 1 lux at 1 m distance, thus numerically $E = I$, thus at a distance d

$$E = \frac{I}{d^2} \tag{2.3}$$

The *cosine law* relates illuminance of a surface (E) to the illuminance normal to the direction of the light beam (E_n), which depends on the angle of incidence. If the angle of incidence is β, (Fig. 2.8) and the surface area normal to the beam is A_n, then $A > A_n$ thus $E < E_n$

$$A = \frac{A_n}{\cos \beta} \quad \text{and} \quad E = E_n \times \cos \beta$$

Material bodies exposed to light behave in various ways. A sheet of glass is said to be *transparent*, a sheet of plywood is *opaque*. A sheet of 'opal' perspex is *translucent*. (Fig. 2.9).

Light incident on the surface can be distributed three ways: reflected, absorbed or transmitted. The corresponding properties are reflectance (ρ), absorptance (α) and transmittance (τ) and in all cases $\rho + \alpha + \tau = 1$, (as discussed in Section 1.1.2.3 and 1.4.1.3 in relation to solar radiation). All three terms are functions of radiation wavelength, and when applied to the visible wavelengths (light) they may be referred to as 'optical', e.g. optical transmittance or optical absorptance.

Materials which in a small thickness appear to be transparent, may become opaque in a large thickness. The term absorpt**ivity** is a property of the material, indicating the absorption per unit thickness, whilst absorpt**ance** is the property of a body of given thickness or a surface quality.

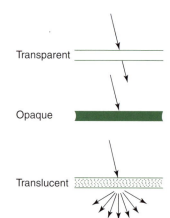

Transparent

Opaque

Translucent

2.9.

Transmission of light.

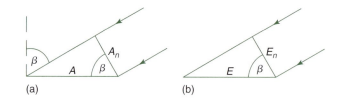

(a)   (b)

2.8.

The inverse square law. A given beam of light on area A_n (normal incidence) is spread over a larger area (A) at oblique incidence, hence illuminance $E < E_n$.

(a) Specular

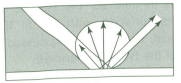

(b) Spread

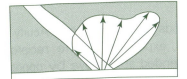

(c) Semi-diffuse

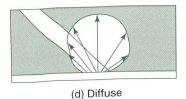

(d) Diffuse

2.10.
Reflective surfaces.

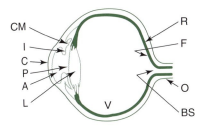

2.11.
Section of the human eye. CM: ciliary muscle; I: iris; C: cornea; P: pupil; A: aqueous humor; L: lens; V: vitreaous humor; R: retina; F: fovea; O: optic nerve; BS: blind spot.

Surfaces may be classified in terms of their reflective properties (Fig. 2.10) as *specular* (a mirror), or *diffuse* (ordinary building surfaces), or transitional: giving a *spread* reflection (basically diffuse, but with some specular component) or *semi-diffuse* (all diffuse, but with some directional bias).

2.2 VISION

2.2.1 The eye and brain

Light is perceived by the eye. Its diagrammatic section (Fig. 2.11) can be compared to a camera:

- aperture, controlled by a light-meter: the pupil, the size of which is varied by the iris (and controlled by the retina), which is the eye's main *adaptation* mechanism
- focusing, controlled by a coupled range-finder: changing the shape of the lens by the ciliary muscles, thus varying its focal length, which is the *accommodation* mechanism
- the adaptability of the retina can only be likened to using films of different 'speed' or ISO (ASA) rating.

The retina incorporates two kinds of nerve endings: cones and rods. A normal eye has some 6.5 million *cones* (in and around the *fovea*), which are sensitive to both quantity and quality (colour) of light, but operate only in good lighting (*photopic vision*). The retina also has some 125 million *rods*, which are more sensitive than the cones, but perceive only quantity of light, do not distinguish colour (*scotopic vision*).

The pupil's response is practically instantaneous. A second adaptation mechanism of the eye is the variation of the retina's sensitivity by varying the photochemical compounds present (e.g. of the *visual purple*). Whilst the pupil's response to changed lighting conditions is almost instantaneous, adaptation of the retina to dark conditions may take up to 30 min, as more visual purple is produced. Adaptation to brighter light is no more than about 3 min, as the visual purple is being removed.

Both adaptation mechanisms respond to the average luminance of the field of vision. Starting from darkness:

at 0.001 cd/m^2	The pupil is wide open and the rods start to operate
at about 3 cd/m^2	The cones start to operate
at 1000 cd/m^2	The pupil closes to its minimum.

Without light there is no vision, but visual perception depends as much on the brain as on the eye. It is largely dependent on recognition. Life is continuous learning, (quickest at the cradle and gradually slowing), new visual images are compared to and built into relationships with images already stored and with percepts from other senses. It relies on memory to such an match realities as near as possible. If the sky component alone is to be determined, the interior of the model can be painted mat black.

Such models can be tested under outdoor conditions, if a representative overcast sky condition is available. Waiting for such conditions would interrupt any testing program, so artificial skies have been developed, which simulate overcast sky conditions, thus allow the testing to be carried out independently of the changing weather, under precisely controlled conditions.

Hemispherical skies can be of two types:

1 a hemispherical translucent diffuser (inside of a structural dome) with the lighting installed behind it (Fig. 2.29)
2 an opaque dome, with a diffusely reflecting internal surface, with the lighting installation below (lighting upwards) all around an annular space (Fig. 2.30).

In all three cases there would be a model table at the centre, with a space around it for the observers, most often with access from below. Some installations allow the selection (by switching) of a sky with uniform luminance or one with the CIE (1:3) luminance distribution.

Many workers in the field prefer the rectangular, mirror type artificial sky. Here all four walls would be lined with mirrors from table height up to the ceiling. This ceiling would be made of a translucent diffusing material, with the lighting installation behind it. The multiple inter-reflections between opposed mirrors would create the effect of an infinite horizon, which is much closer to reality than domes limited to 6–8 m diameter (Fig. 2.31).

Such artificial skies have been developed over 50 years ago and were extensively used by research workers. Indeed, the daylight factor calculation

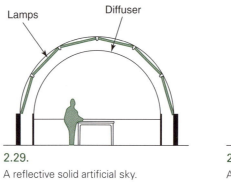

2.29.
A reflective solid artificial sky.

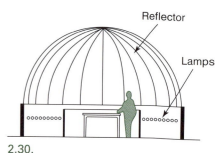

2.30.
A back-lit translucent artificial sky.

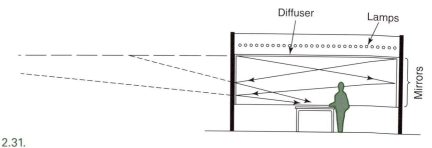

2.31.
A mirror-type artificial sky.

(split flux) method discussed above has been created with the aid of such artificial skies. After the 1958 Oxford conference of the RIBA (which acknowledged the great significance of science in architectural design and education) practically all schools of architecture set up laboratories and built artificial skies. With the rise of post-modern and deconstructivist ideologies and the predominance of formalist attitudes, most of these laboratories fell into disrepair. Only in the last decade – or so – when daylighting came to be recognized as a tool for energy conservation and a contributor to sustainability, have such laboratories been revived to re-gain their role.

The technique of model studies itself is quite simple, as long as the model is well made, its interior reflectances are realistic and light seepage through cracks and joints is prevented. Measure the 'outdoor' illuminance, usually on the top of the model, measure the illuminance 'indoors' at various points and find the daylight factor at each of these points as $DF = (E_i/E_o) \times 100$. Instruments were made to measure illuminance at many points (with miniature light sensors placed at grid-points) and produce the daylight factor automatically. Measurement systems coupled with a PC can display the DF values at grid-points on the screen and generate the DF contours as well as converting these into illuminance (isolux) contours.

2.4.4 Computer tools

Figure 2.32 is a reduced scale summary of a study examining the effect of window size, shape and position on daylight distribution.* It can be seen that the height of the window determines the depth of daylight penetration, whilst the width influences the sideways spread of daylight. This is the result using a very simple computer program, which employs the algorithm of the BRE 'split flux' method. Today a large number of computer programs exist, using a variety of algorithms, the most sophisticated ones based on ray-tracing techniques, which can present the results in photo-realistic internal views, with indication of graded illuminance distribution on room surfaces.

The split flux method of daylight factor calculation is based on the assumption of an overcast sky, originally of uniform luminance, but later using the 'CIE sky' luminance distribution (as eq. (2.5) above). It has been shown (Robledo *et al.*, 1999) that even with overcast skies (cloud cover 7–8 oktas) the zenith luminance itself is changing as a function of solar altitude:

$$L_z = 0.0803 + 10.54597\,a - 0.6364\,a^3 \ \ \text{(in kcd/m}^2)$$
$$\text{where } a = \text{tanALT}$$

The annual variation of L_z (for Madrid) is represented by Fig. 2.33.

The most recent daylight prediction programs include a much more sophisticated sky model and consider not only the diffused daylight entering the room, but also beam sunlight and its internal lighting effects. The lighting would thus vary not only with the location and sky conditions, but also with the time of day.

SUPERLITE can initially calculate outdoor illuminance, then it produces indoor illuminances under different sky conditions. SUPERLINK can predict

---

* In the original each of the 32 room plans were in A4 size.

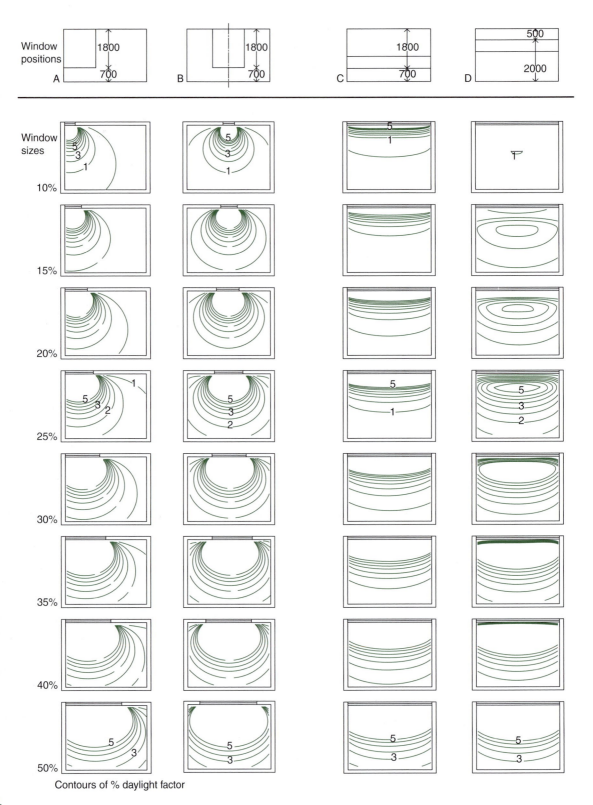

 Contours of % daylight factor

2.32.

A study of daylight distribution. Column A: height fixed, jamb fixed at side wall, width variable; column B: height fixed, centre of window at room centreline, width variable; column C: full width, sill fixed, height variable; column D: full width, head fixed, height variable. Each variant is examined with sizes of 10–50% of wall area (after T. Yamaguchi).

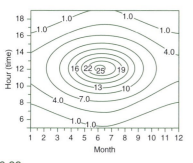

2.33.

Hour × month isopleths of zenith luminance in kcd/m².

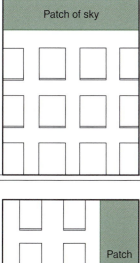

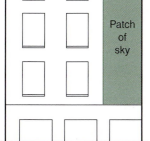

2.34.

The patch of sky visible through a window: either could be acceptable.

lighting energy savings. RADIANCE is perhaps the best known program to produce photo-realistic images representing daylight distribution and it can do this in hourly time-steps. SUPERLITE 2.0 has an integrated CAD model. In several instances daylight simulation is included in a broader design package (e.g. ECOTECT) and some are attached to existing CAD programs (e.g. LIGHTSCAPE to AUTOCAD). PERFECT LITE and LIGHTSOFT are for electric lighting design only (see also Section 1.4.1 for thermal programs).

GENELUX, and particularly DELight are intended for early stages of the design process. The latter has an easy-to-use graphic input/output system. Several of these programs (e.g. ADELINE) have a model that can be used for both daylighting and electric lighting design (see e.g IEA/SHC Task 21 Daylighting Buildings, report: *Survey of simple design tools*, The Fraunhofer Institute, Stuttgart).

A photo-realistic output is certainly an impressive presentation tool, but should only be used as a design tool if its workings, its algorithms and its assumptions are fully understood. Responsibility for the performance of a building lies with the building designer, not with the authors of the program.

2.4.5 Planning for daylight

In densely built-up urban areas the daylighting of one building can be adversely affected by other buildings. The concept of 'right to light' emerged already in the 19th century, especially in relation to row housing: the permissible height was limited as a function of street width. In the second half of the 20th century in the UK this was superseded. The rationale was that a very high tower may be allowed, if the sky is visible to the side of it (Fig. 2.34). Sets of 'permissible height indicators' were devised to facilitate the checking of geometry.

One set can be applied to the front of an existing building (to the sill of the lowest window) to check a proposed building opposite, another set to the boundary or the street centreline. Outside the 'V'-shaped limits (wedges) any obstruction is permitted, but within the wedge height restrictions apply. With a narrow wedge the height restrictions are quite stringent, with a broader wedge these are more lenient. There are three indicators in each set, with 20°, 45° or 90° width of acceptance and any one of these can be used to show compliance.

These indicators are available in a number of scales (1:200, 1:500, 1250) and each set is valid for a particular latitude. Method sheet M.2.5 gives a set (D) of these indicators.

Figure 2.35 shows an example of how these indicators are used. Both the technique and the criteria behind the technique are under continued review, as it is not so much a technical, rather a socio-economic issue.

2.4.6 Control of sunlight

Solar geometry has been discussed in some detail in Section 1.4.1 and method sheets M.1.3 and M.1.4 give all the necessary algorithms. Here the

The existing block, from its ends to points A and B respectively receives enough light, passing by the sides of the proposed block.

The most critical point is C, half-way between A and B.

The most permissive indicator 'D' shows a permissible height of 13 m at point 'x' (measured from sill level of the ground floor at point C).

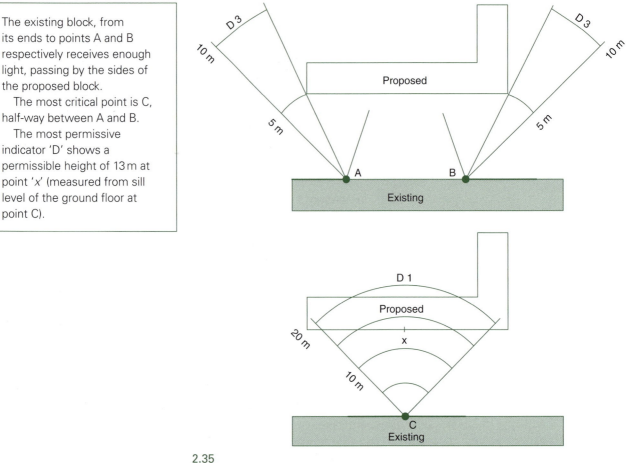

2.35

Use of the permissible height indicators. Short lines on either side of the wedge indicate the limit they may be tilted to.

subject is the lighting effect of solar radiation (often referred to as *beam sunlighting*) and its control.

Climatic data, such as hours of clear sunshine can give an indication of the available resource, or the magnitude of the sunlight problem. Solar irradiation data could be converted to luminous quantities by using luminous efficacy values (such as discussed in Section 2.3.1 and method sheet M.2.1).

In dominantly overcast cool climates most people would welcome sunlight, whenever it is available. Where glare or excessive contrast may be a problem, the designer must consider the situation: are the occupants free to exercise behavioural adjustments? (e.g. draw the blinds or curtains, or move away from the sun-lit area of the room). If not, what are the consequences of direct sunlight?

If it is found that sunlight must be controlled, the first question is: will the sun reach the window considered, or will it be obstructed by external objects (other buildings). The techniques presented in Section 2.3.4 and method sheet M.2.2 are useful in assessing the duration of obstruction and exposure of a selected point. When the critical time is selected, then the extent

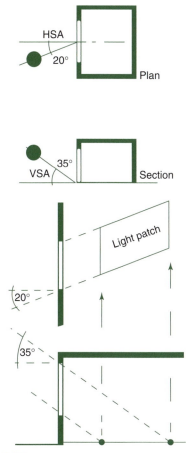

2.36.
Construction of sun penetration: a light patch on the floor.

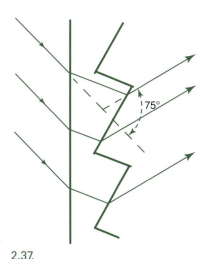

2.37.
Prismatic glass for beam sunlighting with a diversion angle of 75°.

of sun penetration can be examined, assuming that weather conditions are such that there will be sunshine available. This is a purely geometrical task.

The sun's position in relation to the window is to be established first. The horizontal shadow angle (HSA) at the time in question is the azimuth difference between the sun's direction and the orientation (see method sheet M.1.3). The solar altitude (ALT) must be projected onto a plane perpendicular to the window, to get the vertical shadow angle (VSA, as shown e.g. in Fig. 1.49 and method sheet M.1.3). Once these two angles are known the sun penetration, the sun-lit patch on the floor or on the work-plane can be constructed, as shown in Fig. 2.36.

A beam of solar radiation incident on a window pane may produce an irradiance of up to over 450 W/m²:

This depends on geographical latitude and orientation, e.g. in equatorial latitudes, such as Nairobi, an east or west facing wall can receive up to 550 W/m², and a north or south wall only some 250 W/m² whilst at higher latitudes, such as Stockholm, an east or west wall can go up to 200 W/m² only and the south facing one can exceed 350 W/m².

With a glass transmittance of 0.78 the above 450 W/m² would be reduced to 350 W/m². If the luminous efficacy of this is taken as 100 lm/W (an average value) the illuminance produced will be some 35 000 lx. In such a situation the general illuminance is also increased, perhaps to 1000 lx. So the contrast is 35:1. This is too much for comfort. The occupants must be given the option of some control, such as a curtain or blind. It is however likely that irradiance would be controlled for thermal reasons, preferably by some external shading devices, possibly by some adjustable mechanisms.

The use of tinted (heat absorbing or reflective) glasses may provide a remedy, avoid glare and reduce sunlight. The problem is that they affect diffuse light as much as beam light and that their properties are fixed, they have no selectivity in time: perform the same way in winter as in summer, they would reduce daylighting even when it is scarce.

A fixed control should only be used where its necessity is beyond any doubt, otherwise it may be perceived by the users as 'dictatorial'. Some architects adopt the attitude (not just in the lighting context) that they know best what is good for the user. They would argue that one is going to the doctor for advice, not to tell him/her what therapy should be prescribed. Others may perceive this as professional arrogance. It is always useful to allow some degree of control to the user, be it an adjustable thermostat, an adjustable shading device or just a set of blinds.

Even automatic (motorized) louvres have been shown to be disliked by occupants of offices.

2.4.6.1 Beam sunlighting
Beam sunlighting is very useful in areas of the building that are not reached by daylighting through side windows. Several techniques are in use:

1 *Prismatic glass* is often used, normally for the top one third of a window to divert the beam of sunlight (by refraction) upwards, to the ceiling, which will then diffuse it to the rear part of the room (Fig. 2.37).

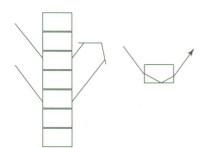

2.38.

Laser-grooved acrylic sheet.

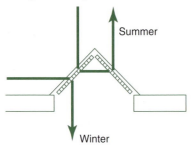

2.39.

Laser-grooved roof light: at low angle the sun is admitted, at high angle excluded.

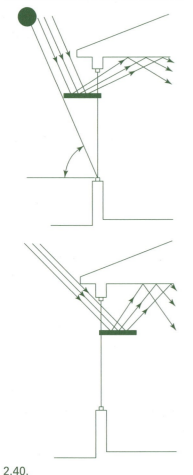

2.40.

External and internal light shelves.

2 *Laser-grooved acrylic sheets*, divided into small elements by laser cuts to some 90% of the thickness, which will serve the same purpose partly by refraction, but mainly by full internal reflection in each element (Fig. 2.38). These have a particular relevance for roof lights in low latitude climates, where the midday sun can be quite a problem. In a prismatic roof light they can completely reject high altitude (near zenith) radiation, but would admit the morning and late afternoon sunlight (Fig. 2.39).

3 *Light shelves* have been used for similar purposes for many years. In its simplest form this would be a horizontal element (an extended transom) across the window at a height of about 2.1 m, with a reflective upper surface, which direct the light up to the ceiling (Fig. 2.40). These would work well in a fairly high room (≈3 m). If mounted externally, they could also serve as a shading device for the lower part of the window, but it may be difficult to keep the top surface clean. The problem is less serious if mounted internally. To allow for the seasonal variation of solar altitude angle some pivoted (internal) light shelves have been used to vary the tilt angle, thus the direction of reflections.

Many varieties of such light shelves exist. Some have a specular top surface, some are diffusing. Partially reflecting semi-transparent materials have also been used. Various clever profiles have been developed to respond to the changing solar altitude. Others are adjustable, to compensate for summer – winter difference in the sun's path. One system provides seasonal adjustment by using a flexible reflective film with a 'V'-shaped shelf (Fig. 2.41).

Beam sunlighting is also used for roof lights. As Fig. 2.42 shows a heliostat (a motorized system, the mirror tracking the sun) and a fixed mirror can direct the solar beam downwards where it may enter the room through a

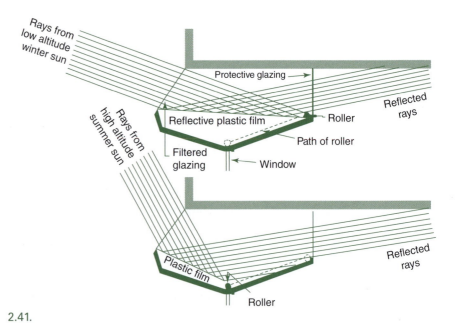

2.41.

A fully enclosed light shelf with a flexible reflective film.

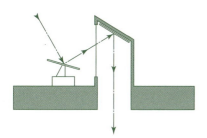

2.42.
Heliostat for beam sunlighting.

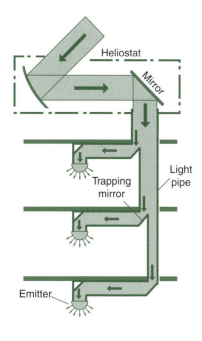

2.43.
Beam sunlighting by heliostat and light pipes.

diffuser. Such a system serving a single storey building (or the top floor of a multistorey building) can have an efficiency around 50%. This means that if a solar beam of 60 klx is incident on the primary mirror of 1 m², of the 60 klm light flux some 30 klm is emitted by the ceiling diffuser, which can produce an average illuminance of 300 lx over a 100 m² area of the work plane.

A system of mirrors and 'light tubes' would allow the use of such systems over several storeys (Fig. 2.43). These light tubes are made of some highly polished material or lined with a reflective film. A light tube of an elongated oblong section can have 'tapping off' mirrors at several levels and after each of these its size is reduced.

Such a system can have an efficiency over 25% measured from light incident on the primary collector mirror to that emitted by all ceiling diffusers. This efficiency depends on the quality of the reflective surfaces and on how well the light beam is collimated. Unfortunately the system will work only when clear sunlight is available, so its success very much depends on weather conditions. One must have a stand-by electric lighting system. However, in reasonably sunny climates it can save much operating energy and cost.

A version of light tubes is the 'anidolic ceiling' (non-imaging reflective duct). This has an upward looking 'collector' at the outer end, a 3–4 m long duct within the ceiling space (Fig. 2.44) and a light outlet in the ceiling, to contribute light to the rear part of the room. This can be effective also under overcast conditions, as it 'sees' the upper part of the sky, which is of a greater luminance.

The idea of using optical fibres to convey light of some concentration has been suggested by a group of students in 1975. Figure 2.45 is reproduced from their original sketch. Since then several research teams worked on such ideas and recently a group reported on a precision-engineered mini dish (200 mm diameter) connected to an optical fibre conductor of 1 mm diameter, which successfully produced a concentrated beam of 11 kilo-suns (11 000 suns!) conveyed to a diffuser at a distance of 20 m. The technique certainly has a future.

2.4.7 The daylight utilization factor

DUF brings in the time factor for the performance analysis of daylighting/sunlighting and various control systems (Robbins, 1986). The space (room) considered is divided into control zones: the area nearest to windows is zone 1 and the one receiving least daylight/sunlight is the highest number. The analysis is carried out for each zone separately. A design illuminance is set (E_d). The time considered is the working day, 8:00–17:00 h. The term duf_r is the fraction of this period when daylight can 'replace' (obviate the need for) electric lighting (Fig. 2.46), when the internal illuminance (E_i) without electric lighting is adequate ($E_i > E_d$). The fraction of time when E_i is less than adequate, but can still provide a useful contribution, 'supplementing' the electric lighting is referred to as duf_s and the daylight utilization factor is the some of these two:

$$DUF = duf_r + duf_s$$

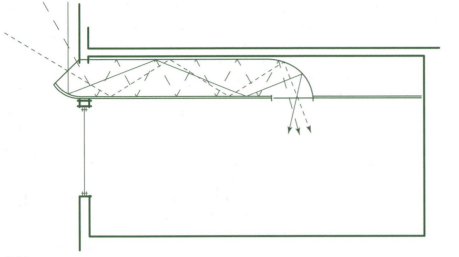

2.44.
A ceiling duct: 'anidolic' ceiling.

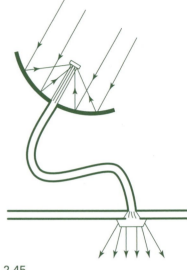

2.45.
A concentrator + optical fibre lighting system.

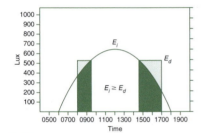

2.46.
Interpretation of DUF: centre part daylight alone, dark shaded: daylight as supplement.

and by definition $duf_r + duf_s + ND = 1$, where ND is the no-daylight fraction. On the basis of this a sophisticated control strategy and economic analysis of the benefits of daylighting can be (and has been) built up.

2.5 ELECTRIC LIGHTING

To clarify the terminology: ***lamp*** is the source of light (bulb or globe are not technical terms). The lamp is usually inside a ***luminaire***, (which in the past was often referred to as a light fitting), although many lamps can be used without a luminaire, just fitted into a lamp holder. *Lamp holders* are the electrical connectors, into which the lamp is inserted or screwed. The generally used ones are the BC (bayonet caps) or the ES (Edison screw), but many other types are available for specialized purposes.

2.5.1 Lamps

Electric lamps make use of two different processes of light generation: *thermo-luminescence* and *electro-luminescence* (gas discharge). The former is made use of by the *incandescent* lamps. These have a thin wire (usually tungsten) filament, with a high resistance, which is heated by the electric current passing through it. These operate around 2700–3000°K temperature. To prevent oxidization of the filament, it is enclosed in a glass container, in vacuum or partial vacuum with some small quantity of inert gas (krypton, argon, or xenon). The life expectancy of these lamps is around 1000 h.

Most of the emission of incandescent lamps (up to 95%) is in the infrared region, i.e. radiant heat. Their luminous efficacy is 10–18 lm/W.

In operation some of the tungsten evaporates and condenses on the inside of the glass bulb, causing a slight blackening. To allow higher temperature operation (and smaller lamp size) some halogen elements (iodine, bromine)

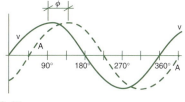

2.47.
The effect of inductive load: the current is delayed.

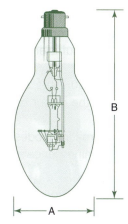

2.48.
A typical mercury lamp, 160W
A = 76 mm, B = 175 mm.

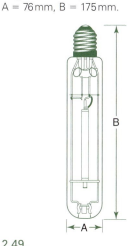

2.49.
A high-pressure tubular sodium lamp (SONT, 70W) A = 71 mm, B = 154 mm.

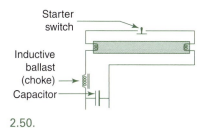

2.50.
Control circuit for a fluorescent lamp.

can be added. These adsorb the tungsten vapour and deposit it back onto the filament. The enclosure of these *tungsten–halogen* lamps is quartz, to withstand higher temperatures and quick changes of temperature. These are available in tubular (double-ended) and single-ended (two-pin) form, both for mains voltage (120–240V) and low voltage (12–24V) versions, from 20W up to 2000W size. Its efficacy is similar to the above: 16–20 lm/W.

Discharge lamps have no filament; light is produced by excitation of the gas or metallic vapours (mercury or sodium) contained in the lamp. They need a device to start the discharge between the electrodes. The discharge is a chain reaction, exponentially increasing, so a device is needed to limit the current, otherwise the lamp would short the circuit. This can be a resistive ballast or an inductive load with a high impedance. If the latter is used, a power factor correction device is needed (see Fig. 2.50).

In direct current $V \times A = W$ (power is the product of current and potential). With alternating current and inductive load (a motor or any electromagnetic coil) would delay the current behind the voltage changes (Fig. 2.47), so the actual useful load (W) is less than the $V \times A$ product. If the full cycle is 360°, the delay or phase angle is ϕ and $\cos \phi$ is referred to as the power factor. *Thus*

$$\text{Power factor} = \cos \phi = \frac{\text{actual useful load (W)}}{\text{apparent load (V} \times \text{A)}}$$

With no phase lag $\phi = 0$, $\cos \phi = 1$, but with heavy inductive load ϕ may be as much as 60° and the power factor can go down to 0.5. Most supply authorities set a limit of 0.9. A correction device is a capacitor connected in parallel, which accelerates the current with respect to voltage.

Mercury lamps (MB) have a very discontinuous spectrum but a high efficacy (up to 85 lm/W). The spectrum can be improved by a fluorescent coating of the inner surface of glass (MBF) lamps. A tungsten filament may improve the red end of the spectrum and serve as the current limiting device (MBT).

Figure 2.48 shows a typical mercury lamp and Fig. 2.49 is a high-pressure sodium (tubular) lamp (SONT), which gives a slightly better spectrum than the low-pressure SOX lamps. Efficacies are 90–140 lm/W.

Figure 2.50 shows a control circuit for a fluorescent lamp, but many others are possible. Fluorescent tubes are actually low-pressure mercury lamps. The discharge is mainly in the UV range. A fluorescent coating on the inside of the tube absorbs this UV radiation and re-emits it at visible wavelengths. The colour of light depends on the composition of this fluorescent coating, hence the many varieties of fluorescent lamps available.

Lamps are characterized by their electrical load (W) and by their light emission, both in quantity and quality. The quantitative measure is their light emission in lumens (the term *lamp lumens* is often used). Data sheet D.2.9 shows some typical values. The qualitative measure is their colour appearance and – more importantly – their colour rendering.

EXAMPLE 2.4

An opal diffuser luminaire is mounted at 1.75 m above the work plane, with its axis vertical and the illuminance at 1 m to one side of the aiming point is to be found (Fig. 2.57) First find the viewing angle:

$$\theta = \arctan \frac{1}{1.75} = 30° \qquad \text{the geometry is such that INC} = \theta$$

and the distance is $d = \sqrt{1^2 + 1.75^2} = 2\,\text{m}$

from the polar curve (Figs 2.53 and 2.54) the source intensity is found as $I_{30} = 230\,\text{cd}$

$$E = \cos 30 \times \frac{230}{2^2} = 50\,\text{lx}$$

For a linear source of light (of 'infinite' length) the illuminance is proportional to the distance, so instead of the inverse square law we have the inverse distance law: $E = \dfrac{1}{d}$

EXAMPLE 2.5

We have a notice board illuminated by a row of tubular lamps from a distance of 2.5 m, which is continuous beyond the edges of the board by the same length as the distance of 2.5 m (thus it can be considered as 'infinite'). The source intensity is read as 150 cd, corrected for a warm white lamp:

$$I = 150 \times \frac{3800}{1000} = 570\,\text{cd}$$

at a point on the board where the angle of incidence is 30° the illuminance will be

$$E = \cos 30 \times \frac{570}{2.5} = 197\,\text{lx}$$

If two or more lamps/luminaires contribute to the lighting of a point, the illuminance from each has to be calculated and these illuminances are simply additive. This is the basis of the *point-by-point method* of lighting design. This is quite simple and manageable for one or two lamps contributing to the lighting of (say) a notice board, but if we have a large room (e.g. an office or a classroom) with many light sources, calculations for the whole work-plane become cumbersome. However the method can provide the algorithm for a computer program.

EXAMPLE 2.6

Given a large office general office of 120 m². From data sheet D.2.6 the required illuminance is 400 lx. We choose fluorescent white lamps in enclosed diffuser luminaires. The total wattage of the lighting will be 120 × 400 × 0.050 = 2400 W. If 40 W fluorescent lamps are used, we need 2400/40 = 60, and with twin-tube luminaires we need 30.

Table 2.6. Lamp power required

Lamp type		$W/(m^2 lx)$
Incandescent	Open enamelled reflector	0.150
	General diffusing	0.175
Mercury	Industrial reflector	0.065
Fluorescent, white	Open trough	0.040
	Enclosed diffusing	0.050
	Louvred, recessed	0.055
Fluorescent de luxe warm white	Enclosed diffusing	0.080
	Louvred, recessed	0.090

For general lighting a rough estimate can be produced by the *watt method*. This is based on a table (such as Table 2.6) which gives the lamp power requirement (W) per unit floor area, per lux illuminance required.

Somewhat similar is the concept of 'unit power density' (UPD) in W/m^2 and long tables give UPD values for different room usages (Robbins, 1996). These are in fact products of recommended illuminance and the watt factors in Table 2.6. For the case of Example 2.6 the UPD is given as 14–25W/m^2, without distinguishing lamp and luminaire type.

The alternative is to use the lumen method of general lighting design.

2.5.4 The lumen method

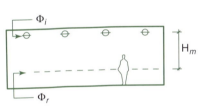

2.58.
Interpretation of flux installed and flux received.

The lumen method (or total flux method) of general lighting design is applicable where a regular array of luminaires produces a uniform lighting over the work plane. The criterion for uniformity is that at the point of least illuminance it is not less than 70% of the maximum. In practice this is provided by limiting the spacing of luminaires to 1.5 times the height of luminaires from the work plane, i.e. the mounting height (H_m).

For a given system the total lumen output of lamps is calculated, which is referred to as the *installed flux* (Φ_i) and the *flux received* on the work plane will be (Fig. 2.58)

$$\Phi_r = \Phi_i \times UF \times MF \quad \text{then the illuminance is} \quad E = \frac{\Phi_r}{A}$$

where MF is the maintenance factor, to allow for the deterioration of the lamp, luminaire and room surfaces. In the absence of more accurate data this is taken as 0.8. UF is the utilization factor and the method hinges on finding the appropriate UF value.

The magnitude of UF depends on the following factors:

1 Properties of the luminaire: an enclosed luminaire or one with less than perfect internal reflectance will have a value much lower than an exposed lamp.
2 The DLOR (downward light output ratio) of the luminaire. Light emitted upwards will reach the work plane only after reflection(s) from room surfaces and some of it is absorbed in these surfaces. A larger DLOR normally means a higher UF.

DATA SHEET D.2.4

Daylight factor: nomogram for the IRC (internally reflected component)

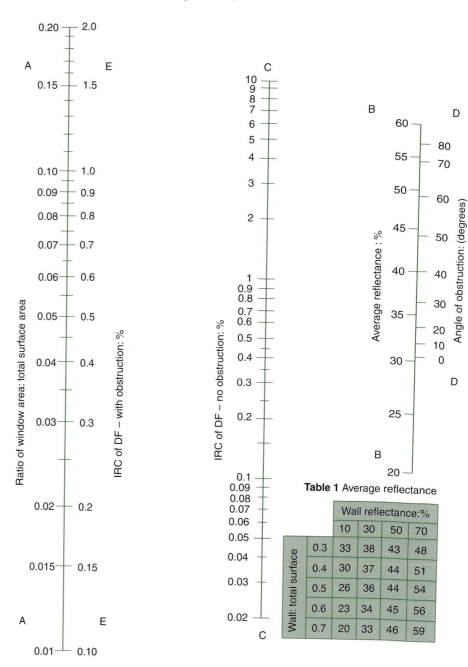

Table 1 Average reflectance

	Wall reflectance:%			
	10	30	50	70
0.3	33	38	43	48
0.4	30	37	44	51
0.5	26	36	44	54
0.6	23	34	45	56
0.7	20	33	46	59

Table 2 D-factors for deterioration of surfaces

Location	Room use	
	Clean	Dirty
Clean	0.9	0.7
Dirty	0.8	0.6

use of the nomogram is explained in Section 2.4.2 and Fig. 2.26

DATA SHEET D.2.5

Daylight factor: the pepper-pot diagram

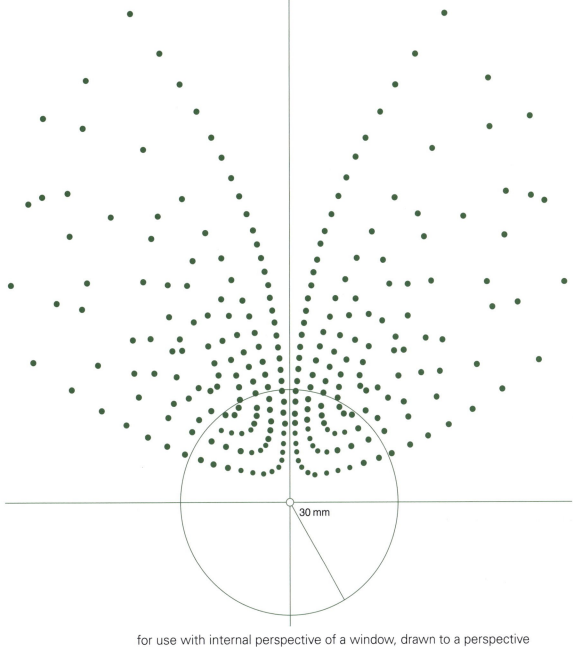

30 mm

for use with internal perspective of a window, drawn to a perspective distance of 30 mm as per method sheet M.2.2.

The 30 mm radius circle indicates a cone of vision of 45° all around (a cone with the height of 30 mm, which is the perspective distance, and the base circle is shown).

DATA SHEET D.2.6

Recommended illuminance and Limiting glare index values

Visual task	Illuminance	Glare index limit
Casual viewing	100 lx	
cloak room, locker, lavatory, bathroom, auditoria, foyer		no limit
boiler or furnace room, bulk store		28
corridor, escalator, stairs		22
hospital ward		13
art gallery (general lighting)		10
Rough task, large detail	200 lx	
store, rough workshop		25
lift, kitchen, dining room		22
pharmacy, library, casual reading		19
lecture room, surgery, telephone exchange		16
Ordinary task, medium detail	400 lx	
reception areas, food shop		22
general office, keyboard work, control panels		19
drawing office, dispensary, laboratory, reading		16
Fairly severe task, small detail	750 lx	
mechanical workshop, fine woodwork, painting, inspection		22
computer room, dressmaking		19
needlework, art room		16
Severe prolonged task, small detail	900 lx	
supermarket display		25
electronic or fine mechanical assembly veneer work		22
instrument factory, fine painting, colour inspection		19
jewel or watch factory, proof reading		16
Very severe prolonged task, very small detail	up to 2000 lx	
sorting, grading of leather, cloths, hand-tailoring, engraving		19
precision instrument or electronic components assembly		16
gem cutting, gauging very small parts		10
Exceptional task, minute detail	3000 lx	
minute instrument work using optical aids		10

These are general recommendations compiled from many sources. The Australian Standard AS1680, as well as the IES Code for Interior Lighting give extensive tables for general lighting and various industrial processes as well as for public and educational buildings.

Recommended spacing of luminaires (for uniformity of general lighting)

Luminaire type	Maximum	End luminaire to wall	Work position next to wall
General diffusing or direct	$1.4 H_m$	$0.75 H_m$	$0.5 H_m$
Concentrating reflector luminaires	H_m	$0.5 H_m$	$0.5 H_m$
Indirect, semi-indirect, (mounted 0.25–0.3 Hc below ceiling)	$1.5 H_c$	$0.75 H_c$	$0.5 H_c$

(H_m mounting height, work plane to luminaire, H_c work plane to ceiling height)

DATA SHEET D.2.7

Luminaire characteristics: polar curves

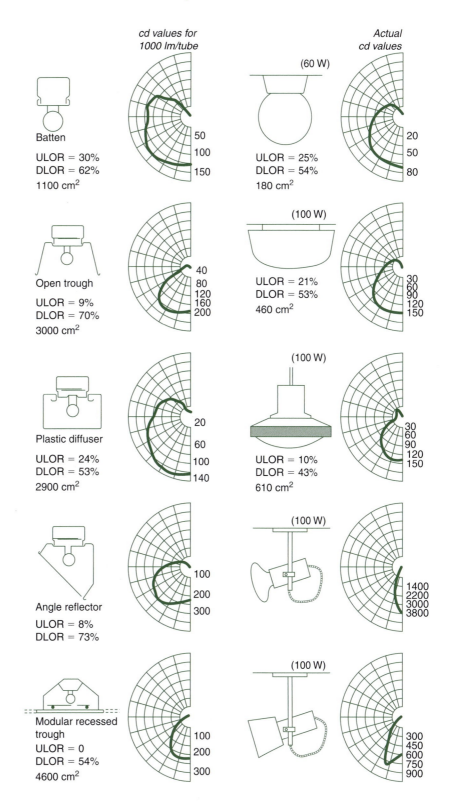

cd values for 1000 lm/tube — *Actual cd values*

Batten
ULOR = 30%
DLOR = 62%
1100 cm²
50 / 100 / 150

(60 W)
ULOR = 25%
DLOR = 54%
180 cm²
20 / 50 / 80

Open trough
ULOR = 9%
DLOR = 70%
3000 cm²
40 / 80 / 120 / 160 / 200

(100 W)
ULOR = 21%
DLOR = 53%
460 cm²
30 / 60 / 90 / 120 / 150

Plastic diffuser
ULOR = 24%
DLOR = 53%
2900 cm²
20 / 60 / 100 / 140

(100 W)
ULOR = 10%
DLOR = 43%
610 cm²
30 / 60 / 90 / 120 / 150

Angle reflector
ULOR = 8%
DLOR = 73%
100 / 200 / 300

(100 W)
1400 / 2200 / 3000 / 3800

Modular recessed trough
ULOR = 0
DLOR = 54%
4600 cm²
100 / 200 / 300

(100 W)
300 / 450 / 600 / 750 / 900

DATA SHEET D.2.8

Utilization factors of typical luminaires

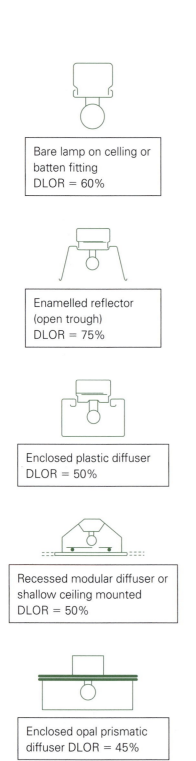

Bare lamp on ceiling or batten fitting
DLOR = 60%

Enamelled reflector (open trough)
DLOR = 75%

Enclosed plastic diffuser
DLOR = 50%

Recessed modular diffuser or shallow ceiling mounted
DLOR = 50%

Enclosed opal prismatic diffuser DLOR = 45%

Room index	Reflectaznce of ceiling and walls								
C:	0.7			0.5			0.3		
W:	0.5	0.3	0.1	0.5	0.3	0.1	0.5	0.3	0.1
0.6	0.29	0.24	0.19	0.27	0.22	0.19	0.24	0.21	0.19
0.8	0.37	0.31	0.27	0.35	0.30	0.25	0.31	0.28	0.24
1.0	0.44	0.37	0.33	0.40	0.35	0.31	0.35	0.32	0.29
1.25	0.49	0.42	0.38	0.45	0.40	0.36	0.39	0.36	0.33
1.5	0.54	0.47	0.42	0.50	0.44	0.40	0.43	0.40	0.37
2.0	0.60	0.52	0.49	0.54	0.49	0.45	0.48	0.44	0.41
2.5	0.64	0.57	0.53	0.57	0.53	0.49	0.52	0.48	0.45
3.0	0.67	0.61	0.57	0.60	0.57	0.53	0.56	0.52	0.49
4.0	0.71	0.66	0.62	0.64	0.61	0.57	0.59	0.55	0.52
5.0	0.74	0.70	0.66	0.68	0.64	0.61	0.62	0.58	0.54
0.6	0.36	0.31	0.28	0.35	0.31	0.28	0.35	0.31	0.28
0.8	0.45	0.40	0.37	0.44	0.40	0.37	0.44	0.40	0.37
1.0	0.49	0.45	0.40	0.49	0.44	0.40	0.48	0.43	0.40
1.25	0.55	0.49	0.46	0.53	0.49	0.45	0.52	0.48	0.45
1.5	0.58	0.54	0.49	0.57	0.53	0.49	0.55	0.52	0.49
2.0	0.64	0.59	0.55	0.61	0.58	0.55	0.60	0.56	0.54
2.5	0.68	0.63	0.60	0.65	0.62	0.59	0.64	0.61	0.58
3.0	0.70	0.65	0.62	0.67	0.64	0.61	0.65	0.63	0.61
4.0	0.73	0.70	0.67	0.70	0.67	0.65	0.67	0.66	0.64
5.0	0.75	0.72	0.69	0.73	0.70	0.67	0.70	0.68	0.67
0.6	0.27	0.21	0.18	0.24	0.20	0.18	0.22	0.19	0.17
0.8	0.34	0.29	0.26	0.32	0.28	0.25	0.29	0.26	0.24
1.0	0.40	0.35	0.31	0.37	0.33	0.30	0.33	0.30	0.28
1.25	0.44	0.39	0.35	0.40	0.36	0.33	0.36	0.33	0.31
1.5	0.47	0.42	0.38	0.43	0.39	0.36	0.38	0.35	0.33
2.0	0.52	0.47	0.44	0.47	0.44	0.41	0.41	0.39	0.37
2.5	0.55	0.51	0.48	0.50	0.47	0.44	0.44	0.42	0.40
3.0	0.58	0.54	0.51	0.52	0.49	0.47	0.47	0.45	0.43
4.0	0.61	0.57	0.54	0.55	0.52	0.50	0.49	0.47	0.45
5.0	0.63	0.59	0.57	0.57	0.55	0.53	0.51	0.49	0.47
0.6	0.21	0.18	0.16	0.21	0.18	0.16	0.20	0.18	0.16
0.8	0.28	0.24	0.22	0.27	0.24	0.22	0.26	0.24	0.22
1.0	0.32	0.29	0.26	0.31	0.28	0.26	0.30	0.28	0.26
1.25	0.35	0.32	0.29	0.34	0.31	0.29	0.32	0.30	0.28
1.5	0.37	0.34	0.31	0.36	0.33	0.31	0.34	0.32	0.30
2.0	0.41	0.37	0.35	0.39	0.37	0.34	0.38	0.36	0.34
2.5	0.43	0.40	0.38	0.42	0.39	0.37	0.40	0.38	0.37
3.0	0.45	0.42	0.40	0.44	0.41	0.40	0.42	0.40	0.39
4.0	0.47	0.44	0.43	0.46	0.44	0.42	0.44	0.42	0.41
5.0	0.49	0.46	0.45	0.47	0.46	0.44	0.46	0.44	0.43
0.6	0.23	0.18	0.14	0.20	0.16	0.12	0.17	0.14	0.11
0.8	0.30	0.24	0.20	0.27	0.22	0.18	0.22	0.19	0.16
1.0	0.36	0.29	0.25	0.31	0.26	0.22	0.26	0.23	0.19
1.25	0.41	0.34	0.29	0.35	0.30	0.26	0.29	0.26	0.22
1.5	0.45	0.39	0.33	0.39	0.34	0.30	0.31	0.28	0.25
2.0	0.50	0.45	0.40	0.43	0.38	0.34	0.34	0.32	0.29
2.5	0.54	0.49	0.44	0.46	0.42	0.38	0.37	0.35	0.32
3.0	0.57	0.52	0.48	0.49	0.45	0.42	0.40	0.38	0.34
4.0	0.60	0.56	0.52	0.52	0.48	0.46	0.43	0.41	0.37
5.0	0.63	0.60	0.56	0.54	0.51	0.49	0.45	0.43	0.40

DATA SHEET D.2.9

Lamp characteristics

Lamp type	Wattage	Ballast	Lumen output
Incandescent (at 240V)			
pear shaped	25W	–	200
	40	–	325
	60	–	575
	100	–	1160
	150	–	1960
	200	–	2720
	500	–	7700
mushroom shaped	40	–	380
	60	–	640
	100	–	1220
Sodium[#]			
SOX (low pressure)	35	20	4200
	55	20	7500
	90	25	12500
SON (high pressure)	70	25	5300
	250	30	24000
Mercury[#]			
MB	80	15	2700
MBI (metal halide)	400	50	24000
MBF (mercury fluorescent)	50	15	1800
	80	20	3350
MBT (mercury/tungsten)	100	–	1250
Fluorescent ('white')			
0.6m	20	5	1050
0.6m	40	8	1550
1.2m	40	10	2800
1.5m	50	20	3100
1.5m	65	15	4400
1.5m	80	15	4850

[#]the smallest lamps in each type are shown. The upper limit is around 200000 lm.

Corrections to the output of fluorescent lamps

Lamp type	Correction	Lumen output of 1200mm 40W
White	1.00	2800
Warm white	0.96	2700
Daylight	0.95	2660
Natural	0.75	2100
Warmtone	0.70	1960
De luxe warm white	0.67	1950
Colour 32 and 34	0.65	1820
Colour matching	0.65	1820
Kolor-rite	0.65	1800
De luxe natural	0.55	1500
Softone 27	0.55	1500
Tricolor 37	0.55	1500
Artificial daylight	0.40	1120

METHOD SHEET M.2.3

Construction of internal perspective (for pepper-pot diagram)

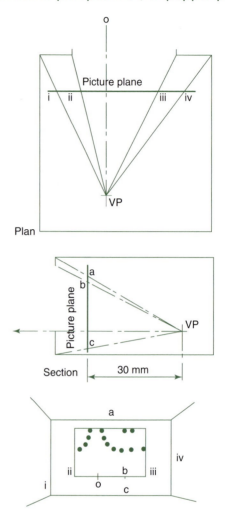

The distance between the point considered (the viewpoint, VP) and the picture plane must be 30 mm, irrespective of the scale of plan and section, whether the picture plane falls inside or outside (for a VP nearer to the window the picture plane will be outside).

Mark the width points (i–iv) an the plan of the picture plane, as well as the O-point. Mark the height points (a–c) on the section, as well as the O-point. Transfer this onto the perspective, left and right, up and down from the O-point.

This is a one-point perspective, and the O-point is also the vanishing point.

METHOD SHEET M.2.4

Glare index calculation

The glare constant is $g = \dfrac{L_1^{1.6} \times \omega^{0.8}}{L_2 \times p^{1.6}}$

L_1, the luminance of the glare source can be found as the source intensity (from the viewing direction) divided by the apparent area of the source.

For example we have a 40W bare fluorescent lamp at a horizontal distance of 4.6 m from the observer and 1.4 m above eye level. The actual distance is $d = 4.8$ m. From data sheet D.2.7 the projected area of this lamp is 1100 cm², i.e. 0.11 m² thus the visual angle (solid angle) subtended by the lamp is $\omega = $ area/$d^2 = 0.11/4.8^2 = 0.0048$ sr

The vertical displacement angle is $\theta = \arctan(1.4/4.6) = 17°$, i.e. with respect to the vertical axis of the luminaire the viewing direction is 73°. The polar curve in data sheet D.2.7 gives a source intensity for this direction of 125 cd for 1000 lamp lumens.

For a 40W warm white lamp data sheet D.2.9 gives a lumen output of 2700 lm, thus the actual source intensity is $I = 125 * 2700/1000 = 337.5$ cd and the source luminance will be

$L_1 = 337.5/0.11 = 3068$ cd/m²

L_2, the background luminance can be estimated from the average reflectance and average illuminance of the field of view. For example if surfaces are about Munsell value 4, then (from eq. (2.2)) $\rho = 4 * 3/100 = 0.12$, and if the illuminance is $E = 400$ lx, then the luminance will be $L_2 = 400 * 0.12 = 48$ asb or $48/\pi = 15.2$ cd/m². If the lamp is directly in the line of vision ($\varphi = 0$), with the vertical displacement angle of 17° the position index (from the table below) is 0.67.

Thus $g = \dfrac{3068^{1.6} \times 0.0047^{0.8}}{15.2 \times 0.67^{1.6}} = 661$

If there were several luminaires/lamps in the field of view the glare constant (g) of each should be found and summarized.

The glare index will be
$GI = 10 \times \log_{10}(0.478 \times \Sigma)$
in this case
$GI = 10 \times \log(0.478 \times 661) = 25$

In terms of the limiting values given in Section 2.5.5, (or in data sheet D.2.6) this is acceptable for an industrial situation, but not for an office.

Horizontal displacement angle (φ)

↓	0	6°	10°	17°	22°	27°	31°	35°	39°	42°	45°	50°	54°	58°	61°	68°	72°
62°		–	–	–	–	–	–	–	—	0.02	0.02	0.02	0.02	0.02	0.02	0.02	0.02
61°	–		—	–	0.02	0.02	0.02	0.02	0.02	0.02	0.02	0.02	0.02	0.02	0.02	0.02	0.02
58°	0.03	0.03	0.03	0.03	0.03	0.03	0.03	0.03	0.03	0.03	0.03	0.03	0.03	0.03	0.03	0.03	0.03
54°	0.04	0.04	0.04	0.04	0.04	0.04	0.04	0.04	0.04	0.04	0.04	0.04	0.04	0.04	0.04	0.03	0.03
50°	0.05	0.05	0.06	0.06	0.06	0.06	0.06	0.06	0.06	0.06	0.06	0.05	0.05	0.05	0.05	0.04	0.04
45°	0.08	0.09	0.09	0.10	0.10	0.10	0.10	0.09	0.09	0.09	0.08	0.08	0.07	0.06	0.06	0.05	0.05
42°	0.11	0.11	0.12	0.13	0.13	0.12	0.12	0.12	0.12	0.11	0.10	0.09	0.08	0.07	0.07	0.06	0.05
39°	0.14	0.15	0.16	0.16	0.16	0.16	0.15	0.15	0.14	0.13	0.12	0.11	0.09	0.08	0.08	0.6	0.06
35°	0.19	0.20	0.22	0.21	0.21	0.21	0.20	0.18	0.17	0.16	0.14	0.12	0.11	0.10	0.09	0.07	0.07
31°	0.25	0.27	0.30	0.29	0.28	0.26	0.24	0.22	0.21	0.19	0.18	0.15	0.13	0.11	0.10	0.09	0.08
27°	0.35	0.37	0.39	0.38	0.36	0.34	0.31	0.28	0.25	0.23	0.21	0.18	0.15	0.14	0.12	0.10	0.09
22°	0.48	0.53	0.53	0.51	0.49	0.44	0.39	0.35	0.31	0.28	0.25	0.21	0.18	0.16	0.14	0.11	0.10
17°	0.67	0.73	0.73	0.69	0.64	0.57	0.49	0.44	0.38	0.34	0.31	0.25	0.21	0.19	0.16	0.13	0.12
11°	0.95	1.02	0.98	0.88	0.80	0.72	0.63	0.57	0.49	0.42	0.37	0.30	0.25	0.22	0.19	0.15	0.14
6°	1.30	1.36	1.24	1.12	1.01	0.88	0.79	0.68	0.62	0.53	0.46	0.37	0.31	0.26	0.23	0.17	0.16
0°	1.87	1.73	1.56	1.36	1.20	1.06	0.93	0.80	0.72	0.64	0.57	0.46	0.38	0.33	0.28	0.20	0.17

← Vertical displacement angles (θ)

METHOD SHEET M.2.5

Permissible height indicators

Scale 1:500

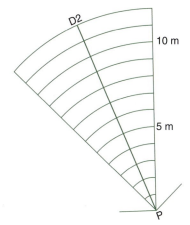

the radius of the highest arc
in each case should be

D1	46 mm
D2	53 mm
D3	79 mm

For use with the method described
in Section 2.4.5
and Fig. 2.34

For this D set the slope of the limiting
plane (within the wedges) is

D1	10°
D2	25°
D3	27.5°

Based on MoHLG Planning bulletin No.5,
*Planning for daylight and sunlight and Sunlight
and daylight*, DoE Welsh Office HMSO, 1971

May be reconstructed for a scale of 1:200
with the following radii:

D1	116 mm
D2	133 mm
D3	198 mm

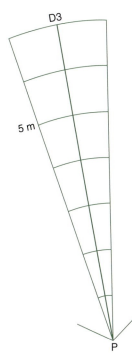

METHOD SHEET M.2.6

Comparison of two alternative lighting schemes

In some situations it may be possible to replace a high level general (electric) lighting system with a low level general lighting supplemented by local lighting where required, e.g. at individual work-stations. This would produce a reduction in electricity use, as illustrated by the following example:

Assume a library reading room of 10 m × 20 m (200 m²) and 2.9 m high, which is to accommodate 20 reading desks. Take surface reflectances as 70% for the ceiling and 50% for the walls.

If the desk height is 0.8 m and the luminaires are 0.1 m from the ceiling, the mounting height will be 2.9 − 0.8 − 0.1 = 2 m, thus the room index becomes

$$RI = \frac{10 \times 20}{(10 + 20) \times 2} = 3.33$$

Use 1.2 m fluorescent tubes in enclosed plastic diffuser luminaires,

From data sheet D.2.8 (first column, interpolating for RI 3.33 between 0.58 and 0.61) the utilization factor is UF = 0.59

Lamp output of (from data sheet D.2.9) 2800 × 0.75 (for 'natural') = 2100 lm

Scheme **A**: general lighting to give work-plane illuminance of 400 lux

flux to be received if maintenance factor is	$\Phi_r = 10 \times 20 \times 400 = 80\,000$ lm $M = 0.8$
installed flux required	$\Phi_i = \dfrac{80\,000}{0.59 \times 0.8} = 169\,492$ lm
number of lamps required	$N = \dfrac{169\,492}{2100} = 81$
installed power:	$81 \times (40 + 10) = 4050$ W
thus power density	$\dfrac{4050}{200} = \textbf{20.25 W/m}^2$

Scheme **B**: general lighting of 100 lux + local lighting to 20 desks combining four of the above equations

	$N = \dfrac{10 \times 20 \times 100}{0.59 \times 0.8} / 2100 = 20$ lamps
installed power:	$20 \times (40 + 10) = 1000$ W
thus power density	$\dfrac{1000}{200} = \qquad 5$ W/m²
+ 20 desk lamps	$\Phi_i = 20 \times 40 = 800$ W
thus power density	$800 / 200 = \qquad 4$ W/m²
Total power density	$\textbf{9W/m}^2$

which is less than half of that required with scheme A
and if we consider that the 20 desk lamps would not be used at all times, the energy advantage is much greater.

PART 3   SOUND: THE SONIC ENVIRONMENT

CONTENTS

SYMBOLS AND ABBREVIATIONS

a	absorption coefficient	NNI	noise and number index
f	frequency (Hz) (or interval of averaging for L_{eq})	NR	noise rating
f_c	octave-band centre frequency	P	sound power (W)
h	height	RT	reverberation time
p	sound pressure (Pa)	S	stimulus or sound source
r	radius	SIL	speech interference level
s	surface area	SiL	sound intensity level
v	velocity	SpL	sound pressure level
Abs	total absorption (m^2 open window units)	SRI	sound reduction index
ARS	assisted resonance system	STC	sound transmission class
C	a constant	R	response
CRT	cathode ray tube	S	stimulus
DIN	deutsche Institut für Normung	TL	transmission loss
I	intensity (W/m^2)	TNI	traffic noise index
L	sound level	V	volume or volt
L_{eq}	equivalent continuous sound level	α	absorptance
M	mass, surface density (kg/m^2)	λ	wavelength
MCR	multi-channel reverberation	ρ	reflectance or density
NC	noise criteria	τ	transmittance

LIST OF FIGURES

LIST OF TABLES

LIST OF WORKED EXAMPLES

LIST OF EQUATIONS

3.1 PHYSICS OF SOUND

Sound is the sensation caused by a vibrating medium as it acts on the human ear. Loosely, the term is also applied to the vibration itself that causes this sensation. Acoustics (from the Greek ακονστικos) is the science of sound, of small amplitude mechanical vibrations.

A simple acoustic system consists of a source, some conveying medium and a receiver. The source is some vibrating body, which converts some other form of energy into vibration (e.g. mechanical impact on a solid body, air pressure acting on a column of air, such as in a whistle or pipe, electrical energy acting on a steel membrane or on a crystal, etc). The word *transducer* is often used for devices converting other forms of energy into sound (e.g. a loudspeaker) or vice versa (e.g. a microphone). The conveying medium may be a gas (e.g. air), which transmits the vibration in the form of longitudinal waves (alternating compressions and rarifications), or a solid body, where lateral vibrations may also be involved (e.g. a string). Figure 3.1 illustrates the longitudinal (compression) waves and their representation by a sine curve.

In buildings we are concerned with *airborne sound* and *structureborne sound*, the latter being transmitted by the building fabric.

3.1.1 Attributes of sound

Sounds are characterized by wavelength (λ in m) or frequency (f in Hz) and the product of the two, the velocity (v in m/s). The latter depends on the transmitting medium. In air it is usually taken as 340 m/s, but it varies with temperature and humidity (faster in warmer, less dense air).

The relevant equations are very similar to those given for light (eq. 2.1):

$$v = f \times \lambda \tag{3.1}$$

from which

$$\lambda = \frac{340}{f} \quad \text{and} \quad f = \frac{340}{\lambda}$$

Note that p (lower case) denotes sound pressure, P (capital) denotes sound source power.

The output (power, P) of a sound source is measured in W (watts). Table 3.1 gives some typical sound power values.

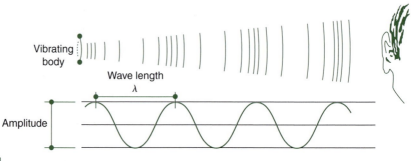

Vibrating body

Wave length
λ

Amplitude

3.1.
Sound waves: longitudinal compression waves and their sinusoidal representation.

Table 3.1. Sound power of some sources

Jet airliner	10 kW (10^4W)
Pneumatic riveter, accelerating motorcycle	1 W
50 kW (electrical) axial flow fan	0.1 W (10^{-1}W)
Large (symphonic) orchestra	0.01 W (10^{-2}W)
Food blender, coffee grinder	0.001 W (10^{-3}W)
Conversational speech	0.00001 W (10^{-5}W)

Frequency is perceived as pitch and the 'strength' of sound is measured either by its pressure, p (in Pa) or by its power density or intensity, I (in W/m^2). The latter is the density of energy flow rate. Sound pressure actually varies within every cycle from zero to positive peak then through zero to a negative maximum, so what we measure is the RMS (root-mean-square) pressure.

The relationship of p and I depends on the conveying medium, but in air under 'standard conditions' (air density of $\rho = 1.18$ kg/m^3 and $v = 340$ m/s) it is usually taken as

$$p = 20\sqrt{I} \tag{3.2}$$

3.1.2 Pure tones and broad-band sound

A sound that can be described by a smooth sine curve and is of one particular frequency, is referred to as a *pure tone sound*. This can only be generated electronically. Sounds produced by instruments always contain some harmonics.

The fundamental frequency itself is the first harmonic. The second harmonic is double that frequency, the third is three times that, etc; e.g. middle *C* has a frequency of 256 Hz. Its harmonics will be:

2nd = 512 Hz
3rd = 768 Hz
4th = 1024 Hz

Most sounds contain many frequencies and are referred to as *broad-band sounds*. An octave extends from f to $2f$ frequency, e.g. from 1000 Hz to 2000 Hz. An octave band is usually designated by its centre frequency (f_c), then the limits are defined as

$$f_{lower} = f_c \times \frac{1}{\sqrt{2}} \quad \text{and} \quad f_{upper} = f_c \times \sqrt{2}$$

Table 3.2 shows the standard octave-band centre frequencies and the octave boundaries.

If the sound is measured in each octave separately (by using 'octave-band filters') then a sound spectrum can be built up, such as those shown in Fig. 3.2.

higher intensities. As a first approximation of auditory response a logarithmic scale has been devised: the *sound level*.

The logarithm of the ratio I/I_0 has been named Bel (after Alexander Graham Bel), but as this is a rather large unit, its sub-multiple the deci-Bel (dB) is used.

It can be derived from intensity or from pressure:

Sound intensity level: $\text{SiL} = 10 \times \log \dfrac{I}{I_0}$ (3.4)

Sound pressure level: $\text{SpL} = 20 \times \log \dfrac{p}{p_0}$ (3.5)

and the reference values have been standardized as the average threshold of audibility:

$I_0 = 1\,\text{pW/m}^2$ (pico-Watt = 10^{-12} W)

$p_0 = 20\,\mu\text{Pa}$ (micro-Pascal = 10^{-6} Pa)

Under standard atmospheric conditions both derivations give the same result, so in practice both may be referred to as sound level (L).

The intensities of two sounds are additive, but not the corresponding sound levels. If sound levels are given, they must be converted to inten-sities, these intensities can be added, then the resulting sound level must be found.

EXAMPLE 3.1

Two sound levels are given: $L' = 90\,\text{dB}$, $L'' = 80\,\text{dB}$. The sum of the two is NOT 170 dB (!)

From eq. (3.4): $I = 10^{-12} \times 10^{L/10}$

thus

$I' = 10^{(9-12)} = 10^{-3} = 0.001$ $I'' = 10^{(8-12)} = 10^{-4} = 0.0001$

$$I' + I'' = 0.0011\,\text{W/m}^2$$

$$L_{\text{sum}} = 10 \log \frac{0.0011}{10^{-12}} = 10 \log(11 \times 10^8) = 10 \times 9.04 = 90.4\,\text{dB}$$

The nomogram given in Fig. 3.4 can be used for adding two sound levels.

Find the difference between the two levels on the upper scale and add this to the larger of the two levels given. To continue the above example: the difference is $90 - 80 = 10\,\text{dB}$. On the nomogram opposite the 10 dB read 0.4, so the sum will be $90 + 0.4 = 90.4$.

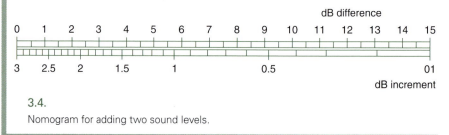

3.4.
Nomogram for adding two sound levels.

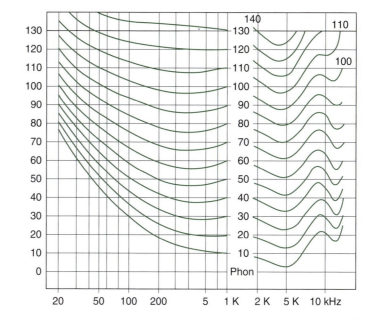

3.5.

Equal loudness contours: definition of the phon scale.

The next step in quantifying the auditory response recognizes that the sensitivity of the ear varies with the frequency of the sound. It is most sensitive to about 4 kHz (4000 Hz). Sensitivity to various pure tone sounds has been plotted on a (logarithmic) frequency graph, giving the *equal loudness contours* for pure tone sounds (Fig. 3.5). These curves are designated by the sound level at 1 kHz and define the loudness level (phon) scale (i.e. the sound level and loudness level scales coincide at 1 kHz frequency).

For example, take the 30 phon curve. This indicates that at 1 kHz a sound level of 30 dB is perceived as of 30 phon loudness level, but 30 dB at 100 Hz would only give 10 phon whilst at 4 kHz it is perceived as of about 37 phon loudness level. Conversely, 40 phon loudness level is produced by (e.g.) each of the following sounds:

at 40 Hz ...   70 dB
at 100 Hz ...   52 dB
at 250 or 1000 Hz or 7000 Hz   40 dB
at 4000 Hz ...   32 dB

i.e. pure tone all sounds along one of these equal loudness contours would be perceived as of the same loudness level.

A true measure of the human ear's sensitivity is thus found, after two adjustments:

1 for logarithmic response to the stimulus, which gave the sound level scale (dB)
2 for the frequency dependence of our ear, which gave the loudness level (phon).

Phon cannot be measured directly, but an electronic weighting network provides an approximation. The effect of 'A' weighting is shown in Fig. 3.6. Sound levels measured with this weighting are referred to as dBA. (The German DIN Standards refer to such a weighted scale as 'instrument phon'.) Other weighting scales also exist, but of no great relevance to architecture. These dBA values are often used to describe a broad-band sound with a single figure index. However, numerous combinations of levels and frequencies may give the same dBA value, thus an accurate description of a broad-band sound can only be given by its spectrum.

3.2 HEARING

Aural perception (from the Latin *auris* = ear) starts with the ear. Airborne sounds reach the eardrum through the auditory tube and it will start vibrating (Fig. 3.7). This vibration is then transmitted by the ossicles (hammer, anvil and stirrup) to the inner membrane of the oval window and through this it reaches the inner ear, the cochlea. Some 25 000 hair-like endings of the auditory nerve are located in the cochlea, which selectively respond to various frequencies and generate nerve impulses, subsequently transmitted to the brain.

These impulses are interpreted by the brain, but the first selection takes place in the inner ear. The ear is thus not only a very efficient microphone but also an analyser. Most of the auditory brain functions involve pattern recognitions, filtering out what is relevant, and interpretation, based on memory, i.e. past experience.

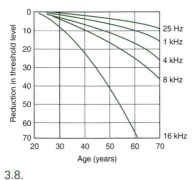

3.7.
The human ear.

3.2.1 The audible range

The human ear is sensitive to vibrations between 20 Hz and 16 kHz, but these limits also depend on the 'strength' of the sound. The audible range of frequencies may also be reduced (especially at high frequencies) by the listener's state of health and definitely by old age. Figure 3.8 shows that at

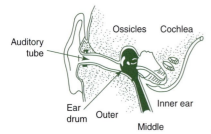

3.8.
Presbycousis: loss of hearing with age.

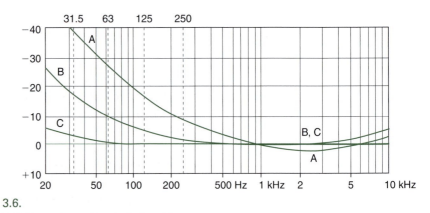

3.6.
Weighings of sound levels: A, B and C.

age 60 people can expect to have a hearing loss of 70 dB at 16 kHz, but only a loss of about 10 dB at 1 kHz.

Figure 3.9 illustrates the range of audible sounds, both in terms of frequency and 'strength'. Strength is measured by three scales: pressure, intensity and sound level. Note that the top and bottom part of the outline corresponds to the equal loudness contours (at 0 and 120 phon). It also shows that there are vibrations below and above the limits: referred to as *infra-sounds* and *ultra-sounds* (infrasonic and ultrasonic vibrations). The bottom of the audible area is the *threshold of audibility* and the top is the *threshold of pain*. Above the latter there may be super-sounds, but there is no specific term for the below threshold sounds. (For calculation purposes both thresholds are fixed in terms of intensity, pressure or sound level, regardless of frequency.)

If pitch is the subjective interpretation of the frequency of a sound, it clearly relates to pure tone (or near pure-tone) sounds. Complex sounds are physically determined by their spectrum, whilst the subjective term for the 'colouring' of a sound of a certain pitch is *timbre*. Several everyday expressions can relate to certain types of sound, e.g. Fig. 3.10 shows a pure tone, a hissing sound and a rumble. The hiss is due to the many high frequency overtones, as shown by the middle curve.

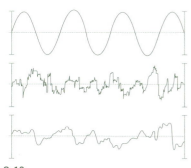

3.10.

A pure tone, a hiss and a rumble (graphic level recordings).

3.2.2 Noise: definition and rating

An attempted definition of noise in objective terms is 'random vibrations, showing no regular pattern'. However, noise is a subjective phenomenon, one person's enjoyable sound may be another's noise. The only meaningful definition of noise is therefore 'unwanted sound'. This is similar to the definition in telecommunications, where the *signal* is distinguished from the *noise*, which is all else.

The term *white noise* is used for a set of vibrations which contains equal amounts of energy in all wavelengths (*per analogiam*: white light, which includes all visible wavelengths of light). It is a common fallacy to believe that white noise would eliminate or suppress noise: it only reduces the intelligibility of such unwanted sound (if it has some information content).

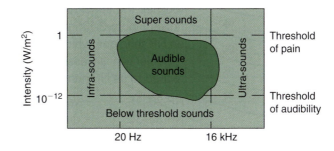

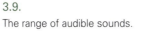

3.9.

The range of audible sounds.

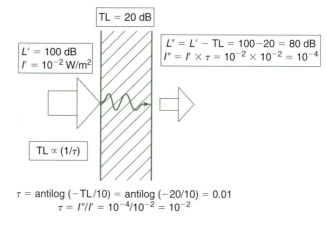

$$\tau = \text{antilog}\,(-\text{TL}/10) = \text{antilog}\,(-20/10) = 0.01$$
$$\tau = I''/I' = 10^{-4}/10^{-2} = 10^{-2}$$

3.22.
An example of expressing transmission two ways.

Similarly to light transmission, sound energy incident on a solid object (such as a partition) would be distributed three ways: part of it can be reflected (ρ), part of it absorbed (α) and the reminder transmitted (τ). The sum of the three components is unity:

$$\rho + \alpha + \tau = 1$$

If the sound intensity on the source side is I', the transmitted (received) sound intensity will be

$$I'' = I' \times \tau$$

but if the sound level on the source side is L', then the sound level on the receiving side will be

$$L'' = L' - \text{TL}$$

thus TL $\propto$ (1/t) (or the loss is proportionate to that NOT transmitted).
The relationship is

$$\text{TL} = 10\log(1/\tau) = 10(-\log\tau) \tag{3.8}$$

conversely

$$\tau = \frac{1}{\text{antilog}(\text{TL}/10)} = \text{antilog}\,\frac{-\text{TL}}{10} \tag{3.9}$$

The mass law states that every doubling of surface density (or unit area mass) of a partition increases the TL by 6 dB and TL $\approx 20\log M$ where M is surface density in kg/m^2.

In practice, due to various imperfections, only 5 dB of TL improvement is likely to be achieved by doubling the mass, or TL $\approx 17\log M$.

Transmission is also frequency-dependent. If a molecule of a body has to vibrate faster (at higher frequency), its dampening effect will be greater. Thus the mass law also states that the TL will increase by 6 dB for every doubling of the frequency. Thus the TL graph as a function of frequency will show an upward slope. This TL will however be reduced by (a) resonance and by (b) coincidence. The first depends on the resonant frequency of the wall. For sounds at this frequency (or its upper harmonics) the TL is very much reduced. The second, coincidence depends also on the angle of incidence of sound, as the incident wavefronts sweep the wall surface. As Fig. 3.23 indicates, (a) is likely to cause problems in buildings at low frequencies, and (b) the high frequencies. The mass law will be fully operative in the medium frequencies only. The purpose of sound insulation improvements is to push the resonance region downwards and the coincidence region upwards.

Data sheet D.3.3 gives the TL values of various building elements for different frequencies and an overall average. Some simple empirical expressions for the average TL of solid, homogeneous elements are:

$$TL = 18 \log M + 8 \quad \text{if } M > 100 \, \text{kg/m}^2 \tag{3.10}$$

and

$$TL = 14.5M + 13 \quad \text{if } M < 100 \, \text{kg/m}^2 \tag{3.11}$$

or for the TL in any octave band
$$TL_f = 18 \log M + 12 \log f_c - 25$$

where f_c = octave-band centre frequency.

The highest achievable TL value is 55–60 dB. When the TL of a partition reaches about 50 dB, the flanking transmission paths become progressively more and more dominant.

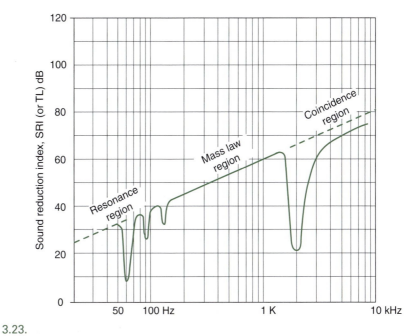

3.23.
A transmission graph showing resonance and coincidence regions.

Method sheet M.3.1 shows the calculation of average TL values for a dividing element consisting of different components, e.g. a partition with a door or a wall with a window. It shows that the 'chain is as good as its weakest link', that, for example, a relatively small opening can destroy the TL of a heavy wall.

For double-leaf walls or partitions (provided that the two leaves are not connected) the TL value will be some 8 dB higher than if the same mass were used in one leaf, e.g.

110 mm brickwork	TL = 45 dB
220 mm brickwork	TL = 50 dB
270 mm cavity wall	TL = 58 dB

This improvement is however reduced at the resonant frequency, and at this frequency the TL of the cavity wall could become less than the solid double thickness wall.

For best effects the cavity should be at least 100 mm as the resonant frequency of this cavity would be lower. With light materials the resonant frequency can be well within the audible range, so the cavity should be wider. The coupling of the two skins by a resonant sound field in the cavity can be prevented by the introduction of some porous absorbent (e.g. a glass wool blanket). This may improve the TL by some 5 dB.

A special case of double walls is a double-glazed window. Here the most important point is to avoid acoustic coupling of the two layers. The cavity should be at least 200 mm wide, otherwise the cavity resonance will be well within the audible range. Airtight closure of both leaves is important and the reveals should be lined with an absorbent material to reduce any cavity resonance. To further reduce the probability of acoustic coupling, the two sheets of glass should be of different thickness thus different resonant and coincidence frequencies.

3.3.2 Control of environmental noise

The main sources of environmental noise would be

a industry
b road traffic
c air traffic.

It is far easier (and far less expensive) to control noise at or near the source than at some distance from it. Often the noise generated is an avoidable by-product of some process. Careful design can eliminate or at least reduce this. Often a mechanical component generates a vibration (which may be below the audible range), which is transmitted, for example, to some sheet metal component, which will vibrate, perhaps at some upper harmonics of the original frequency, and emit sound. It is the task of equipment designers to avoid vibration (e.g. by good balancing) and prevent the transmission of such vibration (e.g. by using flexible mountings or flexible connectors in a duct or pipework).

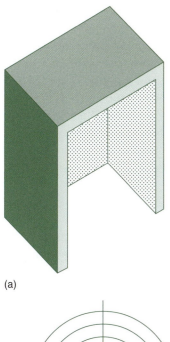

(a)

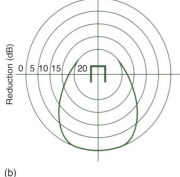

(b)

3.24.
A partial enclosure for sound control and its effect on sound distribution (polar curve).

Impact noise can be reduced at the point where the impact would transmit mechanical energy into the building fabric by, for example, a resilient lining. The most common form of this is the use of carpets with underfelt.

Airborne noise emission from a source can be reduced by some form of (possibly partial) enclosure. A complete and heavyweight enclosure would be the most effective. If it has some openings (e.g. vents), then the inside could be lined with absorbent materials to reduce the sound field. If access is needed (e.g. for an operator of some machinery, a four-sided box can be installed, with one side open, and lined with absorbents. Figure 3.24 shows a possible partial enclosure and its sound reduction effect in directional terms.

The above is of primary importance for industrial noise. For road traffic noise reduction the road user vehicles should be as quiet as possible. As traffic noise is a function of average speed, speed controls can have an effect. Possible road-side barriers will be discussed in the next section.

High-flying aircraft have little effect on environmental noise at ground level. The problem is more acute around airports as aircraft come low to land and even more so at take-off. Only regulatory and planning measures can have desirable effects, such as banning aircraft movements between (say) 23:00 h and 5:00 h, by requiring aircraft to use less than maximum power (thus maximum noise) at take-off (e.g. sound level metering at the end of the runway, with penalties set if a noise limit is exceeded). Planning measures could include, in the first place, locating the airports in non-sensitive areas, e.g. on a peninsula, or where at least the main take-off path is over water or non-residential (e.g. industrial/agricultural) areas.

Planning measures can greatly reduce the noise problem, if zones of noise producing industries are kept separate from noise sensitive, e.g. residential areas. In positioning industries (and other noise sources) the directionality of the source must be taken into account, to point away from noise-sensitive zones and to be downwind from such zones. (*Note*: this should also be done for reasons of air pollution.)

Building design measures would consist of having sealed buildings in the noise-affected area, with good noise insulation, which would imply the use of mechanical ventilation or air conditioning.

The control of community noise, as discussed in Section 3.2.4 above is a regulatory question and very much dependent on reasonableness, a responsible attitude to noise generation and on consensus.

3.3.3   Barriers and sound insulation

Barriers, such as walls, screens or other objects (including buildings) create an acoustic shadow. The attenuation within this shadow depends on the frequency of the sound. Whilst high frequency sounds behave similar to light, at low frequencies much diffraction can occur at the edge of the barrier, which will diminish the shadow effect. One method of predicting this shadow effect requires the calculation of the h/λ (height/wavelength) quotient and determination of the 'diffraction angle' (θ) belonging to the receiver's point (see Fig. 3.25a).

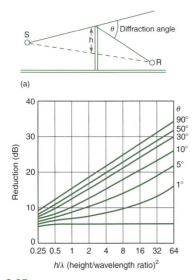

(a)

3.25.

(a) A noise barrier, defining *h* and *θ* and (b) its sound reduction effect.

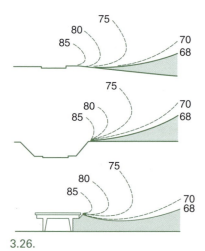

3.26.

Noise contours at roads: on level, in cut and elevated (contours in dBA).

Note that the 'height' is taken only as above the straight line connecting the source with the receiver. The reduction (in dB) can then be read from the graph (Fig. 3.25b). This shows that the effect is much greater with a larger *θ* angle (nearer to or higher barrier) and at larger h/λ ratios (shorter wavelengths). Other methods to estimate the barrier effect are given in method sheet M.3.3.

For any noise barrier to be effective, it should have a surface density of not less than 20 kg/m². A 10 mm thick dense concrete panel, 15 mm fibrous cement sheeting or a 30 mm hardwood boarding would satisfy this requirement.

Noise effects from a road can be lessened by placing it either in a cutting or have an elevated road. Figure 3.26 shows the expected noise contours adjacent such roads.

If a large site is available the first step would be to place the building as far away from the noise source as possible. If possible, any building should be placed outside the 68 dBA contour. The area between the building(s) and the noise source could be heavily vegetated. The noise reduction effect of such 'tree-belts' is given in data sheet D.3.2. Shaping the terrain, e.g. forming a mound or a hill can provide a barrier effect.

In some residential developments near busy roads (e.g. motorways) certain blocks of flats have been designed to act as barrier blocks. These would have all habitable rooms facing away from the noise source road, have service areas on the side facing the road, with very small windows. The best arrangement is if this block is parallel with the road. The difference in noise exposure between the two sides of such a block can be as much as 30 dBA. If the sheltered side is at an angle to the road, the reduction is less, as indicated by Fig. 3.27.

If all these measures are insufficient, then the building envelope itself must be noise insulating. If the building is at the 68 dBA contour, the TL of the envelope should be at least 20 dB, but preferably 25 or 30 dB. Data sheet D.3.3 shows that most wall elements are more than adequate. However, the weakest points are air-bricks, ventilator openings and windows. If the overall noise insulation is not enough, the most economical measures would be to improve these weak points. A single-glazed window, with TL = 22 dB, would be just about enough, but openings should be avoided.

For buildings acoustically more critical, a full spectral analysis should be carried out. This is best illustrated by an example.

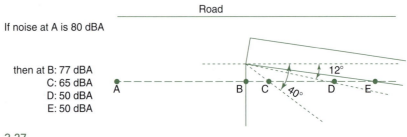

3.27.

A building as barrier and its noise reduction effect.

EXAMPLE 3.2

The analysis can be carried out graphically (Fig. 3.28) or in tabulated form (Table 3.5). A lecture theatre block is to be built near a busy road. The noise spectrum at the boundary (10 m from the centreline of the road) is taken as that shown in Fig. 3.15 (line 1). The site is large enough to allow placing the building at a distance of 40 m from the road. This means two 'doublings' of the distance, i.e. a reduction of 12 dB. The reduced spectrum is line 2. The requirement is that the intruding noise should be no more than NR 25 (from data sheet D.3.1). This is drawn as line 3. The difference between lines 2 and 3 is the noise insulation requirement, and this is now plotted up from the base line (line 4). The next step is to select (e.g. from data sheet D.3.3) a form of construction which would give the required TL values in each octave. It will be seen that for 1000 Hz and above a 110 mm brick wall would be adequate, but the traffic noise is strong in low frequencies. The critical octave will be 125 Hz, thus 220 mm brick must be used. The octave-band TL values of this are plotted and are given in Table 3.5.

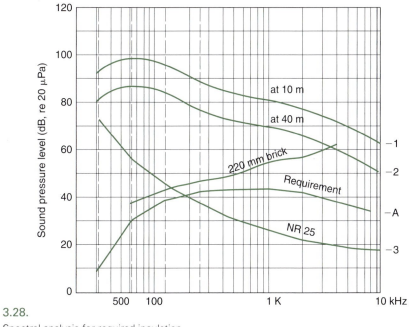

3.28.

Spectral analysis for required insulation.

Table 3.5. Spectral analysis in tabulated form

Octave-band centres (Hz)	63	125	250	500	1000	2000	4000	8000
1 At 10 m from road	98	95	89	85	81	77	71	64
2 At 40 m from road	86	83	77	73	69	65	59	52
3 NR 25	55	44	35	29	25	22	20	18
4 Insulation required	31	39	42	44	44	43	39	34
5 TL of 220 mm brick		41	45	48	56	58	62	

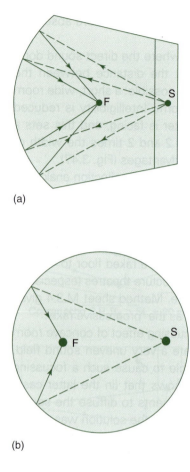

(a)

(b)

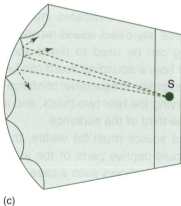

(c)

3.49

Concave shapes: risk of focussing and uneven sound field: breaking up rear wall into convex elements.

As shown by eq. (3.13), the RT depends on room volume and on the total absorption. If the volume is given, the required total absorption can be found by inverting the same equation:

$$Abs = \frac{0.16V}{RT} \tag{3.15}$$

A large part of the Abs will be the sum of the products of each component surface area (s) multiplied by its absorption coefficient (a). Another significant part may be what is referred to as 'room contents', which includes at least people and seats, but (at high frequencies) also room air. Data sheets D.3.4 and D.3.5 give the absorption coefficients of many materials as well as the total absorption values of some room contents. Method sheet M.3.2 shows a worked example of RT calculation for the design of room finishes. Note that values averaged for all frequencies are to be avoided, and the calculations should be carried out for at least three frequencies (at two-octave distances). A number of simple computer programs are available to carry out such calculations, which may involve numerous trial-and-error loops and may be quite lengthy if done manually.

It is not too difficult to achieve the desirable RT for a particular room use and assumed occupation. If the room is to be used for different purposes or if it is to work well for different occupancy rates, some variable absorbers may have to be used. It is customary to design an auditorium for between 2/3 and 3/4 of the seats occupied. To compensate for the absence of human bodies, the underside of tilting seats is made absorbent, but this cannot match the absorption of a human body. With a lesser occupancy the RT will be longer and with a full house it will be longer than the ideal. To compensate for this, a range of different surfaces of variable absorption can be provided. In the simplest case this can be just drawing a (heavy) curtain over a reflecting wall surface, but rotating or reversible panels can also be used,

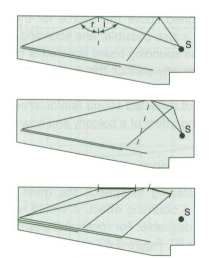

3.50

Sound reinforcement by reflections. S: speaker or source.

3.51

Acoustic shadow caused by a balcony and a way to avoid it.

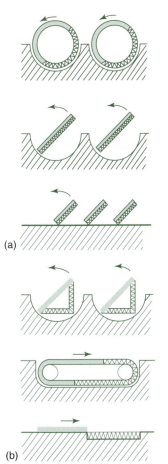

(a)

(b)

3.52.
Systems to provide variable absorption.

such as those shown in Fig. 3.52. Some electrical system to serve the same purpose will be discussed in the following Section 3.4.4.

3.4.3.1 Acoustic quality

Acoustic quality can be quite elusive. It can happen that all four requirements listed in Section 3.4.1 appear to have been satisfied and the acoustic qualities of the room are still unsatisfactory. It is relatively easy to provide for good listening conditions for speech, but to ensure full enjoyment of music is not an easy task. Many 'acoustic experts' have burnt their finger. Some, even today, suggest that good acoustics is an act of god. Beyond the four requirements discussed above, it is difficult even to define what constitutes good acoustics. An attempt should be made at least to define some of the terms used.

Definition means that the full timbre of each instrument is heard clearly, so that each would be individually distinguishable and also that successive notes can be distinguished even in a fast passage (up to 15 notes per second). The term *clarity* is often used with the same meaning.

Blend is not the opposite of definition, although it implies that a whole orchestra is perceived as a homogeneous source and the sound is not fragmentary.

Balance is the correct loudness ratio, as perceived at any point in the auditorium, both between different frequencies and between different parts of the orchestra. It implies that the room will not selectively influence the sound.

Fullness of tone is the term used synonymously with warmth, full body, sonority or resonance. It is absent if an instrument is played under open-air conditions. It is the perception of the whole range of harmonics, but also the persistence of these harmonics for a few milliseconds. What the room does to the orchestra is similar to what the body of the violin does to the vibrations of the string.

In auditorium design very often too much emphasis is placed on the calculation of RT. This can be calculated quite accurately and in a clear-cut way. It is important, but it is not the only criterion. The location of absorbent and reflective surfaces is at least as important. If one side is more reflective than the other, the sound diffusion will suffer and even our binaural location sense may be deceived, may come into conflict with the visual. This may be most disconcerting for audience at the rear of the hall, where the reflected sound may dominate over the direct one. For example, large glazed areas on one side can cause a distortion of the spectrum. Glass is highly reflective for high frequency sounds, but it may absorb up to 30% of low frequency components, acting as a panel absorber. People at the back may lose the bass component.

Generally it is better to use absorbers in relatively small areas, alternating with reflective surfaces. In historical auditoria good diffusion was achieved (often perhaps inadvertently) by the highly ornamented and sculptured surfaces. In some modern auditoria, with large plain surfaces an uneven and ill-balanced sound field has been produced.

There are now great expectations that electrical/electronic measures can be relied on to compensate for the lack of good room acoustics. I am yet to be convinced about this.

3.4.4 Electroacoustics

The trend in cinema design is to rely increasingly on the electrical sound system: in the room itself provide as much absorption as possible (to get the shortest possible RT), as all resonance, reverberation and other acoustic effects can be produced electronically and included in the sound track. This arrangement is probably where electroacoustics started.

There are three items normally discussed under this heading:

1 sound reinforcement systems
2 acoustic correction systems
3 acoustic measurements.

The first two will be discussed in this section in some detail, but the third one only briefly, as sufficient for architectural purposes.

3.4.4.1 *Sound reinforcement*

Sound reinforcement is definitely necessary in auditoria seating more than 1500 people ($\approx$8500 m^3), but it is desirable for rooms seating more than 300 people ($\approx$1500 m^3). If the room has less than perfect acoustic qualities, or an intruding noise is louder than the recommended NR (e.g. in data sheet D.3.1) then these limits will be much lower.

A reinforcement system has three main requirements:

1 it is to provide an adequate sound level uniformly over the whole auditorium, so that there are no 'deaf spots' or loud areas
2 it must not add any noticeable noise
3 it should preserve the characteristics of the original sound, both in frequency composition and localization.

Such a system consists of three main parts:

1 a microphone
2 an amplifier
3 loudspeaker(-s)

These may be connected by 'hard wiring' or may rely on high frequency radio transmitter/receivers.

Ribbon or *moving coil microphones* are based on electrodynamic effects, use a permanent magnet, which needs no polarizing potential; their output is fairly large, thus they do not need a preamplifier. Disadvantages: they are rather bulky and their frequency response is limited. Rarely used these days.

Condenser microphones are widely used; they have a good flat response across all audible frequencies and over a wide range of sound levels. Their electrical output is small, so they need a preamplifier, as well as a static polarizing charge of some 100V.

Crystal microphones rely on the piezoelectric effect and need a preamplifier. They are less vulnerable than the former ones and they can be placed in a liquid (to serve as a hydrophone).

There are many different solutions for a microphone assembly, with different directionality characteristics. For sound measurement omnidirectional

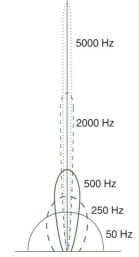

3.53
Directionality of speakers at various frequencies.

50 Hz
250 Hz
500 Hz
2000 Hz
5000 Hz

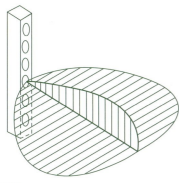

3.54
A column of speakers constrains the distribution vertically, but not horizontally.

(spherical) microphones are used, but these are undesirable in an auditorium, as they pick up the sound of loudspeakers and may generate a feedback effect: a howling, screaming noise. Directionally selective microphones are much preferred.

Amplifiers are not our subject, but it should be remembered that an oversized amplifier used at partial capacity gives a much better sound than a less powerful one stretched to its limits.

The average sound power in a medium sized room, without sound reinforcement, due to one human voice is some 3×10^{-6}W, but a loud voice can reach 3×10^{-3} (0.003) W. The electrical-to-acoustic power conversion efficiency of loudspeakers is 0.03–0.05. To match a loud voice the speaker power would need to be $P = 0.003/0.03 = 0.1$W. A safety factor of 10–30 is usually applied to compensate for distribution deficiencies and to avoid using the speaker near its limits. Table 3.6 gives suggested electrical power for speakers, in terms of watt per 100 person audience.

Ordinary box-mounted speakers tend to distribute low frequency sound almost spherically, but they have strong directional properties for higher frequencies (Fig. 3.53). 'Column speaker', i.e. 6–10 individual speakers mounted in a line produce strong directionality in the plane they share (normally vertical), whilst their sideways distribution is the same as of a single speaker (Fig. 3.54). Emission of the top and bottom speakers 'constrain' the emission of the intermediate ones. This is an obvious advantage (and saving of energy) in open-air situations or in large halls.

Two basic types of speaker systems can be distinguished:

1 high level (central) system, which consists of a few speakers (possibly columns), located near the dais or stage, near the original source, aimed at the audience to give an even coverage
2 low level (distributed) system, which uses many, small output speakers, distributed over the whole auditorium (usually ceiling mounted).

The former is less expensive, readily adjustable and has the advantage that the amplified sound comes from the same direction as the original. It can be disastrous in large, non-acoustic spaces, such as a railway concourse or older airport terminals, where announcements are just unintelligible.

The design of low level systems in auditoria relies on the *Haas effect*. This is the interesting phenomenon that the location (direction) of a source is perceived as the origin of the first sound that reaches the listener. If the same sound arrives with a delay of 10–30 ms (milliseconds) the total sound energy is perceived as if it were coming from the direction of the first. This happens even if the second sound is much stronger than the first.

Table 3.6. Electrical speaker power requirements (W/100 persons)

Venue	For speech	For music	For dance music
High reverberation rooms	0.5	1	2
Low reverberation rooms	1.0	2	3
Open air	1.5	2	3

EXAMPLE 3.3

The Haas effect is made use of by the system shown in principle in Fig. 3.55 (a diagrammatic longitudinal section of an auditorium). There are three rows of low level (low power) speakers. If the distance to a listener at C (the A–C distance) is 40 m, sound travel time will be 0.12 s and if the distance from the loudspeaker at B (the B–C distance) is 7 m, the travel time will be 0.02 s, so the time difference is 0.1 s. The delay system must provide this plus the intended delay of (say) 0.015 s, a total of 0.115 s (115 ms).

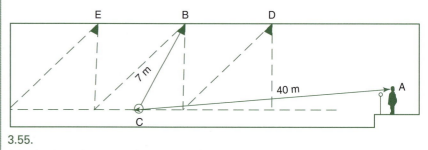

3.55.
A low level speaker system for sound reinforcement,

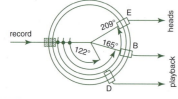

3.56.
A rotating magnetic disc time delay system.

Deliberate time delays in the past were created by a rotating magnetic disc (Fig. 3.56) with one recording head and several pickup heads, where the angular distance provided the time delay. This is now done electronically. The output of each speaker in such a system should be small enough to avoid interference.

The principle is similar to that of PSALI (Section 2.5.6), i.e. to supplement daylighting so that it is hardly noticeable, the daylit character of the room is maintained. Here the sound reinforcement is provided in such a way that the audience is unaware of it.

For public address (and background music systems, if you must have one) the low level system is the only satisfactory solution. In auditoria another advantage of such a system is that the contribution of low power speakers to the reverberant field is imperceptible.

3.4.4.2 Acoustic corrective systems

Acoustic corrective systems have been designed to improve the acoustics of some concert halls. The first such system developed for the Royal Festival Hall (London) was euphemistically referred to as an *assisted resonance system* (ARS). This consists of 172 separate channels tuned to very narrow (4 Hz) frequency bands from 20 to 700 Hz (above 700 Hz the room resonance was satisfactory), each consisting of the following components:

- a condenser microphone in a resonant box or tube (with a very narrow frequency response)
- a preamplifier with gain control and delay mechanism and filters to eliminate any harmonics picked up by the microphone in the resonator (a resonator responds to a particular frequency but also to its upper harmonics)
- a 20 W amplifier
- a speaker of 250–300 mm diameter.

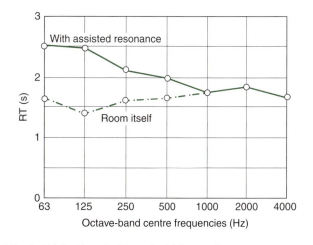

3.57.
RT in the Royal Festival Hall with and without the ARS operating.

A complex switchboard allows the low frequency resonance to be adjusted and balanced. The hall itself, with its short RT for low frequencies was very good for speech intelligibility, but not for large orchestral music. For example in the 125 Hz octave the room RT is 1.4 s, with the ARS it can be increased to 2.5 s. Figure 3.57 shows the spectral variation of the RT in the Royal Festival Hall itself and with the ARS operating.

Multi-channel reverberation (another acronym: MCR) systems are now commercially available and often included in the original design of auditoria (and not as 'correction') to produce variable acoustic properties, e.g. for multi-purpose halls.

Another kind of 'correction' is the design and use of *masking noise systems*. These have been developed and are used mainly in large 'landscaped' offices. Sounds with information content are much more disturbing than a steady hum. A masking noise can suppress the intelligibility of sounds received, but also gives assurance of aural privacy for people talking and do not want to be overheard. 'White noise' has been used for such purposes, but it has been found that a broad-band sound is more effectively masked by a lower frequency noise. Hence the latest trend is to use a 'pink noise' of a continuous spectrum with a slope of 3 dB per octave (*per analogiam*: pink light with continuous spectrum, but slightly biased towards longer wavelengths: i.e. a faint red).

In many practical situations ventilation or air conditioning diffusers are deliberately designed to give a noise of 45 dB at around 1000 Hz, to give a masking effect, but most often masking noise is produced by a generator-amplifier-speaker system.

3.4.4.3 Acoustic measurements

Acoustic measurements are based on a sound level meter, using a condenser microphone. It has a built-in RMS rectifier and a read-out device. It usually has a range selector working in 10 dB increments. The second digit is given by a voltmeter. Most have a set of switchable weighting circuits ('C' weighting is practically linear, see Fig. 3.6). Many have an attached octave-band

DATA SHEET D.3.3

Transmission loss (dB) of some constructions

	Average (Hz)	Octave centre frequencies					
		125 Hz	250 Hz	500 Hz	1000 Hz	2000 Hz	4000 Hz
Walls							
1 110 mm brick, plastered	45	34	36	41	51	58	62
2 150 mm concrete	47	29	39	45	52	60	67
3 220 mm brick, plastered	50	41	45	48	56	58	62
4 330 mm brick, plastered	52	44	43	49	57	63	65
5 130 mm hollow concrete blocks	46	36	37	44	51	55	62
6 75 mm studs, 12 mm plaster boards	40	26	33	39	46	50	50
7 75 mm studs, 6 mm ply both sides	24	16	18	26	28	37	33
8 Same but staggered separate studs and ply	26	14	20	28	33	40	30
Floors							
9 T&G boarding, plasterboard ceiling	34	18	25	37	39	45	45
10 Same but boards floating on glass wool	42	25	33	38	45	56	61
11 Same but 75 mm rock wool on ceiling	39	29	34	39	41	50	50
12 As 10 + 75 mm rock wool on ceiling	43	27	35	44	48	56	61
13 As 10 + 50 mm sand pugging	49	36	42	47	52	60	64
14 125 mm reinforced concrete slab	45	35	36	41	49	58	64
15 As 14 + floating screed	50	38	43	48	54	61	65
16 150 hollow pot slab + T&G boar233ds	43	36	38	39	47	54	55
Windows							
17 Single glazed, normal	22	17	21	25	26	23	26
18 Double 4 mm glass, 200 absorber reveals	39	30	35	43	46	47	37
19 Same but 10 mm glass panes	44	31	38	43	49	53	63
Partitions							
20 Two sheets 10 mm ply, 38 mm cavity		20	25	23	43	47	
21 Same + 10 kg/m² lead on inside faces		25	31	38	57	62	
22 Same but also fibreglass absorber in cavity		29	42	49	59	63	
23 Studs, 10 mm plasterboard both sides		16	35	38	48	52	37
24 Same + 13 mm fibreglass under plasterboard		22	39	46	56	61	50
25 Same but staggered independent frames		34	40	53	59	57	58
26 75 mm studs, 2 × (5 mm hardboard)		12	21	25	40	46	48
27 Same but 2 × (13 mm softboard)		15	25	37	51	51	51
28 100 mm studs, 2 × (5 mm hardboard)		9	19	28	39	51	60
29 Same but 2 × (6 mm hardboard)		13	30	32	38	41	44
30 200 mm hollow concrete blocks		35	35	40	47	54	60
31 100 mm precast concrete panel		36	39	45	51	57	65
32 110 mm brick, 2 × (12 render, 50 × 12 battens, 12 softboard with bonded 6 mm hardboard)		35	43	54	65	73	80
Doors							
33 50 mm solid timber, normally hung	18	12	15	20	22	176	24
34 Same but airtight gaskets	22	15	18	21	26	25	28
35 50 mm hollow core, normally hung	15						
36 Same but airtight gaskets	20						
37 Double 50 mm solid timber, airtight gaskets, absorbent space (lobby)	45						
Sheets							
38 50 mm glass wool slab (26 kg/m²)	30	27	23	27	34	39	41
39 Corrugated fibrous cement (34 kg/m²)	34	33	31	33	33	42	39
40 25 mm plasterboard (2 × 12.5 laminated)	30	24	29	31	32	30	34
41 50 mm plasterboard (4 × 12.5 laminated)	37	28	32	34	40	38	49

DATA SHEET D.3.4

Absorption coefficients (a) of materials and components

	Octave centre frequency		
	125 Hz	*500 Hz*	*2000 Hz*
Building materials			
Boarded underside of pitched roof	0.15	0.1	0.1
Boarding on 20 mm battens on solid wall	0.3	0.1	0.1
Exposed brickwork	0.05	0.02	0.05
Clinker concrete exposed	0.2	0.6	0.5
Concrete or tooled stone	0.02	0.02	0.05
Floor: cork, lino, vinyl tiles, wood blocks (parquetry)	0.02	0.05	0.1
25 mm cork tiles on solid backing	0.05	0.2	0.6
13 mm softboard on solid backing	0.05	0.15	0.3
Same but painted	0.05	0.1	0.1
13 mm softboard on 25 mm battens on solid wall	0.3	0.3	0.3
Same but painted	0.3	0.15	0.1
Floor: hard tiles or cement screed	0.03	0.03	0.05
Glass in windows, 4 mm	0.3	0.1	0.05
Same but 6 mm in large panes	0.1	0.04	0.02
Glass or glazed ceramic wall tiles, marble	0.01	0.01	0.02
Plastering on solid backing (gypsum or lime)	0.03	0.02	0.04
Plaster on lath, air space, solid backing	0.3	0.1	0.04
Plaster or plasterboard ceiling, large air space	0.2	0.1	0.04
Plywood or hardboard on battens, solid backing	0.3	0.15	0.1
Same but porous absorbent in air space	0.4	0.15	0.1
Exposed water surface (pools)	0.01	0.01	0.02
Timber boarding on joists or battens	0.15	0.1	0.1
Common absorbers			
25 mm sprayed fibres on solid backing	0.15	0.5	0.7
Carpet, e.g. Axminster, thin pile	0.05	0.1	0.45
Same, medium pile	0.05	0.15	0.45
Same, thick pile	0.1	0.25	0.65
Carpet, heavy, on thick underlay	0.1	0.65	0.65
Curtain, medium fabric, against solid backing	0.05	0.15	0.25
Same but in loose folds	0.05	0.35	0.5
25 mm glass wool on solid backing, open mesh cover	0.15	0.7	0.9
Same with 5% perforated hardboard cover	0.1	0.85	0.35
Same with 10% perforated or 20% slotted cover	0.15	0.75	0.75
50 mm glass wool on solid backing, open mesh cover	0.35	0.9	0.95
Same with 10% perforated or 20% slotted hardboard cover	0.4	0.9	0.75
3 mm hardboard, bit felt backing on 50 mm air space on solid wall	0.9	0.25	0.1
Two layers bituminous felt on 250 mm air space, solid backing	0.5	0.2	0.1
25 mm polystyrene slab on 50 mm air space	0.1	0.55	0.1
50 mm polyurethane foam on solid backing	0.25	0.85	0.9
25 mm wood wool slabs on solid backing	0.1	0.4	0.6
Same but on 25 mm battens	0.15	0.6	0.6
Same but plastered, mineral wool in cavity	0.5	0.2	0.1
Proprietary absorbers			
6 mm fibrous cement sheet on battens	0.23	0.5	0.2
Burgess perforated metal tiles, 38 mm glass wool	0.15	0.7	0.8
Caneite, 20 mm softboard tiles on solid wall	0.15	0.45	0.8
Celotex 13 mm perforated tiles on solid wall	0.1	0.4	0.45
Same but on 25 mm battens	0.1	0.45	0.4

METHOD SHEET M.3.4

Progressive rake and principles of optical acoustics

The purpose of raked seating is to ensure uninterrupted sight-lines of the speaker (or e.g. the bottom of a projection screen) for all members of the audience. At the same time the rake should not be more than necessary.

On a longitudinal section of the auditorium locate the F (focus) point, usually 0.8–1 m above stage level. Locate a vertical line representing the first row of seating and draw such vertical lines at distances corresponding to row spacing, for each row of seats in the auditorium.

Mark the notional eye level (point E) for the front row at 1100 mm above the floor. Mark a point P at 100 mm above E. Draw a line from the F point to this P and extend it to the second row. Its intersection with the vertical will give the second E point. Repeat this for the second to the third row, and for all rows. This will locate the eye level for each row, and for each eye level measure 1100 mm down, to determine the floor level for that row.

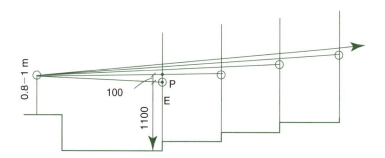

In an auditorium with a flat floor (where the source and listeners are at about the same level) the setting out of a ceiling reflector is quite easy. For example if it is decided that the rear half of the listeners should receive reinforcement reflected from the ceiling, take the distance between the source and the furthest listener, and halve that distance to locate the edge of the sounding board furthest from the stage. Repeat for the mid-point, and the halving of that distance will give the edge of the sounding board nearest to the stage. The horizontal ceiling between the two points should be treated as a sounding board.

With raked seating there are two possibilities:

1 The distance between the source and the rear seating row can be halved to mark the edge of the sounding board. As the 'sound ray' incident on the board and that reflected are not symmetrical, the angle between the two should be halved and the sounding board must be at right angles to this halving line. The sounding board will have to be slightly tilted.

2 If the sounding board is to be kept horizontal, then the position of the edge of sounding board furthest from the stage (the reflection point R) can be found as follows:
  – the horizontal distance between the speaker (S) and the rear row of the audience (A) is d
  – the level difference between A and S is L
  – the ceiling height from point S is h
  – the horizontal distance between S and R is b
  – then b can be determined we have two triangles, where the angle of incidence and angle of reflection at the point R must be the same, say α, then
  $\tan(\alpha) = b/h = (d - b)/(h - L)$
  d, h and L are known; say $d = 18\,\text{m}$, $h = 5\,\text{m}$ and $L = 1.5\,\text{m}$, then b is to be determined
  $b/5 = (18 - b)/(5 - 1.5)$, from which $3.5b = 5(18 - b) = 90 - 5b$
  $8.5b = 90$, thus $b = 90/8.5 = 10.6\,\text{m}$

  – repeat the same for the edge of sounding board nearest to the stage.

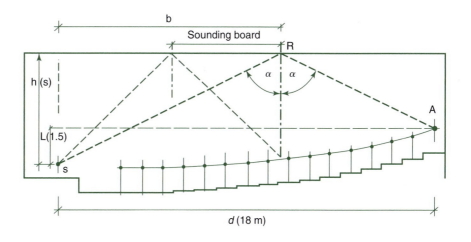

PART 4   RESOURCES

CONTENTS

SYMBOLS AND ABBREVIATIONS

c	velocity of light
v	velocity
A	area, ampere
AC	alternating current
BCA	building code of Australia
BMAS	building materials assessment system
BRE	Building Research Establishment
BREDEM	BRE domestic energy model
BREEAM	BRE environmental assessment method
C	coulomb or capital energy
CHAPS	combined heat and power solar (system)
CHP	combined heat and power
CoP	coefficient of performance
CSIRO	Commonwealth Scientific and Industrial Research Organisation
DC	direct current
DG	distributed generation
DHW	domestic hot water

(Continued)

SYMBOLS AND ABBREVIATIONS   (Continued)

DSM	demand side management	NREL	national Renewable Energy Lab. (Colorado)
E	energy	O	operational energy
ETC	evacuated tubular collector	OTE	ocean thermal electric
EU	European Union	OTTV	overall thermal transfer value
GPO	general purpose outlet	P	power
HDR	hot-dry rock	PER	process energy requirement
IEA	International Energy Agency	PV	photovoltaic
LCA	life cycle analysis (or assessment)	SEDA	sustainable development authority (of NSW)
LCC	life cycle cost	SSM	supply side management
LDC	less developed country	STE	solar thermal electric
LEED	leadership in energy and environmental design	TETD	total equivalent temperature difference
		UNCED	UN Conference on Environment and Development
M	mass		
MEC	model energy code (USA)	UNEP	UN Environment Program
MRET	mandatory renewable energy target	V	volt
NatHERS	nationwide house energy rating scheme (Australia)	VAWT	vertical axis wind turbine
		Ω (omega)	ohm, resistance (electrical)
NFFO	non-fossil fuel obligation	ϕ (phi)	phase angle
NHER	national home energy rating (UK)		

LIST OF FIGURES

(Continued)

LIST OF FIGURES   (Continued)

LIST OF TABLES

4.1 ENERGY

Energy is the potential for performing work and it is measured in the same unit: J (joule). Energy flow rate is measured with the unit W (watt), which is the flow of 1 J per 1 second (J/s). Watt also measures the ability to carry out work (J) in unit time (s), i.e. power. As energy and work have the same unit (J), so power and energy flow rate have the same physical dimension, thus the same unit (W).

An accepted energy unit is the Wh (watt-hour), i.e. the energy that would flow if the rate of 1 W were maintained for 1 hour. As there are 3600 seconds in an hour, 1 Wh = 3600 J or 1 kWh = 3600 kJ = 3.6 MJ. Table 4.1 lists the prefixes used with any SI unit, both sub-multiples and multiples.

A number of other energy units are still in use (some powerful specialized users refuse to adopt the SI), but in this work all these are converted to SI units, to achieve comparability and allow a sense of magnitude of numbers to develop. Some conversion factors are given in Table 4.2.

4.1.1 Forms of energy

Energy cannot be created or destroyed (except in sub-atomic processes), but it can be converted from one form to another. Some often encountered forms of energy are reviewed in the present section.

Table 4.1. Multiple and sub-multiple prefixes for SI units

Sub-multiples				Multiples			
deci-	d	10^{-1}	0.1	deca-	da	10	10
centi-	c	10^{-2}	0.01	hecto-	h	10^2	100
milli-	m	10^{-3}	0.001	kilo-	k	10^3	1000
micro-	μ	10^{-6}	0.000001	mega-	M	10^6	1 000 000
nano-	n	10^{-9}	0.000 000 001	giga-	G	10^9	1 000 000 000
pico-	p	10^{-12}	0.000 000 000 001	tera-	T	10^{12}	1 000 000 000 000
femto-	f	10^{-15}		peta-	P	10^{15}	1 000 000 000 000 000
atto-	a	10^{-18}		exa-	E	10^{18}	

Table 4.2. Some obsolete energy units still in use

barrel (of oil)	brl	6×10^9 J	6 GJ	1667 kWh
tonne oil equivalent	TOE	4.1868×10^{10} J	41.868 GJ	11 630 kWh
megatonne oil equivalent	Mtoe	4.1868×10^{16} J	41.868 PJ	11.63×10^9 kWh
tonne of coal equivalent	TCE		29 GJ*	8056 kWh
kilo-calorie	kcal		4.1848 kJ	1.16 kWh
British thermal unit	Btu		1.055 kJ	0.293 kWh
calorie (gramme-calorie)	cal		4.1848 J	1.16 Wh

*some sources use 26 GJ (7222 kWh): it depends on the quality of coal taken as the basis based on IEA (International Energy Agency) Statistics (2002), which uses Mtoe as the basic unit.

Heat, as a form of energy has been discussed at length in Part 1.
Mechanical energy can take two main forms:

Kinetic energy is possessed by a body in motion and it is proportionate to the mass of the body (M) and to the square of its velocity (v):

$$E_k = \frac{1}{2} M v^2$$

An everyday example of such kinetic energy often made use of is the wind. If the density of air is taken as $1.2\,kg/m^3$ and thus the mass flow rate is

$$M = A \times 1.2\,v \; (m^2 \times kg/m^3 \times m/s = kg/s)$$

then the power of wind over a swept area A is

$$P_k = 1/2 \times A \times 1.2\,v \times v^2 = 1/2\,A\;1.2 \times v^3$$
$$(kg/s \times (m/s)^2) = kg.m^2/s^3 = W)$$

therefore it is said that the power of wind is proportionate to velocity cubed.

Potential energy (or positional energy) is possessed by a body which would be free to fall over a vertical distance (height, *h*), i.e. height relative to a reference level

$$E_p = Mgh$$

where g is the gravitational acceleration, $9.81\,m/s^2$

$$(kg \times m/s^2 \times m = kg.m^2/s^2 = J)$$

An example of such potential energy in everyday use is water in an elevated dam, e.g. with a level difference of 100 m $1\,m^3$ (1 kL) of water would have the potential energy

$$E_p = 1000 \times 9.81 \times 100 = 981\,000\;J = 981\;kJ$$

and if this $1\,m^3$ water flowed in 1 s, it would have a power of 981 kW.

Chemical energy is also a relative quantity. Chemical bonding of molecules represents a certain amount of stored energy, that was needed to produce that compound from its basic constituents. Chemical operations requiring energy (heat) input are termed *endothermic* and those that release energy are *exothermic*. Fuels are compounds with high chemical energy content that can be released by combustion (an exothermic process). Some heat input may be required to start the process (ignition) but then the process is self-sustaining. The energy that could thus be released is the *calorific value* of that fuel, measured in Wh/m^3 or Wh/kg. From the viewpoint of energetics (the science of energy) fuels are referred to as *energy carriers*.

Electrical energy. The presence of free electrons in a body represents a charge, an electric potential. These tend to flow from a higher potential zone to a lower one. The unit of electric charge is the coulomb (C). The rate of electricity flow (current) is the ampere (amp, A):

$$A = C/s \quad \text{conversely} \quad C = A \times s$$

A potential difference or electromotive force (EMF) of 1 volt (V) exists between two points when the passing of 1 coulomb constitutes 1 J

$$V = \frac{J}{C}$$

Electric current will flow through a body if its material has free or dislocatable electrons. Metals are the best conductors (silver, copper, aluminium), which have only one electron in the outermost electron skin of the atom. In gases or liquids electricity may flow in the form of charged particles, ions.

Even the best conductors have some resistance to electron flow. The unit of this is the ohm (Ω), the resistance that allows the flow (current) of one ampere driven by 1 volt.

$$\Omega = \frac{V}{A} \quad \text{conversely} \quad A = \frac{V}{\Omega}$$

The rate of energy flow in the current (or electric power) is the watt (W)

$$W = V \times A$$

a unit which is used for all kinds of energy flow.

The above is valid for direct current (DC), i.e. when the current flows in one direction. Alternating current (AC) is produced by rotating generators, where the resulting polarity is reversed 50 times per second, i.e. at the frequency of 50 Hz (in most countries, except in the USA, where it is 60 Hz). With AC the above relationship is influenced by the type of load connected to the circuit. It is true for a purely resistive load, such as an incandescent lamp or a resistance heater. Here the variations of the current are synchronous with the voltage variations (Fig. 4.1a). With an inductive load, such as a motor or any appliance incorporating an electromagnetic coil, the current is delayed with respect to the voltage variations (Fig. 4.1c). If one complete cycle is 360° the delay is measured by the phase angle φ and the actual power will be

$$W = V \times A \times \cos \phi$$

The term $\cos \varphi$ is referred to as *power factor*. If the phase lag is 90°, then cos 90° being 0 (zero), there will be no current flowing. This delay can be corrected by introducing a capacitor, which has the opposite effect (Fig. 4.1b). This has been discussed in relation to electric discharge lamps in Section 2.5.1. For this reason the power of AC is referred to as VA or kVA (rather than W or kW).

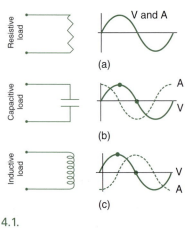

4.1.

Resistive, capacitive and inductive loads end their effect on current.

4.1.2 Energy sources

From the 18th century onwards **coal** was the most important energy source, it can be said that our industrial civilization has been built on coal. Oil production

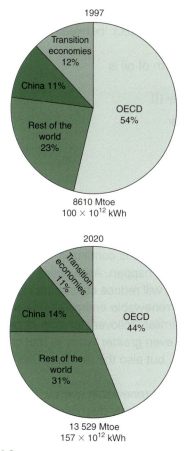

1997

Transition economies 12%

China 11%

OECD 54%

Rest of the world 23%

8610 Mtoe
100×10^{12} kWh

2020

Transition economies 11%

China 14%

OECD 44%

Rest of the world 31%

13 529 Mtoe
157×10^{12} kWh

4.2.

World energy supply by region: 1997 data + 2020 forecast.

started early 20th century and with the introduction of the internal combustion engine as used in cars, trucks, aeroplanes but also in stationary applications its use has rapidly grown. By 1966 oil production exceeded coal (in energy terms) and by 2012 it is expected that gas will also exceed coal. The most worrying fact is that the rate of discovering new oil reserves is rapidly decreasing: from a peak of 49×10^9 barrels p.a. (1960) to 6×10^9 (1995). Figure 4.2 shows the world's energy supply by region, comparing the 1997 data with the forecast for 2020 and Fig. 4.3 indicates the growth of primary energy supply since 1970, with projection to 2020, by form of fuel (expressed in Mtoe, megatonnes oil equivalent: 1 Mtoe = 11.63 TWh).

Oil production by regions is shown in Fig. 4.4, as well as the total, from 1930 to the middle of this century. Demand will exceed supply and production will decline. This is referred to as 'rollover', i.e. from a buyers' market to a seller's market. Such rollovers have already occurred in some regions, e.g. around 1970 for the USA and Canada, and in 1986 for the UK and Norway. The 'big

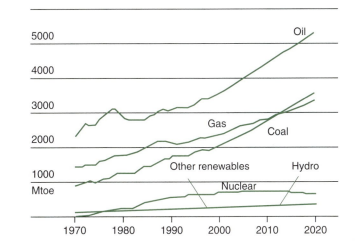

4.3.

World primary energy use by sources in Mtoe; each curve is to be read from the base line, note that the Hydro and Other curves overlap.

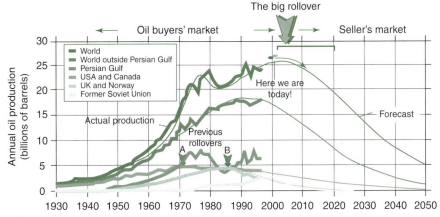

4.4.

History and forecast of world (and regional) oil production. A: USA and Canada, B: UK and Norway (Aus. Energy News, Dec. 2001).

the national total electricity production. In Australia some 130 plants exist, with an aggregate output of 1500 MW (most of these are in the 1–10 MW range) and a similar capacity is now being installed.

A CHAPS (Combined Heat and Power Solar) system has been developed at the ANU (Aus.University) for domestic use. It has two shallow parabolic trough mirrors (2 m^2 each) with a double-axis tracking system and a row of PV (photovoltaic) cells at the focal line, which are water cooled by pumped circulation. This contributes hot water to a DHW system and generates electricity. The output of PV cells would be drastically reduced at elevated temperatures, this system avoids such overheating. The peak output of the system is 700W.

4.1.3.2 Fuel cells

Fuel cells were first constructed around the middle of the 19th century, but it is only recently that they became practical sources of electricity and are increasingly used. A fuel cell is essentially a device that converts the chemical energy of some fuel directly into electricity. In principle it is similar to the dry-cell battery, but while in the latter the finite quantity of ingredients are built in, here the fuel and oxygen are supplied continuously. Fuel cells are used in spacecraft, with liquid hydrogen and oxygen input, using platinum electrodes. In terrestrial applications methanol, petroleum products, natural gas and LPG can serve as fuel, relying on air as oxidant.

Today various fuel cells are commercially available in sizes from 1 kW to some 200 kW. Some are suitable for cogeneration, i.e. the heat produced can also be utilized. Such CHP fuel cell systems have achieved over 70% efficiency. In most modern fuel cells the electrodes are porous metal or carbon structures and some form of catalyst is used. Recently the Australian CSIRO (Commonwealth Scientific and Industrial Research Organisation) developed a ceramic fuel cell using natural gas as fuel. The development of cars powered by fuel cell-operated electric motors are at the prototype stage and large scale production is expected in a few years' time.

As these lines are being written, the world's largest fuel cell symposium is taking place in London, organized by Elsevier. The five major subject areas to be discussed are:

1 transportation, hybrids, auxiliary power units; commercialization
2 commercial/industrial and large stationary fuel cells
3 residential and small portable fuel cells
4 consumer electronics and micro fuel cells
5 fuels for fuel cell applications.

4.2 RENEWABLE ENERGY

The term includes all energy sources which are not of a finite stock, but which are continually available. This would include solar and wind energy and hydro-electric systems, as well as others, such as geothermal or tidal energy, biomass and methane generation. The following Table 4.6 shows the contribution of renewable sources to the world energy use.

Table 4.6. The share of renewables (2002 data)

Total primary energy supply	*124.475 × 10^{12} kWh*	*13.8%*
of which renewable sources	*17.15 × 10^{12} kWh*	
contribute		
of this	hydro	16.5%
	solar, wind, geothermal	3.7%
	combustibles (firewood, wastes, etc.)	79.8%

A US DoE report shows that in 1999 the world total renewable energy production was 227×10^9 kWh and the largest producers were:

- USA 83×10^9 kWh
- Japan 25
- Germany 15
- Brazil 10
- Finland 10

Over the last 9 years the growth rate was 6.5% p.a. in the US, but over 30% in the EU countries.

In the UK, under the 1989 Electricity Act *non-fossil fuel obligations* (NFFO) for electricity generation have been introduced, together with a fossil fuel levy (of some 11%). The income from this is used to subsidize renewable energy systems. Nuclear energy was considered as renewable, but since 1998 the EU does not allow subsidization of nuclear energy.

The most important sources of renewable energy are the sun and wind, but all (except geothermal) are derived from solar energy. Table 4.7 attempts to summarize the technologies and purposes of using solar energy in direct or indirect form.

4.2.1 Solar energy

Solar radiation is the driving force of all terrestrial energy systems. Indeed, all plant material and living body matter, all oil, gas and coal in fact constitute accumulated solar energy. Here the present day use of solar energy is to be discussed. Table 4.7 summarizes the various technologies and purposes of solar energy utilization. Indirect uses, such as wind, hydro and ocean energy will be discussed later, after a brief review of direct forms of utilization. Three main conversion processes can be distinguished: thermal, electrical and (bio-) chemical. The last one of these includes natural processes, i.e. the growth of plants and algae (also referred to as biomass production), as well as artificial reversible chemical reactions. For conversion into electricity the two main routes are photovoltaic and thermo-electric devices. The direct thermal applications include the most diverse systems. It is useful to distinguish low temperature applications and concentrating devices producing high temperatures. The latter would include various solar cookers, concentrators to produce mechanical work and solar-thermal-electric (STE) systems.

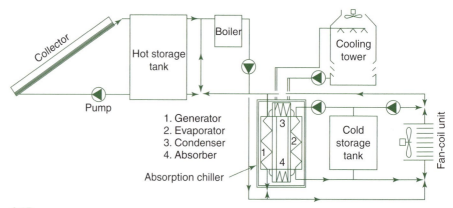

4.15.

A solar powered air conditioning system.
- The collection circuit is: solar collector-hot store-pump.
- The heating circuit is: hot store-(possibly boiler)-pump-fan-coil unit and back to store.
- The chiller circuit is: hot store-(possibly boiler)-pump-absorption chiller generator (1) and back to store.
- The chilled water circuit is from evaporator (2) (possibly cold store) to fan-coil unit and back; if there is no cooling demand, the cold store is cooled. If there is no sun, any cooling demand is satisfied from the cold store.

auxiliary heater may be gas or oil fired or an electric immersion heater, but even an old fashioned fireplace with a back-boiler.

In climates where there may be a risk of freezing of the water in the collector panels or pipework, a 'drain-down' system is often used, emptying the collectors for frost-risk periods, e.g. for overnight. Alternatively some ethylene glycol may be added to the recirculating water. Because of the toxic nature of this compound, any connection to the DHW system must be through a double-wall heat exchanger.

Figure 4.15 shows a solar air conditioning system based on an absorption type (LiBr/H_2O: lithium bromide/water) chiller system. The principles of absorption chillers have been discussed in Section 1.6.3.2, where an ammonia/water system has been described. Here H_2O is the refrigerant and LiBr is the absorbent.

For best performance the tilt angle of solar collectors should be the same as the latitude (this would receive the most beam radiation, whilst a lesser tilt would receive more of the diffuse radiation), but may be biassed for the dominant need: steeper for winter heating and flatter for summer cooling. The orientation should be due south (northern hemisphere) and due north (southern hemisphere). Local climatic conditions may influence this, e.g. if foggy mornings are usual, the orientation should be slightly to the west. In equatorial locations the seasonal variations should dictate the tilt angle.

Solar collectors may use air as the heat transport fluid and fans to drive the circulation instead of pumps. Such solar air systems are often used for space heating, (one advantage is that there is no risk of freezing overnight), but also for many industrial purposes, such as crop drying or timber drying. A crushed rock (or pebble) bed can be used as heat storage. Figure 4.16 shows a solar air heating system and its ductwork.

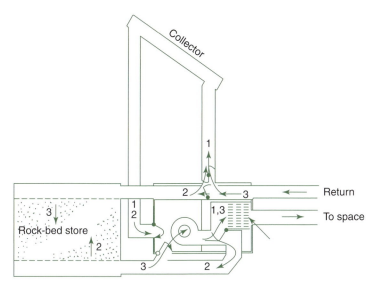

4.16.

A solar air-heating system.

1 Collector to space circuit (possibly auxiliary heater)

2 Collector to rock-bed heat storage

3 Storage – (possibly auxiliary heater) – to space

The double outline indicates a prefabricated unit: the fan, auxiliary heater and all dampers.

4.17.

Flat plate solar collector production of the world, 1982–2003 (in MW$_{thermal}$).

4.18.

A large array of ETCs.

Air heater flat plate collector panels can also be used for industrial purposes, such as crop or timber drying. Figure 4.17 shows the annual production of flat plate collectors in terms of rated MW (thermal) output. In 2006 the EU collector output reached 2.1 GW$_{th}$, bringing the total installed capacity to 13.5 GW$_{th}$.

A relatively recent development is the use of evacuated tubular collectors (ETCs). These employ a glass tube of 75–100 mm diameter, which houses a copper strip absorber. The selective surface of this reduces radiant losses and the vacuum in the tube largely eliminates convective heat loss, thus quite high temperatures and high efficiencies can be achieved (Fig. 4.18).

The heating of swimming pools may use huge quantities of energy and because only low temperature heat is required, the use of electricity or gas for this purpose is considered by many as downright 'immoral'. An inexpensive (low efficiency) solar heating system will do the job quite well. Often an unglazed collector, consisting of black HDP (high-density polyethylene) strips with multiple water-ways will do the job. Ordinary PVC pipes are used as headers and the pool filter pump could drive the circulation.

It has been shown that in Australia salt production uses more solar energy than all other applications put together: the evaporation of sea-water from shallow ponds, with the salt being left behind and scraped up with heavy machinery.

Figure 4.19 shows a range of passive systems used in buildings. This type of systematic categorization was fashionable 20 years ago. Now we consider that the distinction between a 'passive solar system' and a thermally well-designed building is almost impossible. All houses are potential solar collectors, their success or failure depends on the design. Indeed some of these systems have been discussed in Section 1.5.1.1 in the context of thermal design of buildings, under the heading of passive control of heat flows.

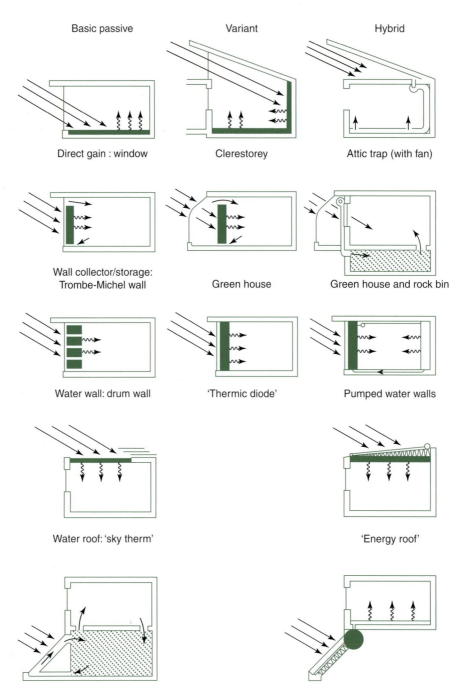

4.19.

Main types of passive solar systems.

- The direct gain window and clerestory is not more than a correctly oriented window and some mass in the floor or wall to absorb and store the solar heat.
- The Trombe-Michel wall and solar greenhouse have been discussed in Section 1.5.1.1
- The drum wall uses water in drums as the heat storage. The thermic diode circulates water by thermosiphon from the outer collector to the inner storage tank in a clockwise direction; a non-return valve at the top stops reverse circulation.
- The skytherm roof is some 200 mm of water in bags; winter: covered by insulating panels at night, exposed to solar input during the day; summer: exposed at night to dissipate heat by radiation to the sky, covered during the day to provide a cool ceiling.
- The thermosiphon air system uses a rock-bed heat storage. The water system has a pumped emitter circuit to warm the floor.

Right to sunlight has been discussed in Section 2.3.4 (and method sheet M.2.2) in the context of lighting of buildings. From the point-of-view of solar energy utilization this can become a serious problem in legal and economic terms. To put it simply: if I invest in a solar system (whether it is active or passive or PV) and later my neighbour builds a tall block that will overshadow my collectors, do I have some legal protection? The issue is acute in urban (even suburban) situations, especially for small scale, domestic installations.

Several states (e.g. New Mexico) had introduce legislation, modelled on the old 'right to water' law, essentially the first user establishing the right to the source. Soon it had to be repealed as it led to unreasonable (even vexatious) claims, e.g. a cheap home-made collector mounted at ground level would prevent my neighbour of erecting any substantial building.

Knowles (1977) did important work on this, developing the concept of 'solar envelope', which led to solar access legislation (e.g. in California, see Thayer, 1981).

4.2.1.2   High temperature thermal systems
The best flat plate collectors can heat water (or air) to over 90°C, but much higher temperatures can be produced by concentrating collectors. These all use some mirror, either as a single curvature parabolic trough or as a double curvature 'dish'. The former has a linear focus, the latter a point (or near-point) focus. These usually operate at 500–800°C temperatures and can produce superheated steam. Areas of several hectares may be covered by such collectors for the purposes of electricity generation. These are often referred to by the generic term STE or solar-thermal-electricity systems. Figure 4.20 is a diagram of a field of parabolic troughs with a central boiler/turbine house (see also Fig. 4.21).

A particular type STE system is referred to as the 'power tower', which has a large field of individually steerable mirrors, all focussed on a central receiver mounted on top of a tower (Fig. 4.22). Large-scale prototypes of both the power tower and a field of parabolic troughs have been built both in California and for the EU in Spain and feed electricity into the grid (Fig. 4.23). STE generators are all high temperature systems.

4.20.
A field of parabolic troughs connected to a central boiler/generator house.

4.21.
A large scale concentrating trough system.

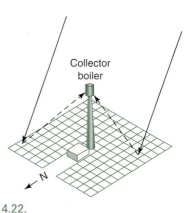

4.22.
A 'power tower' system: a field of mirrors with a central tower-mounted boiler and the generator house.

Collector boiler

N

4.23.
A 11 MW power tower system in Spain with a 115 m high tower.

4.24.
A 'big dish' concentrator.

Conservative governments tend to brush aside solar and wind power as incapable of providing 'base load' power. The fact is that STE plants in the order of hundreds of MW are in operation and a GW size plant is at the planning stage. It is seriously suggested that even the most industrialized countries could eliminate coal-fired power generation, without resorting to nuclear power (Fig. 4.24).

4.2.1.3 Photovoltaic systems

PV cells are used for direct conversion to electricity, relying on some semiconductor. The most widely used ones are silicon cells, which may be single crystal (grown as a cylinder and sliced into thin wafers), polycrystalline or amorphous silicon. Single crystal cells in commercial production exceeded 24% conversion efficiency, but polycrystalline cells, with their 15–19% efficiencies are much less expensive. These have been used in large arrays, mounted on a framework at ground level, but recently the building-integrated PV systems became widely used.

Several governments have large-scale programs. Germany launched its 'thousand solar roofs program' some 10 years ago and a follow-up 100 000 solar roofs program is in progress. The USA launched its 'million solar roofs' program (although that includes flat-plate thermal collectors). Australia gives a direct subsidy of $5 per Wp (peak watt) to any domestic scale PV installation (the size of PV installations is usually given in terms of their rated peak power, watt, peak (Wp) under standard irradiance.

Figure 4.25 shows the growth of annual PV module production of the world since 1976 (the three main producer countries + the rest of the world. The cost of such modules moved in the opposite direction: in 1974 it was about US$ 120 per Wp, and now it is around $4–5 per Wp (Fig. 4.26).

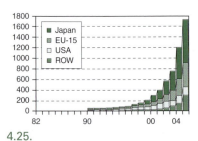

4.25.
The world's PV cell production in MWp.

4.26.
A 1.6 MW PV system for Google's HQ in San Rafael, CA a roof over a parking area.

4.27.
A high solidity pumping wind mill.

Whilst silicon solar PV cells dominate the present day market, many other semiconductors produce a photovoltaic effect and have been used experimentally, such as

gallium arsenite – GaAs
cadmium sulphide – CdS
cadmium telluride – CdTe
germanium – Ge
selenium – Se

Today there are some promising developments in other directions. Titanium oxide (TiO_2) cells, using an organo-metallic dye are said to be much cheaper and produce an output higher than the Si cells, especially at low levels of irradiance, thus they can be used also for indoor purposes.

4.2.2 Wind energy

This seems to be at present the most competitive of the renewable alternatives and the most widely used (perhaps with the exception of domestic solar water heaters). Apart from the traditional windmills, slow moving devices having large 'sails', (e.g. in Crete and in the Netherlands, but used already in China and Babylon over 2000 years ago) two types of wind devices have been used for well over a hundred years, those with horizontal axis and those with vertical axis. In the horizontal axis types we have high solidity rotors (Fig. 4.27), (i.e. the frontal view of the rotor is almost all solid) used primarily for water pumping and the low solidity (propeller) type, used for electricity generation (Fig. 4.28). In the vertical axis type we have the high solidity Savonius rotor (Fig. 4.29) and the low solidity rotors, developed by Darreius, also referred to as 'egg-beaters' (Fig. 4.30). Up to the 1970s most propeller-generators were in

4.28.
Propeller type wind generators (aerogenerators).

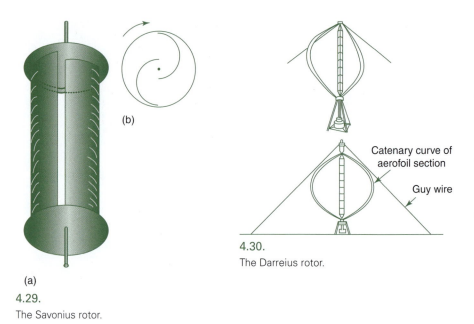

4.30.
The Darreius rotor.

Catenary curve of aerofoil section

Guy wire

(b)

(a)

4.29.
The Savonius rotor.

4.31.
A large scale wind farm with 1 MW turbines.

the order of 1–2 kW and since then this type became the most developed into large units, 500 kW to 1.5 MW sizes. The largest one so far is the Nordex N80 unit, with a rated output of 2.5 MW and a rotor radius of 80 m (Fig. 4.31).

A 5 MW wind turbine (Beatrice) is being installed in the deep waters of Moray Firth (N/E Scotland) as part of an EU project. The installed wind generating capacity in the world has increased from less than 1 MW in 1980 to more than 50 GW in 2005 (see Table 4.9) and the electrical energy produced has grown from 1 GWh to 50 TWh (10^{12} Wh) per annum. Figure 4.32 shows the annually installed wind generating capacity since 1996 in the five largest user countries.

In the UK there are operating wind generators with a total output of 422 MW$_e$ (2001 data), current and planned projects will bring this up to

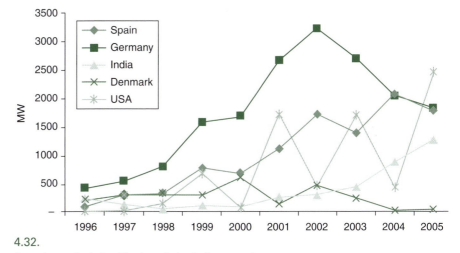

4.32.

Annual rate of wind turbine installation in five countries.

Table 4.9. Installed wind generating capacity (2005)

Germany	18 445 MW
Spain	10 027
USA	9181
India	4253
Denmark	3087
Italy	1713
UK	1336
China	1264
Netherlands	1221
Japan	1159
Total	50 350 MW

2000 MW capacity. The UK target is that by 2010 renewables should contribute 10% of the total electricity production.

The world's total installed capacity reached 75 GW in 2006. An increasing proportion of this consists of off-shore wind-farms, much favoured as over the water surface the wind is much less turbulent than over the land. *WindForce 10*, an international alliance set the target for 2020: 20% of all electricity produced should be by wind generators. The Australian target is very conservative: only 2%, although the Federal Senate voted to increase the MRET (Mandatory Renewable Electricity Target) to 5% by 2020, the government is still undecided.

Recently a new VAWT (vertical axis wind turbine) became available, which is suitable for roof mounting; a low solidity device, serving the individual consumer. It is available in 1.2–2 kW outputs, with 0.8–1.5 m diameter and with suitable current conditioning, it may be used as a grid-connected device. (A stand-alone system would need back-up storage batteries to ensure availability of power when there is no wind.)

The 'world's largest' wind farm operates at King Mountain, near McCamey, Texas, which consists of 160 turbines, each of 1.3 MW capacity, a total of over

200 MW. Apparently Texas legislation requires that 1.5% of electricity be produced from renewable sources by 2003, rising to 3% by 2009. There seems to be a much smaller, but significant market for small wind turbines. The above VAWT is a good example, but three others should be mentioned:

1 'Air 403' of Southwest Windpower of the USA, 400W, 1.15 m. diameter, with three narrow blades
2 'Rutland 913' of Marlec, UK, 90W, 0.9 m diameter, with six blades
3 'Enflo Systems 0060/05' of Switzerland, 500W, a 5-bladed rotor of 0.6 m diameter, within a 0.8 m diameter tubular diffuser.

All three are rated with a 12.5 m/s wind speed and all three can be grid-connected with a suitable inverter and power conditioner.

4.2.3 Other renewables

The growing of trees is biomass production and burning of such wood is the most ancient for of biomass energy conversion. The burning of bagass (sugar cane residue) is the same process, to generate steam and produce electricity. Many other conversion techniques are available.

4.2.3.1 Methane gas

Methane gas (CH_4) generation can be considered as biomass conversion. Essentially this is the anaerobic digestion of farm by-products, e.g. straw and manure. The *carbon–nitrogen ratio* of the feedstock is important. Too much carbon (plant matter) will produce much CO_2 and little CH_4 (Figs 4.33 and 4.34). Some manure will help to restore the C/N ratio to the optimal 25 to 35. The methane generated is easily stored (e.g. in gasometers) and can be used in burners.

Large-scale use is possible in sewage treatment plants, where enough methane may be generated and collected to produce steam, to drive turbines and generate electricity in the order of tens of MW.

In the UK the installed methane-based electricity generating capacity is some 13.4 MW.

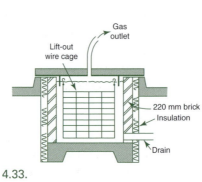

4.33.
A methane generator for solid input.

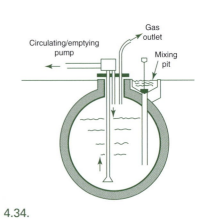

4.34.
A methane generator for liquid input.

A recent development is the capture and use of methane generated in waste dumps. The dump, when full, can be covered by a polythene film, before the usual layer of earth is put on. Significant amounts of gas may be collected over many years and used for electricity generation.

These systems have the added benefit of reducing the greenhouse effect. Methane is a greenhouse gas with an effect about forty times as great as CO_2 (partly because it persists much longer in the atmosphere). It would be produced anyway and dissipated into the atmosphere. If it is oxidized (burnt) it is reduced to water and some CO_2.

4.2.3.2 Energy crops

Agriculture can produce many plants (biomass) which then can be converted into practically useable forms of energy. A significant success story is the production of ethanol (alcohol) from sugar cane in Brazil. There are cars produced for the use of ethanol instead of petrol (gasoline), but it has been shown that any car can use up to 30% ethanol mixed with the petrol fuel. It may have a slightly lower calorific value than petrol, but it has better ignition properties, so the consumption is about the same as of pure petrol. In the USA corn is used for ethanol production to such an extent, that shortages of corn becomes a concern. Sorghum (Indian millet) and miscanthus are also used for ethanol production.

In Australia ethanol production is the saviour of the sugar cane industry, when there is a glut of sugar supply on the world markets. Car manufacturers and the petroleum lobby mounted a scare campaign (the risk of engine corrosion) against ethanol, but a mix of 10% is now accepted. Ethanol has a long history: in the 1920s and 30s in Europe almost every petrol station offered a mix marketed as 'motalco' (motor-alcohol).

Bio-diesel is another liquid fuel produced from biomass. The most favoured product is rape-seed oil, but many other vegetable oils can be treated to serve as diesel fuel. In some countries producing crops for conversion to fuel is such a profitable business that agricultural food production stated to suffer. A new phrase created for this activity is 'growing fuel'.

Figure 4.35 indicates the various sources of biomass, the conversion processes and the final products of biomass conversion.

4.2.3.3 Sea and earth

Sea and earth energy sources are also available and systems for their utilization are in various stages of development.

Ocean energy may be utilized by a number of techniques. Tidal flow can be made to drive turbines and such systems are feasible in geographically favourable locations, where the tidal variations are large. If a barrage is constructed e.g. across a river estuary, both the incoming and the outgoing tide can be made use of.

Numerous ingenious mechanical solutions have been proposed to make use of **wave energy**. No doubt that the energy available in waves is huge, but none of these systems is a clear winner yet and very few large-scale installations are in operation.

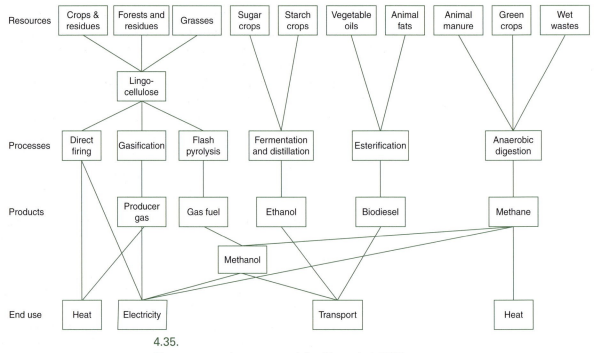

4.35.
Biomass conversion processes (after Diesendorf, 2007).

Table 4.10. Summary of geothermal electricity production (2005)

	Installed (MW$_e$)	Annual output (GWh/year)
USA	2534	17 840
Philippines	1930	9253
Mexico	953	6282
Indonesia	797	6085
Italy	791	5340
Japan	535	3467
New Zealand	435	2774
Iceland	202	1483
Costa Rica	163	1145
El Salvador	151	967
Kenya	129	1088

Ocean-thermal energy (OTE) represents a completely different approach. It makes use of the temperature differences between deep water layers (several thousand metres) and the surface layers. The grade of such energy is not very large, but the quantities are huge. Attempts are made to drive various heat engines with this temperature difference.

Geothermal energy is the heat of the interior of the Earth. It can be made use of in several ways. Surface utilization is possible at hot springs or geysers. The first geothermal power plant was set up in Italy, in 1913, with a capacity of 250 kW. Plants of increasing size have since been constructed (mostly after the 2nd World War) in many countries, as summarized in Table 4.10. Notable

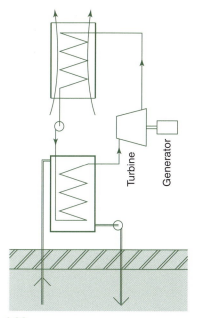

4.36.
Principles of an HDR plant.

examples are Rotoroa in New Zealand and Yellowstone in Wyoming, USA. The world's 'most efficient' geothermal system is said to be in Indonesia at Darajat (near the Mt Kendang volcano, in Central Java), producing 81 MW of electricity. A second similar unit is under construction.

In Australia the heat of deep layers is recovered through bore-holes delivering hot water or by the 'hot-dry rock' (HDR) technology: pumping water down a bore-hole and recovering hot water at quite high temperatures (Fig. 4.36). A 13 MW unit is in operation in the Cooper basin and a 100 MW plant is in preparation. Here at a depth of 3.5 km solid granite is found at over 250°C temperature. Each of these methods may produce steam to drive turbines, or below boiling-point temperatures to drive some form of heat engines, such as 'screw-expanders'.

Low-grade geothermal energy can also be made use of. Temperature of the earth at a depth of 2–3 m is practically constant all-year-round, at about the annual mean air temperature of the location (or slightly warmer). A pipe coil buried at this depth can produce warm water at about this temperature. A similar method saves earth-works by drilling a large number of bore-holes and place a U-pipe in each, to serve the same purpose, to act as a heat source. A heat pump (see Section 1.6.1.1 and Fig. 1.97) can step-up the temperature to a level useful for space heating (at least 30°C). This system is sometimes referred to as an 'active earth-coupled system', or an 'earth-source heat pump' system. Some versions of such installations can also serve as a heat sink, when the heat pump is used in reverse, as a cooling technique.

Over the last 30 years renewable (mainly solar and wind) electricity generation experienced very high growth rates, albeit from a very low base in 1971 (practically nil in 1970). This is summarized in Table 4.11. The EU has proposed a binding target of 20% of the total energy consumption to be obtained from renewable resources.

4.2.4 Energy storage

This is a major issue with most renewable energy systems, because of the mismatch in timing of supply availability and the demand. The storage requirements may be short term (e.g. the 24-hour cycle) or long term (inter-seasonal). Much work has been devoted to the latter, especially in cold winter climates (e.g. Scandinavia) to store heat collected in the summer to be available in the

Table 4.11. Growth of renewable electricity production (as % of national total generation)

	2000 (%)	2030	
		Extrapolation (%)	With new initiatives (%)
USA and Canada	2	7	11.5
Europe	3	11	25
Japan, Australia and New Zealand	2	5	7.5

winter. Such storage must be inexpensive. Underground heat storage in either man-made containers or in natural formations, even in the aquifer, seems to be the most promising.

Energy can be stored by pumping water up to an elevated reservoir, to be used to drive a turbine when needed. Producing compressed air is an alternative, which can drive a turbine or a reciprocating engine for recovery of energy. Kinetic energy storage is provided by large flywheels, accelerated as an input and driving a generator as recovery.

Low-grade heat can be stored in the building fabric, often without any extra cost, in elements which are provided for other purposes, such as a concrete floor slab or various masonry walls. It is up to the architect or designer to realize this potential as and when needed.

Short-term storage of low temperature heat is well developed in storage type hot water (H/W) systems or block-(unit-) heaters for space heating. Electricity produced by PV or wind generators can be stored in rechargeable batteries, but these are expensive and their useful life is limited (maximum 10 years). Much research effort is devoted to alternative battery systems, but the (improved) lead-acid batteries are still the most reliable. If the generators (PV or aerogenerators) are connected to the grid, the grid itself will take on the role of energy storage.

Many countries now regulate the status of grid-connected 'small producers' of electricity. The local electricity supply company (or authority) must buy the electricity offered by such a small producer. This may be a house owner who has some PV devices on the roof or a small aerogenerator in the backyard. It may be a company owning and office block or some industry who have similar devices, or even a farmer who has a micro-hydro generator on his property. Two-way metering is installed. The electricity company may pay the generator only the wholesale price, but charge the normal retail rate for what is consumed. However, in most cases the price is the same both ways.

An interesting new development is the introduction of 'time-of day metering'. The reduced cost of off-peak electricity is well established. Now the day may be divided into several time bands, each band attracting a different rate. Very high price will apply at periods of peak demand. This is very much in favour of PV system owners in hot, clear-sky climates. The peak demand is due to air conditioning, occurring at the hottest part of the day, usually in the early afternoon hours. But this is also the time of peak production by the individual PV system and the electricity fed back to the grid will attract a similarly high price.

4.2.4.1 Reversible chemical reactions

Reversible chemical reactions are some of the most promising technologies for the long term storage of high-grade energy.

Ammonia (NH_3) is one of the candidates. With high temperature input it can be split into nitrogen and hydrogen (thermal dissociation), the two gases are separately stored and may be made to re-combine (in the presence of some catalyst) at will, which is a highly exothermic process.

Electricity (DC) may be used to split water into H and O. That hydrogen can be stored or piped to where needed and it can be used in internal combustion

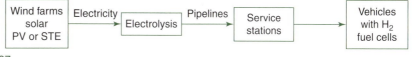

4.37.
Renewable hydrogen production.

engines or in fuel cells to produce electricity. Indeed the 'hydrogen economy' is one of the most promising technologies for the future. Hydrogen is a very good energy carrier and it can be used as input for fuel cells and thus converted directly into electricity. The only emission from these processes is H_2O), i.e. some water vapour. The 'hydrogen economy' is feasible (and desirable) only if the electricity used for electrolysis is generated from renewable resources. The diagram (Fig. 4.37) shows that hydrogen can be generated using renewable energy and it is the most useful energy carrier which produces no greenhouse gas emissions.

Professor Bockris (of Adelaide) 30 years ago visualized large areas of the Australian desert used for PV-based devices, producing DC current, to be used for electrolysis of water to produce hydrogen, that can be piped to the major cities. Problems to be solved were then identified as hydrogen embrittlement of steel (pipes or tanks) and the explosive nature of hydrogen. The former has been solved by various coatings of the inside of tanks or pipes and it can safely be stored in the form of metal hydrides, or stored and transported in liquefied form under a pressure of 200–300 kPa.

It is particularly attractive for aircraft fuel, as its energy content per unit mass is much higher than of liquid fuels (see Table 4.20).

Recently the NREL (National Renewable Energy Laboratory, Colorado) started a project to use wind-generated DC electricity to produce hydrogen, and use this either as fuel for internal combustion engines or in fuel cells for direct production of electricity.

A number of other reversible chemical and electro-chemical reactions have been or are being examined, tested and developed.

4.2.4.2 Phase change materials

Phase change materials, in addition to any sensible heat change can make use of their latent heat of phase change. The latent heat that was necessary for an upward change will be released during the corresponding downward change.

The simplest application is in ice storage: making ice by a compression chiller using cheap off-peak electricity, which requires the extraction of heat, (some 335 kJ/kg) and using this ice for air conditioning (cooling) during the day, giving a cooling effect again of some 335 kJ/kg (93 Wh/kg). Here the phase change ('transition') temperature is 0°C. Table 4.12 lists some materials with transition temperatures possibly useful in building applications.

In many instances paraffin wax has been used for thermal storage. Apparently the transition (melting point) temperature of this can be set by cutting the chain molecule to the appropriate length. Such phase change materials are often used in conjunction with passive solar heating systems.

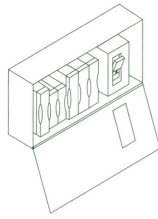

(a)

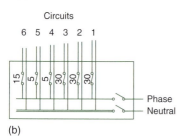

(b)

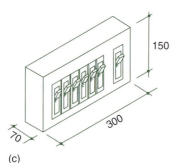

(c)

4.38.

A fuse-board consumer unit and one with circuit breakers.

numbers on the outside, such as the odometer in cars or combination locks on briefcases, but the latest development is the use of a digital (liquid crystal) display.

In the past the consumer unit included a series of fuses (rewirable or cartridge type), which would melt (burn out) in case the current exceeding a set limit. Nowadays automatic circuit breakers are used almost exclusively (Fig. 4.38). There is usually one main circuit breaker for the whole supply, then the wiring splits into several circuits, say 2 lighting and 2 power-point circuits, each with its own circuit breaker. The stove and the H/W system would have their own separate circuits. Circuit breakers are labelled according to the current they permit before cutting out, such as 5, 8, 15, 20 or 30 A (amperes).

Whilst circuit breakers protect the installation against overload (which could cause fire), earthing (or 'grounding' in North America) is used as a safety device to protect the user (shock protection). If the insulation is faulty and the conductor becomes exposed or the metal body of the appliance becomes 'live' and touched by the user, a current will flow through the route of least resistance. The earth wire, connected to metal parts is usually a multi-strand copper conductor, uninsulated, leading to an electrode buried in the ground. This has (we hope) a lesser resistance than the human body, so it takes the bulk of the current, unless the human body is well 'earthed', e.g. bare feet on a wet floor. In this case the 240V supply may produce a lethal current through the body.

Earth leakage circuit breakers are increasingly used, which would be tripped as soon as there is any current going through the earth wire or if the current in the active wire differs from the neutral.

Wiring within a house (or apartment) is usually in double-insulated 3-core PVC cables. The live or active conductor and the neutral are insulated separately and with a bare copper wire for earthing added, the whole is covered by a PVC sheathing. These are often referred to as TPS (thermoplastic sheathed) cables. In exposed flexible cables the earth wire is also insulated. The colour of the insulated cores is now standardized, but some old cables of different colour are still in use, as shown in Table 4.15.

Whilst these cables can run freely in a framed/sheeted wall or floor and can be embedded in a concrete slab, it is better practice to install conduits (with a draw-wire) which would allow re-wiring, should the need arise.

In a larger project an electrical consultant would design the system, in a single house this is usually left to the licensed electrician, but in both cases the architect/designer would set the 'human interface', the location of switches, light points, GPOs (general purpose outlets = power points) and any fixed appliances (e.g. cookers or H/W cylinders). The requirements can be shown

Table 4.15. Standard colours of electrical cables (insulated cores)

Conductor	Standard colour	Old colour
Phase (line, active, live)	Brown	Red
Neutral	Blue	Black
Earth (bare or)	Green + yellow stripes	Green

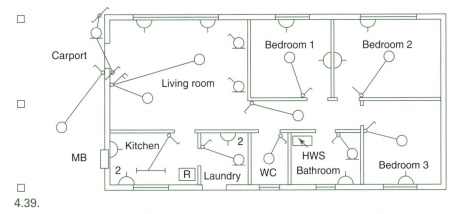

4.39.

An electrical plan: location of lamps, switches, etc.

on a plan, which is not a circuit diagram, (such as Fig. 4.39) using the standard electrical symbols (Fig. 4.40). The architect (in consultation with the client) would normally select the luminaires. It is important to consider the luminous characteristics of these (light distribution, surface luminance thus risk of glare, size of lamps to be used, see Part 2, Section 2.5) and not to select them purely on the basis of 'looks'.

Luminaire (ceiling)	○
Wall mounted luminaire	
Luminaire with switch	
Fluorescent luminaire	
Same, twin-tube	
Switches, 1, 2, 3-pole	
Two-way switch	
Socket outlet	
Switched socket outlet	

An appliance   R
  eg: HWS hot water service
      R   electric range (cooker)
      EF   exhaust fan
      AC   air conditioner

Boards   MSB
  eg: MB   meter board
      MSB main switchboard
      DSB distribution board
      CP   control panel

Dimmer switch	
Telephone outlet (wall)	▽
Telephone floor outlet	▽
Electric bell	

4.40.

Electrical location symbols.

4.3.2.2   *Gas supply installations*

Where piped gas supply is not available, gas can be purchased in bottles or cylinder. These must be located outside and a pipe must be carried to the points of use. Bottled gas is often used for cooking and has been used for refrigerators (to drive absorption cooling machines). For larger users, e.g. space heating, gas would be adopted only if piped reticulation is available.

From the gas mains a *service pipe* would connect to the meter (Fig. 4.41) and then the pipe may branch out to e.g. the cooker, the H/W system and the central heating boiler. These boilers are available now in a form which looks like a slightly fat radiator panel and can be installed in any habitable room. A larger H/W system or central heating boiler must have a flue (Fig. 4.42). Boilers may be located next to an external wall and have a *balanced flue*. (e.g. Fig. 1.97, which shows a gas-fired convector unit.) At one stage it was very popular to install gas burners into old open fireplaces, even in the form of artificial 'logs', to imitate a wood fire or glowing artificial embers to look as a coal fire, perhaps including a flickering light. These may well be 'mood elements' (for some) but are very inefficient heating devices.

The main concern with gas installations is the risk of leakage. Any small amount of gas leaking out would form an explosive mix with air and could be triggered by a small spark, e.g. from an electric light switch. An argument against the use of gas, citing the many catastrophic gas explosions and fires that regularly occur is usually countered by referring to the equally (if not more) numerous fire disasters caused by electrical faults. The morale of this discussion is that there are risks with any form of energy system, gas or electric or even with open solid fuel fireplaces; the house may be

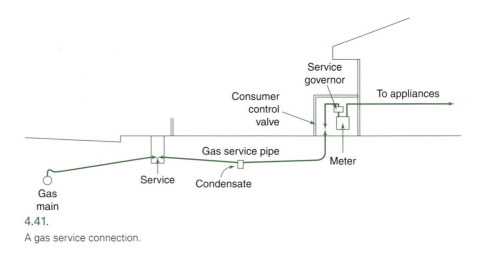

4.41.

A gas service connection.

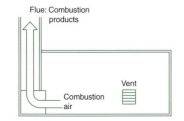

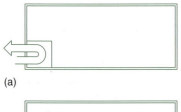

(a)

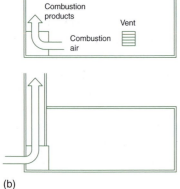

(b)

4.42.

Possible flue arrangements for gas heaters.

burnt down in a fire started by a candle,-all the designer, the supplier and the installer can do is *risk minimization*. Instructions for use should be supplied with any such system, but the ultimate responsibility should be with the user.

4.3.2.3 Energy rating of buildings

Energy rating of buildings began in the early 1980s. Several authorities in many countries realized that regulations are not enough to achieve a reduction in energy use. California introduced a building energy code in 1978 and it set a pattern for a two-pronged approach: *prescriptive* or *performance-based* regulations. The former would prescribe in detail many attributes of the proposed building and its components (such as thermal insulation) whilst the latter would set the 'energy entitlement' (per unit floor area) for different building types and a number of climate zones. An applicant for a building permit may elect to comply with the prescriptive part or else (s)he must prove, by using an approved computer simulation program (such as those discussed in Section 1.4.4.1) that the proposed building will not exceed its annual energy entitlement.

Such *simulation programs* are also used for producing a star rating for a house (or a plan), which can then be used as a marketing tool. The first such scheme in Australia was released in 1986, as the FSDR (Five Star Design Rating) scheme. Its 'simulation engine' was the CSIRO thermal response and energy simulation program CHEETAH. This was further developed and officially adopted in 1993 as NatHERS (Nationwide House Energy Rating Scheme). Its use is voluntary, but several authorities require that such a rating be carried out and disclosed if and when the house is put on the market (e.g. based on the *Trade Descriptions Act*). Some authorities stipulate that any design for a new house must be shown to achieve at least a 3-star rating (on a scale of 0 to 5 stars). In one instance recently this has been increased to 4 stars.

An alternative to simulation is a *point-scoring method*, where even the non-professional person can answer a series of (mostly multiple-choice) questions about the house and each answer results in a certain number of points.

The number of points awarded for each building attribute had been determined by an extensive simulation-based parametric study. Categories are set in terms of the number of points achieved, for awarding a number of stars (see e.g. data sheet D.4.1). Several states (both in Australia and in the USA) have such methods and the Danish *Positive List Method* is similar.

A survey of the international scene identified some 30 similar rating schemes in operation, most of them in various states of the USA. The EU Council Directive 93/76 required member states to develop and implement *energy certification* of buildings. This may be based on an energy audit of existing buildings or on computer simulation of a planned building.

The French QUALITEL scheme is based on a qualitative assessment but it includes energy use prediction. The Portuguese RCCTE (Regulations on the thermal behaviour of building envelopes) is a combination of prescriptive building regulations and an energy rating. The maximum allowable energy use is set and building data can be fed into a spreadsheet, that will predict the expected energy use. If this is below the set limit, a building certificate will be issued, giving a rating on a scale of fair/good/excellent. The implementation of this system is at present voluntary, but it is intended to become compulsory in the future.

In the UK, based on the BREDEM method, (see Section 1.4.4.1) the Open University developed the MKECI (Milton Keynes Energy Cost Index) and a modified version of this is NHER (National Home Energy Rating) system, which is the basis of the computer program *Home Rater*.

In Germany the Bauhaus University (Weimar) proposed a 'building passport', a significant part of which would be the energy rating (Fig. 4.43). This was adopted by the EU directive: from 2006 onwards, any building between Finland and Portugal, when sold or rented must have such a 'passport'. In Germany this was administered by the DENA (Deutsche Energie-Agentur) and an 'Energiepass' has been introduced for houses and residences. Householders can obtain the services of an authorized person to do an energy audit and issue an energy-pass. The crucial part of this is the annual energy consumption expressed in kWh/m^2. Older, unimproved houses would be in the 400–550 kWh/m^2 range, while new houses should not exceed 100 kWh/m^2, but should preferably be 30–60 kWh/m^2. (Compare these values with those given in data sheet D.4.1.)

On the basis of this (and a qualitative assessment of sustainability) the house would be awarded an 'efficiency class' on an 8-point scale, labelled from A (best) to I. Such rating strongly depends on the life expectancy of the building, which is e.g. some 25 years in Japan, 50 years in the USA and 75 years in the UK. This energy-pass becomes an important piece of information for the owner or a prospective buyer.

A similar system operates in Denmark since 1997, with the name: 'Energiemærke'. It must be obtained at every point of sale for a house, but the rating must be carried out annually for larger buildings, based on actual energy use records.

Such energy ratings often become the basis of compulsory regulations.

Some building control authorities (esp. in South-East Asia) use the OTTV (overall thermal transfer value) concept to prescribe the thermal characteristics

4.43.

… and what's yours using per square metre? Source: German Energy Agency (dena).

of the building envelope. This can be considered as an average U-value for the whole of the building envelope, including solar radiation effects. Its calculation is based on the following equation (the sum of three components: envelope gain, window conduction and window solar gain, divided by the total area):

$$\text{OTTV} = \frac{A_w U_w \text{TD}_{eq} + A_f U_f \text{DT} + A_f \text{SC} * \text{SF}}{A_t}$$

where
A = area of each element
A_t = total envelope area
U = U-value of each element
TD_{eq} = equivalent temperature difference
$\text{DT} = T_o - T_i$ (averages)
SC = shading coefficient
SF = solar factor (W/m^2)

and the subscripts
w = walls
f = fenestration (windows)

The calculation of the TD$_{eq}$ is quite involved (it makes an allowance for solar input). It is a derivative of the TETD/TA (total equivalent temperature differential) method (ASHRAE, 1972), where TA indicates time-averaging. The method heavily relies on tables presenting empirical (simplified) values and is falling into disrepute. Furthermore the SF concept is no longer in use (see Section 1.4.1.3).

Most countries now have energy-related building regulations. In the UK one of three methods can be used to satisfy such regulations:

1 *the elemental method*: each element is to achieve the prescribed U-values and window sizes are limited to 22.5% of the floor area,
2 *the 'target U-value' method*: a weighted average U-value is prescribed and calculations must show that it is achieved; provisions against thermal bridging and infiltration control must be demonstrated,
3 *the energy rating method*: which includes ventilation/infiltration as well as SWH (service water heating).

The U-value requirement is fairly stringent: a maximum of 0.25W/m^{2}K is allowed for roof and 0.45W/m^{2}K for walls.

The New Zealand system is similar, only the terminology is different. The three methods distinguished are Schedule method, Calculation method and Modelling method. The last of these requires the use of a building thermal response and energy use simulation program. The insulation requirements are not as stringent as in the UK: even in the coldest of the three climatic zones distinguished the prescribed value is R2.5 for roofs and R1.9 for walls, which corresponds to U-values of 0.4 and 0.52 respectively.

The BCA (Building Code of Australia) distinguishes eight climatic zones, from the hot-humid North, to the 'alpine' zones of the cool-temperate Tasmania and the south/east mountainous area (of NSW and Victoria). The stated 'performance requirements' are qualitative only, which can be satisfied either by following the deemed-to-satisfy provisions ('acceptable construction') or by 'alternative solutions' which are shown to be equivalent to the former, either by a recognized computer program (such as NatHERS mentioned above) or by 'expert opinion'. Generally the requirements are fairly timid. The stated aim is not to achieve 'best practice' but only to eliminate 'worst practice'. Insulation requirements (except for the mountainous areas) are R1.9 (U = 0.52) for walls and the (quite respectable) R3.7 (U = 0.27) for roofs. An interesting point is that for roofs in the northern zones downward heat flow is taken as critical, whilst upward heat flow is controlled in the south.

A version of NatHERS is AccuRate, which includes a cross-ventilation routine. It is intended for use in the hot-humid climates of Northern Australia where houses are operated in the fully open mode, relying on the apparent cooling effect of air movement produced by cross-ventilation or ceiling fans.

In the USA almost each state differs, but many adopt the MEC (Model Energy Code) as the basis of regulations. The MEC also allows three routes to compliance:

1 following the prescriptive package
2 the trade-off approach and
3 the software approach.

The IECC (International Energy Conservation Code) is referenced at many levels, which regulates the building envelope as well as HVAC (heating, ventilation and air conditioning), SWH (service water heating) and lighting installations. It is called 'international', but it appears to be a USA code. It references ASHRAE and IES (Illuminating Engineering Society) standards and divides America into 38 climate zones.

4.3.3 Energy conservation

The term refers to the conservation of conventional, non-renewable energy sources and many would prefer the term *rational use of energy* applied to all forms of energy. Energy use in buildings is determined by four sets of decisions:

1 **setting of environmental standards**: attempts at conservation do not mean a 'lowering' of standards, but the setting of reasonable standards, e.g. Not setting the thermostat at 25°C for winter, when 22°C would be adequate, and not cooling the building to 22°C in the summer, when 27°C may be quite comfortable, i.e. rely on the adaptability model of thermal comfort. Similarly in lighting: an illuminance of 800 lx would require twice as much energy as 400 lx, and the 400 lx may be quite adequate for most office-type tasks.
2 **building form and fabric**: the effect of these has been discussed quite extensively in Part 1.
3 **environmental control installations**: in this area we have to rely on engineering advice to a large extent, but often the architect can influence design decisions and achieve greater efficiencies, avoid the wastage of energy (e.g. use more efficient motors, Fig. 4.40). Examples of this may be the choice of compact fluorescent lamps rather than incandescent, or

making sure that the air conditioning condenser unit is not exposed to solar heat input.

4 **choice of energy source: including renewables**: the decision for such often rests with the client and it may be based on economic considerations. These will be discussed in Section 4.5.6, but the architect should consider the possibilities, examine the feasibility of a chosen technique and advise the client accordingly.

A possible list of energy conservation measures has been suggested at a recent conference:

Building	Installations
– daylighting	– controls of HVAC systems
– shading	– energy-efficient HVAC
– natural ventilation	– economizer cycle
– insulation	– exhaust air heat recovery
– thermal mass	– energy-efficient lamps
– solar air (pre-) heating	– reduced duct leakage
– improved windows	– photovoltaics
– air infiltration control	– solar water heating
– passive solar heating	– solar/wind generators

The list is by no means comprehensive, but it includes most of the main measures. A few additional issues are mentioned below, that the architect may keep in mind and advise the client or may remind the consulting engineer.

The efficiency of electric motors varies between quite broad limits, especially for smaller motors (72–96%), as shown in Fig. 4.44. If energy is to be conserved, the use of high efficiency motors should be a requirement. Their initial cost may be slightly higher, but in terms of LCC (life cycle cost) analysis they are quite superior.

In an electricity supply system it is not only the overall load and consumption that is critical, but also its timing. The generation of peak-time electricity is far more expensive than the supply of base load. As the system must be capable of satisfying the peak demand (even if that occurs only for a short period) there is much generating capacity which lies idle most of the time. It can take up to 12 hours to start up a steam turbine generator set, thus there is no point in stopping them during off-peak periods. They are often referred to as *spinning reserve*.

Suppliers are anxious to level out the load, especially by *demand side management* (DSM). This includes various pricing strategies, such as

- off-peak tariff, much cheaper than normal, for purposes not time-dependent, such as storage type DHW system or storage type 'block' heaters or indeed 'ice storage' systems for air conditioning (here a large volume of water would be frozen overnight, using cheap electricity, and the next day it would provide chilled water for air conditioning, i.e. making use of the latent heat of fusion of ice)

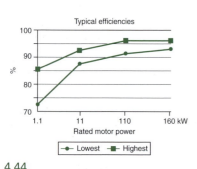

4.44.

The efficiency of electric motors.

- interruptible supply: the supplier can send out a high frequency signal through the supply cables to trigger a switch in the consumer's meter box, which can cut off (or switch back) non-essential circuits at peak periods
- two-part tariffs, where the consumer pays a flat rate for all electricity used (energy rate) but also pays according to the peak load reached during the billing period (power rate). In some cases, where such metering and registering of peak power is not available, there may be a charge according to 'total connected load'
- the latest development is digital metering, which allows the use of 'time-of-day' tariffs: higher prices at peak periods, lower prices in the off-peak 'troughs'.

A single consumer may have at least two meters, one for the 'normal' consumption (lighting and power points) and one for a 'special tariff' for off-peak DHW and space heating (block or unit heaters) or for interruptible supply. In office and commercial buildings a large tank of water may be frozen overnight, using cheap off-peak electricity and the following day the melting of this ice (an endothermic process) would provide chilled water for the air conditioning system.

Attempts for levelling out energy use rate at the individual consumer level have been made in the 1960s and 1970s, by the so-called *load shedding* systems. All electric loads in the house would be ranked into an order of priority and grouped into separate circuits. A maximum load would be set and when that were to be reached, the lowest priority load would be 'shed', i.e. that circuit switched off. Such systems are now available in an electronic version, named IHG (Intelligent Home Gateway).

Some electricity supply companies also promote demand side management in order to reduce the total demand, to obviate the need for building new generating plants. California e.g. saved the construction of an 1000 MW plant by DSM measures, such as technical advice to consumers, funding of feasibility studies, subsidizing or even direct funding of more efficient equipment, such as compact fluorescent lamps.

Supply side management (SSM) systems include various arrangements to utilize surplus capacity at off-peak times (by large buffer storage systems) and make use of this at peak periods, such as

- pump-back systems, which can be used if the grid has some hydro-electric generation components: the surplus capacity can be used to pump back from a lower level (small) reservoir up to the main reservoir, to be re-used to drive the turbines at peak periods
- other storage devices, which include batteries, reversible chemical reactions (e.g. ammonia dissociation), compressed air, flywheels and superconducting magnetic energy storage (SMES),
- distributed generation (DG), which means the incorporation into the grid a multitude of small-scale generators, from micro-hydro or wind turbines to building-mounted PV systems. This is often considered as using the grid as storage, which is feasible because of the favourable diversity factors of the many small generators (e.g. wind is usually strongest when there is no solar radiation).

Energy conservation and substitution of renewable energy resources is imperative not only because of the finite availability of oil and coal, but also because of the atmospheric pollution, primarily CO_2 emissions due to their use. The magnitude of greenhouse gas emissions is not directly proportional to energy use, but certainly energy use is responsible for most greenhouse gas emissions. This can be well illustrated by statistics from the Australian Government, shown in Table 4.16 as percentage of all energy use and emissions by government properties and activities.

4.4 WATER AND WASTES

4.4.1 Water

The human body requires a minimum of 1 L of water per day for its normal functioning. The usual amount of intake is some 2 L/day, in the form of food and drink. The per capita water consumption (Table 4.17) in a large city can be as much as 2000 L (2 kL = 2 m³). How is the remaining 1998 L used?

The answer is that it is used mostly by industry and commerce, but also for some other purposes (on average):

residential buildings – 44%
industry – 22%
commerce – 18%
health facilities – 5%
parks and streets– 7%
urban fringe agriculture – 4%

Table 4.16. The relationship of energy use and greenhouse emissions

End-use	Energy consumption (%)	Greenhouse emissions (%)
Buildings	46	54
Defence establishments	37	40
Transport	15	5
Other	2	1

(WOGER: Whole Government Energy Report, Canberra 2002).

Table 4.17. Per capita (national average) water use

	L/(pers.day)
Africa	10–40
South America, Asia	50–100
France	135
(Cote d'Azur	239)
Germany, Austria	250–350
North America, Japan	400–600
Australia	500–800

In residential buildings alone the per capita use can be up to 800 L/day. This domestic consumption approximately divides as:

ablution and sanitation – 36%
cooking, washing up, laundry – 23%
household gardens – 41%

Obviously there are large variations with the type of accommodation unit (house and garden, or high-rise apartment block) and with the climate. In a dry climate more is used for gardening. A domestic swimming pool can lose 5–10 mm of water per day by evaporation, depending on the weather (more on a dry, hot and windy day) which on a $50\,m^2$ pool may add up to 250 to 500 L/day. In some cities of Australia severe water restrictions are current (due to the unprecedented draught): the limit is 140 L/(pers.day), above which penalty rates apply.

The commercial use is made up of components such as

offices –   120 L/pers.day
hotels –   1500 L/room.day
restaurants –   10 L/meal served
laundry –   40 L/kg of washing

All our fresh water is the product of solar energy. It causes evaporation, largely from ocean surfaces, and starts the hydrological cycle. Vapour laden air and clouds are carried by winds (which themselves are produced by differential solar heating). Precipitation (rain, snow) will also occur over land areas. Some of this may run off and form streams and rivers, some may be retained by the soil, some may percolate into porous subsoil strata. We may tap any of these sources, but all this water comes from precipitation.

Dry land areas of earth receive (on average) about 1000 mm rainfall per year, but this may vary between some 200 mm (e.g. in North Africa) and 2600 mm (in western parts of India and Central America). It also varies from year-to-year. An annual variation of ±20% is considered as highly reliable. Some desert areas may receive rain once in 10 years.

Gaining water can take many forms, from collecting roof water in tanks to large dams collecting run-off from their catchment area. Near-surface ground water may be obtained through shallow wells. Deeper water-bearing strata may be tapped by bore-holes. Natural springs may be made use of. Rivers can provide water by surface pumping, by wells near the flow-bed or by construction of dams to form water reservoirs. The problems are both the quantity and the quality of such supply.

River valley authorities or other water resources management bodies may exercise strict control both over the allocation and use of the available water and over the possible sources of water pollution. In some instances the whole catchment area of a water reservoir is controlled. It is a continuing struggle for both preserving the quality and to justly divide the water available among potential users. Water used for agricultural irrigation is a huge quantity and the right to use it is often disputed.

Potable water (for human consumption) must satisfy the following criteria:

- It must be clear, free of any suspended clay or silt. Many natural sources provide *turbid* water. Turbidity can be controlled by filtering.

- It must be without taste or odour. Taste and smell are caused by foreign matter, which should not be present in the water.
- It must not contain chemicals in dangerous or harmful quantities. Maximum permissible levels (in ppm i.e. parts per million) are established for many possible substances. Frequent analysis should ensure that these limits are not exceeded.
- It must be free of bacteria and other micro-organisms. Minute quantities of some are tolerable, but these should be checked by frequent counts. Most common one is the *bacillus coli*, which causes *enterocolitis*. A count of 100/mL is the acceptable limit.

Waterworks are usually operated by local authorities or water boards, being consortia of several such authorities. These include pumping, filtering and water treatment facilities. Sand filters can remove solid particles down to about 0.1 mm size. As most bacteria adhere to the surface of such particles, these will also be removed. Bacteria on their own are about 1 µm in size, and cannot be removed by filtering. If such bacteria are found after filtering, the water must be disinfected, most often by adding chlorine of 1 ppm ($1 \, g/m^3$). At the draw-off points chlorine should not exceed 0.2 ppm, as this could add an undesirable taste. Ozone treatment is equally effective, it is without taste or harmful effects, but it is expensive.

Long distance pipelines are designed for continuous flow from the source to local service reservoirs. The function of these is to even out the fluctuations of demand. In some countries (e.g. in the UK) many authorities 'pass the buck' to even out the flow in the local pipework: any residential unit is allowed only a 13 mm pipe connection and one tap on this service in the kitchen, all other outlets must be served from a high level storage tank or cistern to serve as a buffer. At peak times these may be almost emptied and will be refilled only slowly, through a float-valve.

4.4.1.1 Water supply

Water supply in buildings must be available for the following purposes:

- domestic: drinking, cooking, toilet flushing, as well as both hot and cold supply for baths, showers, basins, kitchen washing up and laundering
- fire-fighting: automatic sprinklers and hydrants (for use by the fire brigade) and hose reels (for occupants' use)
- environmental plant: air washing and humidification, evaporative cooling and heat transport (incl. cooling towers)
- external: garden hoses and sprinklers, car washing, etc.
- manufacturing: process cooling and industrial process water for a multitude of purposes.

The design and installation of the water system is often left to the licensed plumber, to serve all fittings indicated by the architectural plans. In larger buildings a consulting engineer may do this work. It is however the architect's task to show what fittings are to be installed and where. A few small points are worth remembering:

1 Grouping all the 'wet' areas would reduce both the water and the drainage pipework necessary.

2 It is both wasteful and irritating when opening a hot tap one has to wait for the hot water to arrive after discharging the cold water content of the 'dead leg' pipe. This is wasting much water, but also energy. After a short use of the hot water the dead leg pipe is full of hot water and will lose its heat in a short time, even if the pipe is insulated. In a residential unit it is the kitchen where a small amount of hot water is used quite frequently. It is therefore advisable to have the H/W system near the kitchen.

3 In a hotel or hostel type building a whole series of draw-off points may be served by a hot water loop. The hot water is slowly circulating (a small pump may be used) and it is available as soon as a tap is opened. The piping in this case should have a good insulation. Even then some heat may be lost, but much water would be saved. This has been mentioned in Section 1.6.2 (hot water supply) and shown diagrammatically in Fig. 1.109.

4 In buildings of more than 1 or 2 stories it is useful to have a tank full of 'fire reserve' water at the highest level. In many places this is a statutory requirement. Where service water storage is also a requirement, the two can be combined by using the piping arrangement shown in Fig. 4.45.

5 Up to the middle of the 20th century the piping was often installed on the outside of the building (often such piping was an afterthought, or a later addition in 'modernization'). Even in London's relatively mild winters this often lead to the freezing of water in the pipe and – as water expands as it freezes – this often caused cracks in the pipes and consequent leakages. Today all pipes are located internally, but it is useful not to 'bury' pipes in the building fabric, but place them into service ducts or make them accessible by other means (e.g. using removable cover plates). Plumbing repairs may cause consequential damage much more costly than the plumbing repair itself. Even the best pipework is unlikely to be trouble-free for more than some 30 years, whilst even the cheap and flimsy buildings would have a life expectancy of at least three times that.

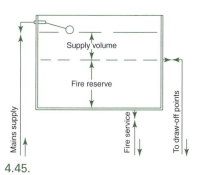

4.45.
Combined supply header and fire reserve tank.

4.4.2 Wastes

Our civilization, particularly our towns and cities produce a huge amount of waste. This includes solid, liquid and gaseous wastes and the following is to examine these in turn.

4.4.2.1 *Gaseous wastes*

Gaseous wastes today mostly consist of motor vehicle emissions and the discharge of power stations and heavy industry. In the past it consisted mostly of visible smoke, mainly fly ash, soot and (with internal combustion engines) some metallic particles: lead, mercury, cadmium. The thousands of smoking chimneys of residential districts, the chimney stacks of industries and railway steam engines were the prime causes of air pollution, especially of the London fogs and the sooty, grimy blackness of industrial cities.

The UK 'Clean Air Act' of 1956, the 1963 Act of the same name in the USA (and similar legislation in many other countries) radically changed the situation. Fuels were changed, new technologies were introduced, controlling agencies were established by governments and emissions were drastically reduced. Catalytic after-burners reduced motor vehicle emissions and power stations started building super-tall chimney stacks (up to 300 m). The latter helped the local atmosphere, but produced long distance effects, such as the sulphuric rains in Scandinavia caused by the tall chimney emissions of North of England power stations.

It is interesting to note how our understanding and our reactions change. In the 1950s all blocks of flats in Sydney had to have an incinerator (!), to reduce domestic solid wastes. Now these are banned and the air is much cleaner. Today buildings emit very little (if any) gaseous wastes, but emissions are only shifted: electricity consumption in buildings is responsible for huge amounts of CO_2, NO_x (sodium oxides) and SO_x (sulphurous oxides) emissions.

Much can be done to reduce such emissions. The use of various catalysts (platinum, aluminium) over the last decade reduced gas turbine emissions of sulphur, nitrogen and carbon monoxide from 25 to 2 ppm.

From the point-of-view of global warming CO_2 emissions are the largest problem, but some other gases have, on a unit quantity basis, a much greater global warming potential (GWP). If CO_2 is taken as GWP 1, a few others are:

- methane (CH_4) –   21
- nitrous oxide –   290
- CFC11 –   1500
- CFC12 –   4500

Agriculture, notably the cattle industry (intestinal methane production or 'enteric fermentat' of cows) is the greatest producer of methane.

4.4.2.2   Liquid wastes

Liquid wastes from buildings are largely the product of our sanitary arrangements. Since the 19th century our disposal systems, both sanitary fittings and the supporting pipework have improved tremendously. Up to the 1950s the *two-pipe system* was generally used, separating the waste water pipes (the discharge of baths, showers, basins, kitchen sinks and laundry tubs) and the 'soil' pipes (servicing WC pans, urinals and slop hoppers). Subsequently the *one-pipe system* took over and the installations were much simplified.

Today, at least at the domestic scale, it is taken as desirable (and beginning to be adopted) to separate the 'grey water', what was earlier referred to as 'waste water' and to make use of it, for flushing the toilet, watering the garden, or hosing down the driveway. This would obviously need a storage tank and separate pipework. The 'black water', the effluent discharged by soil fittings, must be connected to the public sewerage system to be treated at 'sewage farms'. In less densely built-up areas, or for isolated houses this effluent may be treated within the site, in septic tanks.

These domestic scale septic tanks and the public sewage treatment plants are based on the same principles. Figure 4.46 shows the section and plan of a domestic septic tank. The first chamber is just a holding tank, sometimes referred to as the liquefying chamber, where *anaerobic bacteria* decompose organic matter (consuming some 30% of organic solids), which constitutes the *primary treatment*. Methane (CH_4) and CO_2 are produced and must be

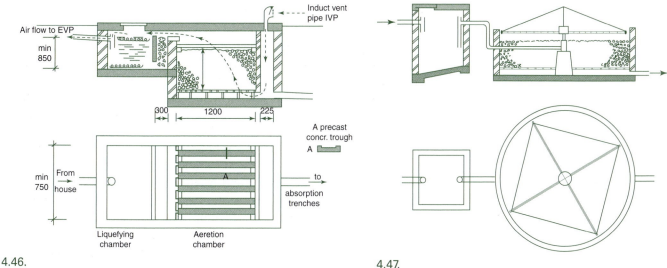

4.46.
A built-*in-situ* domestic septic tank.

4.47.
A rotary aeration facility.

vented to the atmosphere. A slightly modified set-up may allow the methane to be collected and used as a fuel (see Section 4.2.3, under biomass conversion). In some large-scale sewage treatment plants the methane collected is used to generate electricity in the MW order of magnitude. One plant in Sydney operates a methane-based CHP system, producing 3 MW electricity and 3 MW of thermal energy.

Secondary treatment is provided in the aeration chamber which (in this case) is a series of trays allowing the effluent to be sprinkled over a gravel (or crushed rock) bed, where on the surface of gravel particles *aerobic bacteria* breed (Fig. 4.46). These will consume a further 60% of organic matter. Good ventilation of this chamber must be ensured from an induct vent pipe, (IVP) through the aerobic chamber to the educt vent pipe (EVP). An alternative to this chamber (for larger systems) is an open, circular gravel bed with a slowly rotating spraying system (Fig. 4.47) to distribute the effluent from the anaerobic tank.

The effluent at this stage is rich in phosphates and nitrates: a good fertilizer. It may be used for watering, but it must not be allowed to enter natural waterways, as it may cause algae blooming. These have a large BOD (biochemical oxygen demand), deoxigenate the water, which may thus no longer be able to support aquatic life and may become abiotic.

A *tertiary treatment* of sewage (a more complicated process and not practicable at the scale of an individual house) may remove phosphates and nitrates and produce a marketable fertilizer. The solid residue (sludge) of the primary and secondary treatment may be dried and incinerated. The ashes left may be used for land fill ('concentration and confinement') or loaded on barges and dumped at sea ('dilution and dispersal').

4.4.2.3 Solid wastes

Solid wastes, (refuse or trash) normally collected by garbage trucks (using a variety of mechanized systems). The average waste produced is about 1 kg/pers.day in the UK, 1.5 kg/pers.day in Australia and up to 2.5 kg/pers.day in the USA. The collection, handling and disposal of this is quite a problem. Garbage tips have been created in disused excavations, quarries or clay pits, filled, compacted and covered with earth. In flat areas quite large garbage hills have been created, covered with earth and landscaped. However, we are running out of space for the creation of such garbage dumps.

Large-scale incinerator plants have been built, some of which can be used to generate steam and drive an electricity generation system. Local authorities are quite desperate in trying to reduce the bulk of such wastes. Various levels of recycling arrangements have been introduced. At the simplest level residents are asked to separate the recyclable and non-recyclable wastes, in other cases paper, glass, metals and plastics are collected separately, and directed to various recycling plants. The paper recycling industries are now quite significant, but only a few plants are commercially successful. Most require some public assistance, at least to get started.

The possibility of collecting methane gas generated in garbage dumps has been mentioned in Section 4.2.3.1 (methane gas as biomass conversion). The disposal of toxic industrial waste is quite a problem, but beyond the scope of this work.

4.5 SUSTAINABILITY ISSUES

4.5.1 Historical background

Environmental degradation was already the main concern of the Stockholm UNEP conference in 1972. Barbara Ward and Rene Dubos (1972) well summarized the situation in their book: *Only one earth.* In the following year the OPEC oil embargo brought home the realization of the finite nature of our fossil fuel supplies. The three main problem areas identified were

1 population explosion
2 resource depletion
3 environmental degradation.

Already in 1973 the RIBA (the then president Alex Gordon) initiated the LL/LF/LE (long life, loose fit, low energy) movement. The philosophical basis of this was that it would be ecologically beneficial to erect buildings which last, which are designed in a way to remain adaptable for changed uses and which use little energy in their operation. The term 'sustainability' did not exist then, but it was a programme for sustainable architecture.

The extreme view was that any 'development' would harm the environment, but it was recognized that the LDCs (Less developed countries) do have the right to develop, as the ideal of equity demands it. The argument was resolved by accepting the necessity for development, as long as it is sustainable. The Brundtland report (1987) introduced the term and gave the definition as:

> Sustainable development is development that meets the needs of the present without compromising the ability of future generations to meet their own needs.

The latter point has been labelled as 'inter-generational equity'.

In 1987 the Montreal protocol agreed on the phasing out of organo-fluorides, which are affecting the ozone layer and as a consequence admit more UV irradiation (whilst also contributing to the greenhouse effect). The Intergovernmental Panel on Climate Change (IPCC) reported in 1990 and firmly established that the climate is changing and that this is largely anthropogenic, caused by the emission of greenhouse gases by humanity.

The 'Earth Summit' (1992) UNCED (United Nations Conference on Environment and Development) considered environmental degradation together with resource depletion and broadened the discourse in Agenda 21 and with the 'Rio Declaration' laid down the principles of sustainable development.

Equity for all humanity is one of the aims of Agenda 21, but inter-generational equity is perhaps even more important.

The UN Framework Convention on Climate Change (UNFCCC) called a meeting in Kyoto, which reached a very watered-down agreement in 1997: the reduction of 1990 level of CO_2 emissions by 5% by 2012. The 169 countries ratified the agreement by December 2006, with the notable absence of the greatest emitters: the USA, Australia,* China and India.

Architecture joined the movement by the *Declaration of Interdependence for a sustainable future* at the Chicago Congress of the IUA in 1993 (see Appendix 1). Many national bodies and institutions of architecture adopted this declaration and produced energy and environmental policies. As an example, Appendix 2 presents the Environment Policy of the RAIA (Royal Australian Institute of Architects). Such declarations and policy statements are fine words only, but even if not immediately effective, they have a significance: they imply a commitment which individuals must recognize at the risk of being 'politically incorrect', they must pay at least lip-service to these and with frequent repetitions they do become the accepted norm. Even if an individual fails to act accordingly, at least he/she will have a guilty conscience about it.

4.5.2 Philosophical basis

Some authors (e.g. Radford and Williamson, 2002) argue that the notion of sustainability, (thus sustainable architecture) is a social construct, that it implies an action plan, therefore it must have an ethical basis. A good rational materialist would suggest that this is back-to-front: the physical need for survival must dictate a new ethics, an environmental or ecological ethics. In Marxist terms: the rest of it is 'superstructure'. In Maslow's hierarchy of human needs (see box in Section 1.2.2) the physical/biological needs are at the top.

Some studio/design teachers argue that teaching environmental science has no place in architecture courses, or at best it is a side-issue. The counter-argument is that environmental/architectural science deals with questions of survival, whilst they talk about the icing on the cake. They are playing the violin whilst Rome is burning. They do not realize the urgency of fire-fighting.

Ethical systems may be based on some (alleged) 'divine' proclamation or pronouncement (e.g. the ten commandments of Moses) or some speculatively

---

*Australia recently signed the Kyoto protocol.

derived notion of duty (such as Kant's *categorical imperative*), or some other set of values shared by the group, by a professional body or by society as a whole. Most such differing ethical systems are built on shifting sand. Conflicts arise not just between different nations, different social systems, different religions (or other irrational belief-systems) but also within a liberal democratic society, e.g. between different interest-groups. This is a question of horizon. Individual survival and well-being depends on societal survival. The survival of societies depends on the existence of our global eco-system. It is suggested that, if humanity is to survive, our behaviour must be governed by a globally based environmental ethics.

Over three decades ago humanity's survival was recognized to be threatened by the three trends mentioned above (in Section 4.5.1). Within the third of these, environmental degradation, global warming became the dominant threat. Local environmental problems are important, but must be seen in the context of the global problem, the problem of survival.

This concern for humanity's survival has been accused of being 'anthropocentric', implying that this is 'speciesism', just as bad as racism, that it is our duty and obligation to protect nature, the fauna and flora. Terms like 'duty and obligation' implies some external dictate or command. There is no need to postulate any such a dictate. We can unashamedly profess to be anthropocentric, whilst realizing that we are part of a global system and the preservation of that system, of bio-diversity, of the natural environment is in our selfishly perceived best interest.

This environmental ethics dictates that our behaviour, our actions must serve, and certainly not harm, the sustainability of our habitat. It is thus a very pragmatic and rational ethics.

4.5.3 Social implications

A diagram (Fig. 4.48) proposed by Meadows & Meadows (1972) indicates that the vast majority of people are primarily concerned with the here and now (vertical spatial scale, horizontal time scale), partly because they have to struggle to survive to the next day, but partly also because of a very limited vision and understanding. Few people have a broader horizon and a longer term view. Even those who have a global perspective and look at the distant future must think of the next minute and the next step, most of the time. However, that next step should be governed by the global view.

'Globalization' is a highly controversial issue. It is an unavoidable necessity, but its meaning must be clarified. Is it the 'Workers-of-the-world unite!' slogan of the 'dictatorship of the proletariat', or does it mean the unrestrained global market of multinational corporations? Globalization, as it happens today, is in fact extremely short-sighted. Its driving force is the individual, or small group (shareholders') interest, short-term profit. This may be acceptable, if it is within the framework set by far-sighted governments which represent the people. Acceptable, as long as it is realized that there are measures of value other than money. Acceptable, as long as these are not in conflict with the global interest of humanity's survival.

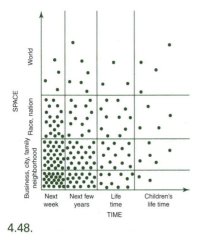

4.48.
Human horizons.

Dictatorships are often envied for being able to produce quick and significant results, changes without procrastination, but lasting and beneficial changes can only be based on consensus. It has been said that democracy is a luxury, which a large part of the world can ill-afford. It is painfully difficult to achieve such a consensus and international cooperation is even more difficult, as shown by the Kyoto agreement. After more than 10 years it has not been ratified by the world's largest producer of CO_2, (the USA) and the largest *per capita* producer (Australia).

However, there is no other way. Globalization, in the sense of democracy with international cooperation is the only possibility to avoid global destruction. The role of a national government is to ensure the well-being of its people without harming others, in harmony with the global eco-system. Anything else would be suicidal.

There are millions of conflicting interests, interest-groups at work. These can be resolved and channelled in the direction of the global interest by information, education, enlightenment. There are encouraging signs. Information is influencing public opinion and politicians depend on the public opinion. Within this context, is it possible to enlighten and influence our own profession?

4.5.4 What can architects do?

Buildings and associated uses are responsible for a large part of the environmental load caused by humanity:

- 42% of all energy consumption
- 40% of all atmospheric emissions
- 30% of all raw materials used
- 25% of water usage
- 25% of solid wastes
- 20% of liquid wastes.

All these can be strongly influenced by architects and designers.

The main practical question is how the above noble ideas can be translated into actions at the level of everyday reality. Design may be constrained by clients and regulatory authorities. However architects work at many levels and may influence the development process. Architects may be employed by client organizations. As facility managers may influence the client on building needs. They may be involved in site selection and feasibility studies. They may assist in formulating the brief, which may involve a series of background studies concerning organizational and social aspects, as well as ergonomics and environmental requirements.

The process from briefing to design is an iterative one. The architect may ask for clarification of the brief and may influence the client by expert advice. The conceptual design is often separated from the detailed design of the fabric and contract documentation. It may even be done by a different architect or firm of architects. Supervision of the building work and contract management is a distinctly separate task. Even if the whole process is carried out by one firm, different individuals may specialize on certain tasks.

Many building companies employ their own architects. Many architects specialize in interior design for shops, for shop front design or office interior 'fit-out'. Some become writers, critics, journalists, educators or theoreticians.

Architects may work for local authorities and may have an influence on town planning and urban design, may have various regulatory tasks. They may have a role in the building approval process, which is not just a yes/no task, it may involve negotiations with the designer and developer to modify the proposal in the interest of the 'public good'.

At each of these levels environmental issues are involved and must be considered. Early decisions may have unforeseen consequences: they may preclude later, environmentally sound decisions. Every action may have environmental consequences. Environmental and sustainability issues are survival issues, thus must have top priority and a decisive role. 'Minor' compromises should be avoided as these may add up and render a project completely unsustainable.

Amongst the many roles the architect can play, the one central task is the design of buildings. Design dominates the architectural ethos. However, design is much more than just the 'looks' of the product. Sustainability, how the building works, how it uses resources can be considered under four headings: *site, energy, materials and wastes*.

4.5.4.1 Site

Land is precious, not only in monetary terms. All building activity disturbs the land, the site. Such disturbance ought to be minimized. Undisturbed land, supporting an intact ecology is particularly valuable. If possible, its use should be avoided. This could be a step in preserving bio-diversity. The use of already disturbed, possibly derelict land would be preferable. Rehabilitation of disturbed or neglected land is desirable.

Buildings should fit their environment: if possible, large-scale earth-works should be avoided. If earth-works are unavoidable, the top soil, which is a valuable living system, should be preserved, stored and used in landscaping. All possible steps should be taken to prevent soil erosion, to promote land and soil conservation and, wherever possible, improvement.

Site selection also has planning implications. There is a dichotomy and argument:

- on the one hand the lobby of builders and developers to get land re-zoned for residential development, for subdivision, they claim that the unavailability of land is the cause of housing shortage
- on the other hand planners generally agree that higher residential densities are desirable, to reduce commuting distances and generally all travel needs (thus making feasible a good public transport system), to reduce the cost of piped and wired public services, but also to preserve unspoilt (or agricultural) land and prevent urban sprawl.

The latter argument is more in sympathy with the ideal of sustainability.

Architects may have an influence in this argument, but may also devise solutions to make high density living more acceptable, even desirable.

4.5.4.2 Energy

Energy is used in buildings at two levels:

Operational energy, (O) annually used for heating, cooling, ventilation, lighting and servicing the building. This has been discussed in Section 4.3 above and, indeed, throughout this book.

Capital energy, (C) or energy embodied in the materials and building processes. It is interesting to note that in the early 1970s, when building energy analysis was in its infancy, the O/C ratio was around 5, i.e. the building would use as much energy in 5 years as was necessary to produce its materials and construct it. For a very poorly constructed building the ratio was as little as 2.5 (i.e. 2.5 years). Recent analyses show ratios of 30 to 40. One study even concluded that it was 50.

The reason for this is two-fold buildings have been improved and such improvements would have increased the capital energy (embodied energy), e.g. thermal insulation, but also many plastics and metal products. At the same time the better buildings resulted in a reduced operational energy consumption. In the 1970s efforts were focused on reducing this operational energy use. Now the major concern shifted and attempts are made to reduce the embodied energy.

The embodied energy, or to be precise: the 'process energy requirement' (PER) of some materials is shown in Table 4.18.

There are large differences in published data regarding the embodied energy of materials, partly due to local differences in the industrial processes, but partly also due to the different calculation methods. For example some results published in India show cement as 1.86 kWh/kg (rather than the above 5.6 shown in this Table) and PVC as 44 kWh/kg (instead of the 22.22). The same source (instead of the 9.44 kWh/kg shown for mild steel) distinguishes rods: 7.83, RSJs: 11.9 and RHS 18.14 kWh/kg. In broad terms two methods of calculation can be distinguished:

> the **analytical method** follows the processes from gaining the raw
> material through various stages of manufacture and transportation to

Table 4.18. The PER of some building materials (in kWh/kg)

Air dried sawn hardwood	0.14	Wood particle board	2.22
Stabilised earth	0.19	Plywood	2.89
Concrete blocks	0.39	Glued-laminated timber	3.05
Precast tilt-up concrete	0.52	Medium density fibreboard	3.14
In-situ cast concrete	0.47	Glass	3.53
Precast steam-cured concrete	0.55	Hardboard	6.69
Kiln-dried sawn hardwood	0.56	Mild steel	9.44
Clay bricks	0.69	Galvanized mild steel	10.55
Gypsum plaster	0.80	Acrylic paint	17.08
Kiln-dried softwood	0.94	Zinc	14.17
Autoclaved aerated concrete	1.00	PVC	22.22
Plasterboard	1.22	Plastics in general	25.00
Cement	5.60	Copper	27.78
Fibrous cement	2.11	Synthetic rubber	30.56
Granite slabs	1.64	Aluminium	47.00

Table 4.19. Embodied energy of some building materials (in kWh/kg)

Low <1 kWh/kg	Sand, gravel	0.01
	Wood	0.1
	Concrete	0.2
	Sand-lime brickwork	0.4
	Lightweight concrete	0.5
Medium 1–10 kWh/kg	Plasterboard	1.0
	Brickwork	1.2
	Lime	1.5
	Cement	2.2
	Mineral wool	3.9
	Glass	6.0
	Porcelain	6.1
High >10 kWh/kg	Plastics	10
	Steel	10
	Lead	14
	Zinc	15
	Copper	16
	Aluminium	56

the installation in the final product: the building and adds up all the energy used;

*the **statistical method** examines the particular industry of a country, a state, or a region, attempts to establish the total energy use by that industry as well as its total output; dividing the latter into the former gives the embodied energy per unit mass (or other production unit) (Table 4.19).*

The best data are likely to be the integration of results of the two methods.

Table 4.19 is based on a number of different sources and groups building materials into three broad categories: low, medium and high-energy materials. The comparison between the two tables (18 and 19) is a good illustration of this point. Note also that the numbers in Table 4.18 imply an accuracy which is unlikely to exist.

If an existing building is to be improved, the first step is to carry out an energy audit. This should also follow a dual approach:

1 List all the energy user installations, equipment or appliances, establish their energy use rating (W) and the duration of use (h) to obtain an energy use figure (Wh or kWh). The time-base is normally be 1 year.
2 Summarize all the energy 'imports', electricity and gas bills, any solid or liquid fuel used. For comparability all these should be converted into kWh unit. For this the conversion factors (calorific values) given in Table 4.20 can be used.

Results of the two approaches should be identical; if not then they should be examined and reconciled. Approach (1) should be revealing: show the items that are unreasonably high in energy consumption and should be improved.

Table 4.20. Calorific values of some fuels

Fuel	Energy value	Unit
Light (gas-) oil	10.6	kWh/L
Heavy fuel oil (class G)	11.7	
Natural gas	10.6	
Propane	12.9	
Butane	12.8	
Coal	7.5–8.3	kWh/kg
Brown coal	4.5–6.3	
Coke	7.9	
Methane	15.4	
Mydrogen	34.2	

Some authors distinguish three types of energy audits: preliminary, targeted and comprehensive. A *preliminary audit* involves a walk-through inspection, collection of energy bills; it is quick, it can be used as a feasibility study for a more detailed audit. A *targeted audit* may result from the preliminary study, if it identified some significant shortcomings or selected system, e.g. the lighting installation or the boiler system. It would produce recommendations for upgrading or improvements.

A *comprehensive audit* is the most time-consuming and thorough (but also most expensive) exercise. It would involve tracing the energy flows and may involve extensive measurements. Such an energy audit will also be the basis of an energy management programme. Many countries have standards for the methodology of energy audits (e.g. AS.2725).

4.5.4.3 Materials

Materials selection must be influenced by this embodied energy, but also by a number of other issues affecting sustainability of their use. A typical evaluation system (BMAS = building materials assessment system) uses 14 criteria, as shown in Table 4.21. In using such a table for evaluating a material a score of 0 to 5 is awarded against each criterion, rating its environmental impact. Thus 0 is no impact, 5 is much impact. 'Help' tables are available to assist such scoring. Then each score is squared (to get a better resolution) and the weighting factors (shown in the table) are applied to each score.

The sum of the 14 squared and weighted scores is the 'ecological factor' (EF) of the material. This is not claimed to be more than a qualitative guidance figure. The scoring can be biased and the weighting factors have been established by seeking an 'expert consensus'. However, this is the most comprehensive system for judging building materials from the sustainability viewpoint.

It is worth noting that the criteria are strongly interconnected, e.g. although timber has low of embodied energy, it will have a low eco-rating only if it comes from renewable resources, i.e. if it is plantation timber. If it comes from 'original growth' forests, produced by a clean-felling method, possibly causing soil erosion, its EF will be quite high.

Table 4.21. BMAS: building materials assessment system

Group		Criteria	Weighting	grp.
	1	Damage to the environment in the extraction of raw material	3	
	2	Extent of damage relative to the amount of material produced	2	
	3	Abundance of source or renewability of material	4	
	4	Recycled content	3	12
Manufacture	5	Solid and liquid wastes in manufacture and production	3	
	6	Air pollution in manufacture and production	4	
	7	Embodied energy (energy used for its production)	5	12
Construction	8	Energy used for transportation to the site	3	
	9	Energy used on site for assembly and erection	1	
	10	On-site waste, including packaging	2	6
In use	11	Maintenance required during life cycle	3	
	12	Environmental effects during life cycle (e.g. toxic emissions)	3	6
Demolition	13	Energy use in and effects of demolition at end of life cycle	2	
	14	Recyclability of demolished material	4	6

A simpler method developed by Lawson (1996) gives an 'environmental rating' of various building products on a straightforward 5-point scale:

1: poor,   2: very good,   3: good,   4: fair and   5: poor

See data sheet D.4.2.

4.5.4.4 Wastes

Wastes have been considered in some detail in Section 4.4.2 above and it is apparent from that discussion that architects can have a strong influence on how wastes are disposed of.

In addition, attempts should be made to retain as much of any stormwater on the site as possible: collection and storage of roof water, using soft surfaces rather than paving to promote percolation, the soaking of water into the soil (and replenish the ground water reserve). Reducing the run-off would also help soil conservation: preventing erosion.

4.5.5 Complex rating systems

Many building energy rating systems are in use world-wide, but recently these have been extended to incorporate 'greenhouse rating' and other environmental issues. Greenhouse gas emission is an important measure of sustainability, but it can only be estimated. Energy use can be calculated with reasonale accuracy, and it is often used to calculate CO_2 emissions. It is suggested that at the building level the following conversion factors can be used for various forms of energy consumed:

electricity (average) –   0.72 kg/kWh
solid fuel (coal, coke) –   0.34
fuel oil (paraffin, kerosene) – 0.29
gas (natural) –   0.21

Many building sustainability rating systems have been devised in various countries, but there is no sign of consensus emerging as yet.

In the USA the LEED (Leadership in Energy and Environmental Design) rating system has been created by USGBC (US Green Building Council) and is in operation. It is also available through Wikipedia (the free encyclopaedia on the Web).

The Swedish *EcoEffect* rating method is based on a life cycle analysis (LCA). It considers energy use, materials use, indoor and outdoor environment. The various effects are weighted by using a complicated 'analytical hierarchic process'. It is emphasized that the single figure index produced hides the causes and problems, therefore it must be supplemented by 'environmental profiles', stating the criteria and weightings used.

The UK point-scoring BREEAM[1] (Building Research Establishment Environmental Assessment Method) is broad, but relied on very qualitative judgements.

The European CRISP (Construction and City Related Sustainability Indicators) network includes 24 organizations of 16 countries. It is based on the work of CIB (Commission International du Bâtiment), notably their project CIBW 082. It is aimed at creating a standardized terminology, methodology, measures of sustainability and a data-base.

In Australia ABERS (Australian Building Environmental Rating Scheme) has recently been introduced.

One state government body, SEDA (Sustainable Development Authority of NSW) uses a Building Greenhouse Rating (BGR) system for commercial buildings, awarding 1 to 5 stars for poor to exceptionally good buildings. This would distinguish common services and tenants' energy use and WBR or Whole Building Rating. Its major component is energy use, but it includes greenhouse gas emissions, at least in qualitative terms. Star ratings are based on the following criteria:

1 star: POOR
Poor energy management or outdated systems. The building is consuming much unnecessary energy. There are cost-effective changes that could be implemented to improve energy consumption, cut operating costs and reduce greenhouse emissions.

2 stars: GOOD
Average building performance. The building has some elements of energy efficiency in place and reflects the current market average. There is still scope for cost-effective improvements and minor changes may improve on energy and operating costs.

3 stars: VERY GOOD
Current market best practice. The building offers very good systems and management practices and reflects an awareness of the financial and environmental benefits of optimizing energy use.

---

[1]not to be mistaken for BREDEM (BRE Domestic Energy Model), see Section 1.4.4.1.

Table 4.22. Limits of CO_2 emission for greenhouse rating in $kg.CO_2/m^2$

Stars max:	Darwin					Brisbane					Melbourne				
	1	2	3	4	5	1	2	3	4	5	1	2	3	4	5
Base building	148	124	101	77	53	215	181	146	112	77	225	194	163	132	101
Tenancy	116	96	76	56	36	172	142	112	82	53	160	137	115	92	70
Whole building	264	220	177	133	89	387	323	259	194	130	385	331	278	224	171

4 stars: EXCELLENT

Strong performance. Excellent energy performance due to design and management practices or high efficiency systems and equipment or low greenhouse-intensive fuel supply.

5 stars: EXCEPTIONAL

Best building performance. The building is as good as it can be due to integrated design, operation, management and fuel choice.

The assessment of CO_2 emissions is an important contributor to Building Greenhouse Rating and in some cases limits for rating are given directly in terms of CO_2/m^2, without reference to energy use.

Table 4.22 gives a summary of such numerical limits of CO_2 emissions in terms of CO_2/m^2 on the basis of which the star ratings would be awarded for office buildings. This is very much a function of climate and as an indication, values for three states are shown: Darwin, Northern Territory (a hot-humid climate), Brisbane, Queensland (a warm-humid, temperate climate), Melbourne, Victoria (a cool-temperate climate).

One popular measure of sustainability is the 'ecological footprint'. Originally conceived as a method to compare the sustainability of different populations, or of the lifestyle of individuals. It is rather a measure of the ecological load an object (a project, an establishment, a suburb or indeed a city) would impose on the environment, related to the area of agricultural land that would be required to supply all materials used and energy consumed by that object (Wackernagel *et al.* 1996).

There are many methods of calculating it and there is no consensus. There are almost as many critics of the whole concept as there are users of it. At best it can assist the qualitative comparison of objects not too dissimilar. It may be used as an educational tool. Several self-assessment methods are available on the web. One exercise suggests that a city, such as Sydney would need an area 27 times its actual area. The footprint of an individual is assessed in terms of his/her food, shelter, transport and goods/services use. A reasonably frugal person would have a footprint of some 7 ha, but some may go as high as 30.

4.5.6 Economics

Ecology and economics are often made out to be in opposition to each other. It is worth noting that both words come from the Greek *οικοσ* (oikos), meaning house, habitat or household. The –*logy* ending means *study of...* whilst the –*nomy* ending implies the *law of...* So, ecology is the study of and economy is the laws of our house or housekeeping. Perhaps two sides of the same coin?

There are many instances when a slightly increased capital cost would result in substantial savings in running cost. It may be easy to convince a rationally-minded client when designing his/her own house to spend a little extra money, say on insulation, which will then reduce the heating costs.

Problems may arise when a developer is producing a building for immediate sale, who has no interest in reducing the operating costs. It should be pointed out that buyers now also have a critical attitude and can gauge the added value of an environmentally sound or 'sustainable' building. There is also a prestige value added to such buildings. However if the architect is acting as an advisor to the buyer, (s)he must be able to ascertain whether the building is really good and 'sustainable' or only claimed to be so. Indeed the various energy rating systems (discussed in Section 4.3.2.3) may give an indication of the quality of the house considered.

Assessment of investment proposals is usually based on a cost/benefit analysis, comparing the investment cost with the longer-term benefit. Its outcome very much depends on the chosen 'accounting horizon', the useful life assumed and the limitation of indirect costs and externalities taken into account. Often the crude or simple pay-back period is used in economic analysis or investment decisions.

More sophisticated methods take into account the 'cost of money', i.e. how much interest would need to be paid if the sum to be invested were to be borrowed, or the interest the invested money would earn otherwise, Such a comparison can be done using a discounted cash-flow technique, to find the *present worth* of future savings, to compare it with the capital investment. Both the interest ('discount') rate and any inflation rate must be considered. Method sheet M.4.1 presents the details of this method.

An alternative to present worth calculations is the LCA or life cycle cost analysis. This may include not only the direct cost comparison, but also the maintenance cost of the alternatives and their life expectancy. Very often the appearance, the perceived quality, the prestige value of the alternatives, the expected future re-sale value must also be taken into account. The architect, whether decision maker or advisor, should also be fully aware of locally applicable and current subsidies, incentive schemes, tax benefits which may be applicable to one of the alternatives but not the other.

The economic argument is not necessarily dominant. The Property Council (formerly BOMA, the Building Owners and Managers Association) of Australia found that only 9% of those surveyed believe that environmental and energy issues are irrelevant to their business and for the others the main reasons for implementing environmental and energy management policies are

community relations –   39%
competitiveness –   24%
market opportunities – 23%
shareholder pressure –   5%
it is irrelevant –   9%

On the other hand tenants are keen to have better lighting and thermal conditions (for increased productivity) and to reduce energy consumption (thus operating costs).

The financial balance of such cost/benefit comparisons is often referred to as the 'bottom line'. Recently a new term has been introduced: the 'triple bottom line'. This means an assessment of *social value* and *eco-efficiency* in addition to the conventional economic/financial balance.

DATA SHEETS AND METHOD SHEETS (RESOURCES)

DATA SHEET D.4.1

Annual energy intensity in kWh/(m²y) for various building types*

Schools		
	Nursery	370–430
	Primary, no pool	180–240
	Primary, with pool	230–310
	Secondary, no pool	190–240
	Secondary, with pool	250–310
	Secondary, with sports centre	250–280
	Special, non-residential	250–340
	Special, residential	380–500
	Colleges	230–280
	Universities	325–355
Hospitality	Restaurants	410–430
	Pubs	340–470
	Fast-food outlets	1450–1750
	Motorway service areas	880–1200
	Hotel, small	240–330
	Hotel, medium size	310–420
	Hotel, large	290–420
Shops	Department stores	520–620
	Non-food shops	280–320
	Small food shops, general	510–580
	Small fruit & vegetable shops	400–450
	Variety stores	720–830
	Supermarkets	1070–1270
	Supermarket with bakery	1130–1350
	Banks	180–240
Offices	Small, <2000 m², naturally ventilated	200–250
	Large, >2000 m², naturally ventilated	230–290
	Small, <2000 m², air conditioned	220–310
	Large, >2000 m², air conditioned	250–419
	Computer rooms	340–480
Sports	Sports centre, no pool	200–340
	Sports centre, with pool	570–840
	Swimming pool	1050–1390
Public buildings	Library	200–280
	Museum, art gallery	220–310
	Theatre	600–900
	Cinema	650–780

* 'fair performance range', after CIBSE.

Star-band limits for the Australian NatHERS rating scheme

Number of stars awarded up to these limits in kWh/(m^{2}y)

Stars:	1	2	3	4	5
Darwin	242	94	133	117	103
Brisbane	80	44	33	25	17
Sydney	130	91	58	40	30
Melbourne	119	94	78	64	51
Hobart	205	129	110	86	60

Compare these with the German limits of 100–30 kWh/(m^{2}y) for new houses, as described in Section 4.3.2.3.

DATA SHEET D.4.2

Environmental rating of some materials (on a 5-point scale)

The 5-point rating scale is:
1: poor, 2: very good, 3: good, 4: fair and 5: poor

Any material or product is to be rated for
seven categories or attributes, as shown below
(18 materials presented, but the method can be used for any other material)

	Raw material availability	Environmental impact	Embodied energy	Product life span	Freedom from maintenance	Product re-use potential	Material recyclability
Plantation-grown sawn softwood	4	4	4	3	2	2	1
Hardwood from native forests	2	2	5	4	3	4	1
Wood fibre hardboard	4	4	2	3	2	1	3
Medium density fibreboard (MDF)	5	4	3	3	3	3	2
particleboard (chipboard)	5	4	3	3	3	1	4
plywood	4	4	3	4	3	3	1
glued laminated timber	4	4	4	4	3	4	2
plastics (synthetic polymers)	3	2	3	4	4	1	3
stabilised earth (cement or bitumen)	4	5	4	3	3	1	5
building stone (sawn)	3	2	3	4	4	4	3
clay bricks	4	3	4	5	5	2	3
cement-concrete products	3	3	4	5	5	1	3
fibrous cement (pine fibre)	4	4	3	5	5	1	1
glass	3	3	3	5	4	3	4
steel	4	3	3	4	3	3	5
aluminium	4	1	1	5	4	2	5
copper	2	1	2	5	5	1	5
lead and zinc	2	1	2	5	5	1	5

No attempt should be made to add up these numbers.
The rating is purely qualitative and in the original no numbering is used.
It is simply a convenience or short-hand to identify the qualitative rating.

For example if $i = 6\%$
the increased sum is

$$A = 100 \times (1 + 0.06)^3 = 119.10$$
$$119.1 < 150$$

the present worth of $150 is

$$P = 150 \times (1 + 0.06)^{-3} = 125.94$$
$$125.94 > 100$$

Both suggest that the $150 in 3 years' time is better

For example I want to buy a solar water heater. Price: $2300, less $500 government subsidy, thus net $C = \$1800$. This would save me annually $235 in electricity. My criterion is that it should pay for itself in 10 years (amortization period).
Total saving: $S = 235 \times 10 = 2350$ thus $S > C$, $2350 > 1800$, it is OK.
However, at an interest rate of 8%, $i = 0.08$ the present worth factor would be

$$F = \frac{1 - 1.08^{-10}}{0.08} = 6.71$$

thus the saving is

$$S = 235 \times 6.71 = 1576$$

thus $S < C$, $1576 < 1800$, it is not OK

METHOD SHEET M.4.1

'Present worth' and the discounted cash-flow method

1 The question is which would I prefer: to get $100 now, or $150 in 3 years' time? Or in more formal terms: what is the *present worth* of $150 payable in 3 years? This can be assessed by using the compound interest expression in reverse: an amount invested at **p**resent (P) at an annual **i**nterest rate (i) for a number of years (y) will increase to an **a**mount (A) equal to the invested amount plus the compound interest earned:

$$A = P + (1 + i)^y \tag{1}$$

from which P can be expressed as

$$P = A \times (1 + i)^{-y} \tag{2}$$

where P is referred to as the present worth of an amount A payable (or saved) in y years.

2 If we have a regular annual sum (B, benefit) saved (or payable) annually, the present worth of this will be

$$P = B \frac{(1 + i)^y - 1}{i(1 + i)^y} = B \frac{1 - (1 + i)^{-y}}{i} \tag{3}$$

the latter part of this expression is referred to as the *present worth factor*

$$F = \frac{1 - (1 + i)^{-y}}{i} \tag{4}$$

3 If a capital investment (C) results in an annual benefit (B) then the *simple pay-back period* is the number of years when the accumulated benefits become equal to the investment:

$C = B \times y$, from which y can be expressed as

$$y = C/B \tag{5}$$

Total savings:

$S = B \times F$ where   and F is found from eq. (4)

The investment is worth-while if $S > C$

If the annual inflation is taken into account, and the rate is $r = 0.04$ (from eq. 6)

$$F' = \frac{1}{0.04}\left[1 - \left(\frac{1.04}{1.08}\right)^{10}\right] = 7.85$$

$S = 235 \times 7.85 = 1844.75$

thus $S > C$, $1844.75 > 1800$, it is OK
(marginally)

if the inflationary increase of the annual benefit is also taken into account then (eq. 7)

$$F'' = \frac{1.04}{0.04}\left[1 - \left(\frac{1.04}{1.08}\right)^{10}\right] = 8.17$$

$S = 235 \times 8.17 = 1920$

thus $S > C$, $1920 > 1800$, it is OK
the investment is well worth it

4 In an inflationary climate the anticipated rate of annual inflation (r) must be taken into account. Eq. (4) will become

$$F' = \frac{1}{i - r}\left[1 - \left(\frac{1+r}{1+i}\right)^{y}\right] \tag{6}$$

but if inflation will cause the annual benefit, B, (or operating cost) itself also to increase, then

$$F'' = \frac{1+r}{i - r}\left[1 - \left(\frac{1+r}{1+i}\right)^{y}\right] \tag{7}$$

METHOD SHEET M.4.2

Performance of flat plate solar collectors

If the operation of any system is to be understood, the following three steps are suggested:

1 describe the system
2 identify the mechanisms involved in its operation
3 analyse the operation in order to construct a model of the system.

The flat plate solar water heater collector is used as an example.

1 The collector consists of an absorber plate (usually of copper), with a black surface and thermally coupled waterways (pipes); insulation to the back and edges, with a transparent cover (usually glass) and some sort of casing.
2 The incident solar radiation is absorbed by the plate, which is thus heated and the heat is transferred to the fluid circulating in the pipes, The insulation of back and edges prevents (reduces) heat loss and the glass cover prevents convective losses from the absorber.
3 G is the global solar irradiance (W/m^2).

$Qs = A.G$ is the solar heat input (W) if A is the collector aperture area
$A.G.\tau$ is the radiation transmitted by the glass of τ transmittance
$A.G\,\tau\,\alpha$ is the heat absorbed by the plate of α absorptance
$Qin = A\,G\,F\tau\,\alpha$ is the heat transmitted into the fluid (F = heat removal factor)

if mr is the mass flow rate of the fluid (kg/s) and the fluid temperature increase from inlet to outlet is $T_{out} - T_{in}$, then the useful heat produced is

$$Quse = mr(T_{out} - T_{in})c_p$$

where c_p is the specific heat of the fluid; for water $c_p = 4187\,\text{J/kg.K}$ (1.16Wh/kg.K)
dimensionally: kg/s $\times$ K $\times$ J/kg.K, by cancellations: J/s = W
The collector efficiency will be

$$\eta = \frac{Quse}{Qin} = \frac{mr(T_{out} - T_{in})c_p}{AG}$$

Analytically: the heat input into the fluid is reduced by losses caused by the temperature difference between fluid Tf and outdoor air temperature Ta. Logically the mean fluid temperature should be taken, as Tf = $(T_{in} + T_{out})/2$, then the loss would be U'(Tf − Ta), but as T_{out} (thus Tf) are unknown the difference can be taken as $\Delta T = (T_{in} - Ta)$, and the loss will be modified by F, thus
$Qloss = F\,A\,U'\,\Delta T$
The useful collection will be

$$Quse = A\,G\,F(\tau\,\alpha) - F\,A\,U'\,\Delta T = A\,F[G(\tau\,\alpha) - U'\,\Delta T]$$

For a particular collector η can be determined by testing. The main determinant of η is the term $\Delta T/G$.

If many test points (values of η) are plotted as a function of $\Delta T/G$, a linear function can be fitted, in the form of $y = a - b\,x$, here

$$\eta = A - B(\Delta T/G)$$

where A is the *no-loss efficiency*, when $U' = 0$, (the Y-axis intercept)
and B is the slope coefficient (U')
when $\eta = 0$, i.e. $A = B\,(\Delta T/G)$
we get the *stagnation temperature* (the X-axis intercept)

The 'collector constants' A and B can thus be determined by testing and can then be used in simulation of collector performance under any conditions of temperature and irradiance.

The performance is improved if:

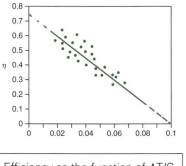

Efficiency as the function of $\Delta T/G$ data points and regression: here: $\eta = 0.75 - 7.5\,(\Delta T/G)$

- τ is increased
- α_{solar} is increased whilst $\varepsilon_{< 100°C}$ is reduced ('low-e' selective surface)
- U' is reduced (lower temperature reduces the ΔT), improves collection efficiency.

REFERENCES

ASHRAE (1997). *ASHRAE handbook of fundamentals*. American Society of Heating, Refrigerating and Air-Conditioning Engineers, Inc, Atlanta.

Atkinson, GA (1953). Tropical architecture and building standards. *Proc. 1953 Conf. On Tropical Architecture*. Architectural Association, London.

Auliciems, A (1981). Towards a psycho-physiological model of thermal perception. *Int. J. Biometeorol.*, 25: 109–122.

Baker, N and Steemers, K (1999). *Daylight design of buildings*. James & James, London.

Bedford, T (1936). *Warmth factor in comfort at work*. Medical Research Council, Report 76. HMSO, London.

Bureau of Meteorology (1988). *Climatic averages*. The Bureau, Australia.

CIE (Commission Internationale de l'éclairage) (1995). Technical Note 117, London.

Danter, E (1960). Periodic heat flow characteristics of simple walls and roofs. *J. Inst. Heat. Vent. Engs.*, July: 136–146.

de Dear, RJ, Brager, G and Cooper, D (1997). *Developing an adaptive model of thermal comfort and preference*. Final report, ASHRAE RP-884, Macquarie University.

Diesendorf, M (2007). *Greenhouse solutions with sustainable energy*. University of NSW Press, Sydney.

Du Bois, D & Du Bois, EF (1916). A formula to estimate (body) surface area if weight and height are known. *Archives of Internal Medicine*, 17: 863–871.

Gagge, AP, Fobelets, AP and Berglund, LG (1986). A standard predictive index of human response to the thermal environment. *ASHRAE Trans.*, 92: 709–731.

Givoni, B (1969). *Man, climate and architecture*. Elsevier, Amsterdam.

Hong, T, Chou, SK and Bong, TY (2000). Building simulation: an overview of developments and information sources. *Building and Environment*, 35: 347–361.

Houghten, FC and Yagloglou, CP (1923). Determination of comfort zone. *Trans. Am. Soc. Heat. Vent. Engs.*, 29: 361.

Humphreys, M (1978). Outdoor temperatures and comfort indoors. *Build. Res. Pract.*, 6: 92–105.

IES (The Illuminating Engineering Society) (1967). *Evaluation of discomfort glare: the glare index system....* Technical Report No.10, The Society, London.

Knowles, R (1977). Solar energy, building and the law. *J. of Architectural Education*, Feb.

Koenigsberger, OH, Ingersoll, TG, Mayhew, A and Szokolay, SV (1973). *Manual of tropical housing and building: pt.1: climatic design*. Longman, London.

Köppen, W and Geiger, R (1936). *Handbuch der Klimatologie*. Borntrager, Berlin.

Lawson, B (1996). *Building materials, energy and the environment*. RAIA, Canberra.

Longmore, J (1968). *BRS Daylight protractors*. Building Research Station, HMSO, London.

Maslow, AH (1984). Higher and lower needs. *J. Psychol.*, 25: 433–436.

Nicol, F and Roaf, S (1996). Pioneering new indoor temperature standards: the Pakistan project. *Energy and Buildings*, 23: 169–174.

Olgyay, V (1953). *Bioclimatic approach to architecture.* Building Research Advisory Board, Conf. Report No. 5, National Research Council, Washington,DC.

Olgyay, V (1963). *Design with climate: bioclimatic approach to architectural regionalism.* Princeton University Press, Princeton, NJ.

Paix, D (1962/1982). *The design of buildings for daylighting.* Bulletin No. 7, Experimental Building Station, AGPS, Canberra.

Phillips, RO (1948). Sunshine and shade in Australia. TS 23, also Bulletin 8, 1963, CEBS, Sydney (Commonwealth Experimental Building Station).

Radford, A and Williamson, T (2002). What is sustainable architecture? *Proc. ANZAScA 2002 conf.* ANZ Arch. Science Assoc., Deakin University, Geelong.

Roaf, S, Fuentes, M and Thomas, S (2001). *Ecohouse: a design guide.* Architectural Press, Oxford.

Robledo, L et al. (1999). Natural light and daylighting research at the School of Architecture, Madrid. In Szokolay, SV (ed.), *Sustaining the Future.* PLEA'99 conf. published by PLEA/Uni of Qld Brisbane.

Sommer, R (1969). *Personal space: the behavioural basis of design.* Prentice-Hall, Englewood Cliffs, NJ.

Szokolay, SV (1980). *Environmental science handbook for architects.* Longman/Construction Press, Lancaster.

Szokolay, SV (1992). *Architecture and climate change.* RAIA. Red Hill, Canberra.

Thayer, RL (1981). *Solar access: it's the Law.* Institute of Government Affairs, Institute of Ecology, University of California, Davis, Environmental Quality series 34).

Vale, B and Vale, R (1991). *Green architecture: design for a sustainable future.* Thames & Hudson, London.

Wackernagel, M and Rees, WE (1966). *Our ecological footprint: human impact on the Earth.* New Society Publishers, British Columbia, Canada.

Yagloglou, CP (1927). The comfort zone for man. *J. Ind. Hyg.*, 9: 251.

FURTHER READING

Allsop, B (1972). *Ecological morality*. Frederick Muller, London.

Anluk, D *et al.* (1995). *The handbook of sustainable building*. James & James, London.

Banham, R (1969). *Architecture of the well-tempered environment*. Architectural Press, London.

Beggs, C (2002). *Energy management and conservation*. Architectural Press, Oxford.

Berge, B (2001). *Ecology of building materials*. Architectural Press, Oxford.

Bockris, JO'M (1974). *The solar hydrogen alternative*. Architectural Press, London.

Burt, W *et al.* (1969). *Windows and environment*. Pilkington/McCorquondale, Newton-le-Willows.

CIBSE (1999). *Guide A: environmental design*. Chartered Institution of Building Services Engineers, The Yale Press, London.

Clarke, JA (2001). *Energy simulation in building design*. Adam Hilger, Bristol.

Cowan, 991Cowan, HJ. *Handbook of architectural technology* (1991). . Van Nostrand Reinhold, New York

Drysdale, JW (1952/1975). *Designing houses for Australian climates*. Bulletin 6, CEBS, Sydney (Commonwealth Experimental Building Station).

Edwards, B (1998). *Sustainable architecture: European directives and building design*. Architectural Press, Oxford.

Fanger, PO (1970). *Thermal comfort*. Danish Technical Press, Copenhagen.

Farmer, J (1999). *Green shift*. Architectural Press, Oxford.

Gagge, AP, Gonzalez, RR and Nishi, Y (1974). Physiological and physical factors governing man's thermal comfort and heat tolerance. *Build Int.*, 7: 305–331.

Givoni, B (1994). *Passive and low energy cooling of buildings*. Van Nostrand Reinhold, New York.

Griffiths, I (1990). *Thermal comfort studies in buildings with passive solar features*. Report to CEC.ENS35090, UK.

Gunn, AS and Vesilind, PA (1986). *Environmental ethics for engineers*. Lewis Publishers, Chelsea, MI.

Hopkinson, RG, Petherbridge, P and Longmore, J (1966). *Daylighting*. Heinemann, London.

Keating, M (1993). *Agenda for change (a plain language version of Agenda 21 and other Rio agreements)*. Centre for Our Common Future, Geneva.

Lawrence, A (1970). *Architectural acoustics*. Elsevier Applied Science, London.

Mackenzie, D (1991). *Green design: design for the environment*. Laurence King, London.

Meadows, DH and Meadows, DL (1972). *The limits to growth*. Club of Rome, Potomac Associates/Earth Island Ltd, London.

Milbank, NO and Harryngton-Lynn, J (1974). *Thermal response and the admittance procedure, BRE. CP 61/74*. Building Research Establishment, Garston.